Leisure in Later Life

A Sourcebook for the Provision of Recreational Services for Elders

About the Authors

Michael J. Leitner is a Professor in the Department of Recreation and Parks Management at California State University, Chico. He received a Ph.D. in Therapeutic Recreation and a doctoral certificate in Gerontology from the University of Maryland. Dr. Leitner has authored numerous published articles on the topic of recreation and aging, and has produced several instructional videotapes.

Sara F. Leitner is an instructor in the outreach program for special populations at Butte College. She received an M.A. in Physical Education from California State University, Chico, with a specialization in exercise and dance for elders. Ms. Leitner was the assistant director of a day care center for the elderly in College Park, Maryland.

Leisure in Later Life
A Sourcebook for the Provision
of Recreational Services for Elders

Michael J. Leitner
Sara F. Leitner

The Haworth Press
New York • London

Leisure in Later Life: A Sourcebook for the Provision of Recreational Services for Elders has also been published as *Activities, Adaptation & Aging,* Volume 7, Numbers 3/4, December 1985.

The Haworth Press, Inc. 10 Alice Street, Binghamton, NY 13904-1580
EUROSPAN/Haworth, 3 Henrietta Street, London WC2E 8LU England

Library of Congress Cataloging-in-Publication Data

Leitner, Michael J.
   Leisure in later life.

   Includes bibliographies and index.
     1. Aged—United States—Recreation. 2. Recreation centers—United States.
I. Leitner, Sara F. II. Title.
GV447.L44 1985   790.1'926'0973   85-17635
ISBN 0-86656-452-7
ISBN 0-86656-476-4 (pbk.)

Dedication

To our parents, Florence and Philip Merenbloom, and Samuel and Lillian Leitner, for their love and devotion.

Leisure in Later Life

Activities, Adaptation & Aging
Volume 7, Numbers 3/4

CONTENTS

SECTION III:
RESOURCES FOR RECREATION PROGRAMS
FOR ELDERS

SECTION IV:
ISSUES IN PROVIDING LEISURE SERVICES
TO ELDERS

Preface

This book is intended to fill the void in the literature for a comprehensive textbook on the topic of recreation and aging. *Leisure in Later Life* is designed to be a useful resource for the provision of recreation services for elders. The book is designed to be used as: (1) a basic textbook for students and instructors of college courses dealing specifically with the topic of recreation and aging; (2) a supplementary textbook for courses in the psychology of aging, social work with elders, therapeutic recreation, adapted physical education, and courses in principles of recreation leadership and programming; (3) a reference text for field work and practicum students working with elders; (4) a reference text for activity directors in nursing homes, recreation leaders in senior centers, adult day care centers, and retirement communities, and other personnel involved in the provision of leisure services to elders; and (5) a sourcebook for the in-service training of volunteers and entry-level recreation personnel working with elders. Therefore, this book is not only intended to be a textbook for courses in recreation and aging, but also a supplementary textbook and resource for students in related areas, and personnel involved in the provision of recreational services for elders. The diversity of the older population is recognized in this book. A diligent effort was made to include information which can be applied to the provision of recreation services for low functioning, high functioning, and moderately impaired elders.

The book has been divided into four sections:

SECTION I.
FOUNDATIONS OF RECREATION SERVICES FOR ELDERS

This section of the book is intended to provide the reader with background information on recreation and aging essential to recreational work with elders in almost any setting. There are four chapters in this section:

Chapter 1: Introduction to Leisure Services for Elders

In this chapter, an overview of the field of leisure services for elders is presented. Topics discussed in this chapter include: research on recreation participation patterns of elders; factors affecting the leisure behavior of elders; trends in the demography of the older population, and the implications of these trends for the provision of recreation services to elders; benefits of recreational activity for elders; and definitions of key terms used throughout the book.

Chapter 2: Recreation Leadership Principles

This chapter focuses on the acquisition of skills needed in order to effectively lead recreational activities with elders. The skills discussed in this chapter are relevant to recreational work with elders in most settings. Chapter two and chapter three both follow a format different from the other chapters in the book. At the beginning of the chapter, a list of learning objectives is presented. Each learning objective represents a particular skill or competency discussed in the chapter. The following format is utilized in the discussion of each skill: (1) a statement of the skill or competency; (2) a problem situation related to the skill; and (3) examples of solutions to the problem, incorporating knowledge related to the skill or competency. This problem-solving approach is utilized to facilitate skill acquisition.

Chapter 3: Program Planning Principles

As in chapter two, a problem-solving approach is utilized. This chapter focuses on the acquisition of skills needed in order to effectively plan recreation programs and activities.

Chapter 4: Program Evaluation

This chapter focuses on providing information on two particular evaluation methods, interviewing, and behavior observation. These two evaluation methods are discussed in detail because of their usefulness in attempting to evaluate the effectiveness of recreation programs for impaired elders.

SECTION II.
SETTINGS FOR RECREATION SERVICES
FOR ELDERS

This section of the book is intended to provide the reader with background information on the various settings where recreation services for elders are provided. This section is designed to help one to understand the differences in approaching recreation leadership and program planning in various settings. There are four chapters in this section:

Chapter 5: Senior Day Care Centers

Topics discussed in this chapter include: background information on adult day care centers in the U.S.; considerations in providing recreation services in adult day care centers; a description of the day care center setting and program participants; and funding sources.

Chapter 6: Senior Centers and Clubs

Similar to chapter five, the topics discussed in this chapter include: background information on senior centers and clubs in the U.S.; considerations in providing recreation services in senior centers; a description of the senior center setting and program participants; and funding sources.

Chapter 7: Nursing Homes

Also similar to chapter five, the topics discussed in this chapter include: background information on recreation programs in nursing homes in the U.S.; considerations in providing recreation in nursing homes; and a description of the characteristics of nursing home residents and their implications for the provision of recreational services.

Chapter 8: Retirement Communities
and Age-Segregated Housing

This chapter follows a different format than the previous three chapters. In addition to examining retirement communities as a setting for recreation programs for elders, the issue of age-segregated housing is explored in this chapter. Topics discussed in this chapter include: the current status of age-segregation in the U.S.; research on elders' preferences for age-segregation; and the desirability of age-segregated living arrangements, including an examination of the recreational advantages of retirement communities.

SECTION III:
RESOURCES FOR RECREATION PROGRAMS
FOR ELDERS

This section of the book is intended to provide information on recreational programs, activities, and techniques which can readily be applied in work with elders in a variety of settings. There are six chapters in this section:

Chapter 9: Intergenerational Activities

The purpose of this chapter is to provide practical information on how to plan and lead successful intergenerational recreation activities.

Chapter 10: Leisure Counseling

The purposes of this chapter are to help the reader understand leisure counseling, and how to use leisure counseling with elders.

Chapter 11: Exercise

The purpose of this chapter is to provide practical information on providing recreational exercise programs for elders in a variety of settings. Topics discussed in this chapter include: benefits of exercise for elders; considerations in leading exercise sessions for elders; instructions for specific exercises for bedridden elders, high functioning elders, and elders with limited mobility; and sample exercise session plans.

Chapter 12: Adapted Dance for Older Adults

This chapter is intended to provide the reader with practical information on how to adapt diverse dance forms for elders of various functioning levels. The topics discussed in this chapter include:

benefits of adapted dance for elders; suggested components of an adapted dance session for elders; and procedures for adapting folk, square, ballet, tap, and modern dance for elders. In addition, numerous sample adapted folk, square, and tap dances for moderately impaired and low functioning elders are presented.

Chapter 13: Recreational Techniques and Activities

The purpose of this chapter is to foster a greater awareness and understanding of some of the diverse recreational activities and techniques which can be used with elders. The activities and techniques discussed in this chapter are: massage; clowning; drama; music; arts and crafts; horticulture therapy; pet therapy; and the uses of humor and laughter with elders. In addition, practical information on how to use these techniques and activities with elders, and resources for further information are provided.

Chapter 14: Recreational Programs and Special Events

The purpose of this chapter is to provide information on recreation programs for elders which can be implemented in almost any community. The programs discussed include: camping; sports programs; and Elderfest.

SECTION IV:
ISSUES IN PROVIDING LEISURE SERVICES TO ELDERS

This section of the book is intended to increase the awareness and understanding of several important issues related to the provision of recreation services for elders. The chapters in this section are:

Chapter 15: The Role of Recreation in Hospice Care

Recreational work with terminally ill elders is an area which has great potential. This chapter is intended to arouse interest in including recreation services as a component of hospice care.

Chapter 16: Recreation and the Rural Elderly

The data on the geographical distribution of elders in the U.S. indicates that a substantial proportion of the nation's elderly live in rural areas. This chapter focuses on the special concerns in providing leisure services to elders who live in rural areas.

Chapter 17: Sexuality in Later Life

Sexual activity can be an exceptionally enjoyable and beneficial leisure activity for elders. Recreation personnel working with elders can make a significant contribution to enhancing the sexual behavior of elders if they are well informed in this area. In this chapter, information is presented on the sexual behavior patterns of older Americans, factors affecting these behavior patterns, attitudes toward sex in later life, benefits of sexual activity for elders, and suggestions for overcoming physiological and psycho-social barriers to sexual fulfillment in later life. This chapter is intended to enlighten students and recreation personnel on this topic in the hopes that better-informed recreation services providers will be able to more effectively foster enhanced sexual behavior and attitudes among elders.

Thus, *Leisure in Later Life* covers a broad range of topics. Both theoretical information and material with clear practical applications are presented in this book. Thus, the book is truly a valuable sourcebook for the provision of recreation services to elders.

Acknowledgements

The authors wish to acknowledge the important contributions of numerous individuals and organizations to the successful completion of this book:

Gloria Leitner, for her contributions to the chapter on sexuality in later life;

Lesley Caunt, for typing the original manuscript;

The Department of Recreation and Parks Management, California State University, Chico for their help and support;

Crestwood Convalescent Hospital and Riverside Convalescent Hospital in Chico, California for photographs;

Paul Shepherd and Ed Ansello for their contributions to the chapter on recreation and the rural elderly;

The Department of Recreation, University of Maryland at College Park, for assistance and support in the initial stages of writing this book; and special thanks to

All of our family and close friends for their inspiration and interest in this project.

Section I:
Foundations
of Recreation Services
for Elders

Chapter 1

Introduction to Leisure Services for Elders

INTRODUCTION

The topic of leisure services for elders is one of growing importance. One reason for the increased concern for leisure services for elders is the continuous growth in the population of persons age 65 and older. This segment of the population has grown from 12.3 million in 1950 to 27.4 million in 1983, and is projected to grow to 35.0 million by the year 2000 ("Spotlight on Older Americans," 1984). Another reason for the increased concern for leisure services for elders is the fact that persons age 65 and older have more leisure time (43 hours per week) than any other age group (National Recreation and Parks Association, 1983).

The purpose of this chapter is to present an introduction to the field of leisure services for elders. The chapter has been divided into the following sections:

1. *Terminology.* In this section, key terms used throughout this book are discussed and defined.
2. *Demography of the Older Population.* In this section, trends and statistics regarding the status of persons age 65 and older in our society are discussed. The implications of these trends and statistics for leisure services for elders are also explored.
3. *Current Status of Recreation Services for Elders.* In this section, numerous research studies on recreation participation patterns of elders and the benefits of recreational activity for elders are discussed in order to clarify the state-of-the-art of leisure services for elders. In addition, factors affecting the recreation participation patterns of elders are discussed in

11

order to understand the influences on recreation participation patterns of elders.

TERMINOLOGY

Terms discussed and defined in this section include: elders; high functioning; limited mobility; low functioning; leisure; leisure services; recreation services; recreation; and therapeutic recreation.

Elders

For the purposes of this book, the term *elder* refers to persons age 65 and older. Although age 65 does not necessarily denote a point in one's life at which dramatic biological, psychological, and/or social changes occur, this book does focus on the provision of leisure services for persons age 65 and older because age 65 is commonly used as the minimum age requirement for many recreational programs for older persons. Other terms used in this book to denote persons age 65 and older include: older persons; older adults; mature adults; senior citizens; senior adults; seniors; elderly; aging; and aged. The term elders is most commonly used in this book because it is both a familiar term and one which is associated with a more positive and respectful attitude toward older persons.

High Functioning, Limited Mobility, and Low Functioning Elders

Throughout the book, discussion on providing leisure services for elders focuses on three major categories of older persons: *high functioning*; elders with *limited mobility* or *moderately impaired*; and *low functioning*. For the purposes of this book, *high functioning* elders refers to those persons age 65 and older in good or excellent health, with unrestricted mobility, and physically, mentally, and emotionally capable of participating in most recreational programs for elders. The terms *limited mobility* and *moderately impaired* are utilized in this book to refer to elders with chronic conditions which restrict their ability to participate in recreational activities involving a great deal of movement or strenuous exercise, but are not necessarily confined to a wheelchair or bed. For the purposes of this book, the term *low functioning* is used to identify bed-ridden or wheelchair-bound elders with chronic conditions which limit their ability to participate in many physically and mentally demanding recreational activities.

Leisure and Recreation

For the purposes of this book, the term *leisure* refers to free or unobligated time, time during which one is not working or performing life-sustaining functions. Although more elaborate theoretical constructs of leisure have been described in the literature by Kaplan (1975), Murphy (1975), Neulinger (1974), and others, the "discretionary time" definition of leisure is used for the purposes of this book because it is easier to use in attempting to identify and categorize different types of behavior.

For the purposes of this book, *recreation* is defined as activity conducted during one's leisure. Again, more complex and elaborate definitions have been discussed in the literature, but a simpler definition is being used for the purposes of this book because it is practical to use in categorizing different types of behavior.

Leisure and Recreational Services, Therapeutic Recreation

The terms *leisure services* and *recreational services* are used interchangeably in this book to identify programs and activities designed to provide enjoyable experiences for people during their leisure. *Therapeutic recreation* is defined as leisure activity designed to facilitate an improvement and/or maintenance of one's physical and/or mental functioning and/or promote developmental growth (Meyer, 1977).

DEMOGRAPHY OF THE OLDER POPULATION

Size and Proportional Representation

As indicated by statistics cited earlier, the number of persons age 65 and older is expected to triple between 1950 and the year 2000 ("Spotlight on Older Americans," 1984). The proportional size of the older population has also grown. According to the American Association of Retired Persons (1984), people 65 and older represented 4.1% of the population in 1900, 11.7% in 1983, and is projected to be 13.0% of the population by the year 2000 and 21.2% by the year 2030. Certainly, this growth in the older population will necessitate a growth in leisure services for elders.

The projections for the growth in size and proportional representation of the older population between the years 2010 and 2030 are based on members of the "baby boom" generation reaching age 65 during those years, and no great changes in medical technology occurring. It is important to keep in mind that advances in medical research, particularly in the areas of cancer and heart disease (two of the most prominent causes of death of people age 65 and older), coupled with a declining birth rate, could conceivably increase the proportional representation of elders in our society by the year 2035 to a much greater level (40%-50%) than is currently projected. In addition, the continuance of the trend toward increasing amounts of leisure for our society as a whole (Weiskopf, 1982) reinforces the notion that a great expansion in leisure services for elders will be needed.

Sex, Age, and Health Status

One characteristic of the older population which has a very significant impact on recreation programs for elders is the higher proportion of women than men among those 65 and older. In 1983, women comprised 59.9% of the 65 and over population, or in other words, there were approximately 150 women for every 100 men among those 65 and older ("Spotlight on Older Americans," 1984). According to the American Association of Retired Persons (1984), the ratio of women to men increases with age, ranging from 124 women for every 100 men in the 65-69 age group, to a high of 241 women for every 100 men in the 85 and older age group. Approximately 79% of men in the 65 and over age group are married, compared to 40% for women (American Association of Retired Persons, 1984).

The predominance of women in the older population is reflected in most recreation programs for elders. In senior day care centers, senior centers and clubs, and nursing homes, recreational activities and programs are often geared primarily to the interests of women, because there are more female participants in the program. This trend has presented a problem for encouraging male involvement in programs, because programs are often perceived by men as being female-oriented. Thus, while recreation programs for elders should attempt to meet the needs of the majority of the older population (i.e., single women), special efforts are also needed in order to encourage men to become involved in recreation programs.

Another characteristic of the older population which has implications for recreation services for elders is that the older population is becoming increasingly older. According to the American Association of Retired Persons (1984), among those 65 and older in 1983, 16.4 million were between 65-74 years old, 8.5 million were between 75-84 years old, and 2.2 million were 85 years old or older. According to Gelfand (1984), the proportion of persons age 75 and older among persons age 65 and older will continue to increase.

The implications of this trend for recreational services for elders are complex. One view is that the increasing age of the older population is reflective of improved health status, thus indicating a greater need for recreation services for high functioning elders. On the other hand, the lowest functioning segment of the older population is the 75 and over age group. Growth in the number of persons age 75 and older might therefore also indicate an increasing need for recreational services for low functioning elders.

With regard to health status, persons age 65 and older are probably healthier than they are commonly believed to be. According to Gelfand (1984), 69% of the elderly report to be in good or excellent health, and only 9% report their health to be poor. According to the American Association of Retired Persons (1984), although most older persons have at least one chronic condition, the majority of elders are able to perform activities of daily living independently. According to the American Association of Retired Persons (1984), the most frequently cited chronic conditions of elders are: arthritis (46%); hypertension (38%); hearing impairments (28%); heart conditions (28%); sinusitis (18%) visual impairments (14%); orthopedic impairments (14%); arteriosclerosis (11%); and diabetes (8%). Thus, the health status of the older population indicates that a great variety of recreational activities and programs can be participated in by most elders, although activities may need modification for many people.

Education and Economic Status

Two positive trends in the older population are improved educational and income levels. The percentage of persons age 65 and older living in poverty declined from 24.5% in 1970 to only 14.6% in 1982 ("Spotlight on Older Americans," 1984). With regard to education, in 1980, persons age 65 and older had completed an average of 10.2 years of education (American Association of Retired Persons, 1984), although 41.6% of the older population had completed only grammar school (Gelfand, 1984). Obviously, the average number of years of education and the percentage of elders who complete four or more years of college will rise significantly over the next few decades. The improved economic status and educational levels of the older population should enable the provision of a broader range of leisure services for elders in the future.

Living Arrangements

Although over one million elders reside in nursing and personal care homes, this figure represents only 5% of persons age 65 and older in the U.S. (Gelfand, 1984). One significant change in the living arrangements of elders has been the increase in the percentage of noninstitutionalized elders who live alone, an increase from approximately 16.5% in 1960, to approximately 33% in 1980 (U.S. Bureau of the Census, 1981). According to Gelfand (1984), this trend is partially due to longevity, but also reflects the improved economic status of elders. With more elders living alone and fewer living with families, the provision of opportunities for intergenerational interaction through recreational programs becomes more of a concern (which is the topic of chapter 9).

It is also interesting to note the geographic distribution of persons age 65 and older. According to Gelfand (1984), rural states such as Iowa, Arkansas, and Missouri had high proportions of elderly residents. Thus, the provision of leisure services to rural elders is an important concern (which is the topic of chapter 16).

CURRENT STATUS OF LEISURE SERVICES FOR ELDERS

Recreation Participation Patterns

The leisure activities of elders are quite diverse. Some of the more commonly participated in activities are: watching television; reading; hobbies; gardening and other home-related activities; spectator sports; camping; physically active recreation such as swimming, jogging, and tennis; visiting friends and relatives; caring for grandchildren; movies and theatre; sexual relations; travel; walking; exercise in general; games; dance; arts and crafts; music; cooking; social gatherings; discussion groups; religious activities; and participation in voluntary associations.

Several studies have been conducted on the leisure activities of older persons (Lambing, 1972; Guttman, 1973; Peppers, 1976; Gordon, Gaitz, and Scott, 1976; Cutler, 1977; Scott, 1977; Babchuk, 1979; McAvoy, 1979; Ward, 1979; Ginsberg, 1981; Creecy, Wright, and Berg, 1982; and Moss and Lawton, 1982). Most of these studies examined the level and type of leisure activities of older persons through the use of self-report questionnaires and/or interviews administered to a state-wide or local sample of older persons. Several of these studies are described in some detail in order to gain a better picture of recreation participation patterns of the aged.

McAvoy (1979) examined the leisure activities of 540 non-institutionalized Minnesotans ages 65 and over. McAvoy found that the five most frequently participated in activities were: visiting friends and relatives; watching television; reading; gardening; and indoor hobbies. These five activities were the ones most frequently participated in by the sample studied, but were not identified as also being the most preferred activities. For example, walking was more preferred as an activity than watching television, yet television viewing was a more frequently participated in activity. A possible reason for this finding is physical limitations which prevent persons from engaging in more physically demanding activities. Indeed, in this study, lack of physical ability was the most commonly stated barrier to involvement in leisure activity.

Lambing's (1972) study of 101 retired black Floridians ages 48 to 105 produced results similar to those of McAvoy's study. Television viewing and reading were also identified in this study as being heavily participated in activities.

Creecy, Wright, and Berg (1982) also examined the leisure activities of black elders in their study of the relationship of social-psychological, activity, and demographic variables to loneliness among a nationwide sample of 479 noninstitutionalized black elders. The authors found that watching television reinforced feelings of loneliness, whereas reading, social contact, and participation in leisure activities in the community, such as involvement in clubs and organizations, relieved feelings of loneliness. It is interesting to compare the results of this study with the findings of Moss and Lawton's (1982) study on the time budgets of older people.

Moss and Lawton (1982) interviewed 535 urban elders in order to examine the time utilization of elders of four different lifestyles. Some interesting findings of this study regarding the time budgets of elders are: (1) between 58% and 66% of the waking day is spent alone; (2) between 75% and 85% of the day is spent at home; (3) between 20% and 23% of the day is spent watching television; and (4) rest and relaxation consumes between 12% and 20% of the day. Thus, Moss and Lawton's (1982) study suggests that many elders spend most of their time in sedentary and solitary activities, with a great portion of that time being spent watching television. This is disturbing, in light of Creecy, Wright, and Berg's (1982) study which indicated that watching television reinforces feelings of loneliness, and that social activities and community activities relieve feelings of loneliness. Based on these two studies, it seems that many elders are spending their time in a way that reinforces feelings of loneliness. Thus, many elders seem to be in need of, or lacking involvement in recreational activities which promote socialization.

In a different light, Gordon, Gaitz, and Scott (1976) discuss the Houston study of leisure activity across the life span. The Houston study examined differences in leisure activities of 1,441 persons in five different age groups. The five age groups studied were labeled as: young adults; early maturity; full maturity; old age; and very old age. Some findings of the study were: older persons had lower levels of general leisure activity; participation in physically active recreation such as tennis, basketball, and swimming declined in relation to advanced age; levels of participation in spectator sports, television watching, and various social activities remained fairly stable across the different age groups studied; and older persons tended to engage more in relaxation/solitude activities than did persons in other age groups.

Caution should be taken in interpreting the results of the Houston study. The Houston study presents cross-sectional data; it is *describing* differences in the leisure activities of different age groups, *not predicting* changes in leisure activity as one gets older. A common error in interpreting research in gerontology is the inference of cause-effect relationships based on correlational data. Rather than inaccurately predicting age-related changes in leisure activity, it would be more useful to understand the factors affecting leisure activity participation patterns of older persons.

Factors Affecting Recreation Participation Patterns

The factors affecting leisure activity participation patterns of elders are numerous and complex. One factor is attitudes toward work and leisure. For some older persons, the Protestant work ethic is a strongly valued belief which inhibits one from participating in various types of recreational activity. Some researchers theorize that the work ethic is becoming less prevalent in modern society (Kaplan, 1975; and Murphy, 1976); if today's youth are indeed more leisure-oriented than the youth at the turn of the twentieth century, then the future aged population (today's youth) might be more leisure-oriented than today's aged population (who were the youth of society at the turn of the twentieth century). Therefore, the aged of the future might have higher levels of leisure activity than the aged population of today.

Attitudes toward old age and aging also affect leisure activity participation patterns of the aged. People that hold negative stereotypes of older persons might be less inclined to engage in recreation activity with older persons than people that have a more positive view of old age. In addition, an older adult that has a negative image of the aged might project this negative image onto himself. Such an attitude can inhibit one from participating in a variety of "youthful" activities. For example, if one believes that elders are incapable of performing vigorous activity, then one might not engage in physically active sports, merely because of advanced chronological age.

Demographic variables such as age, sex, education, socio-economic status, health, race, and cultural and religious background all affect recreation participation patterns of older persons. In particular, health status affects recreation participation patterns in numerous ways. Health problems are often cited as a factor restricting the leisure activities of older persons. In addition, health status influences the type of activity participated in, and the goals and objectives of such activity.

Other variables, such as climate, availability of transportation services, mass media services, proximity to family and friends, technological advances, and the quality, quantity, and type of recreational facilities available all influence the recreation participation patterns of the aged. Also, crime and/or fear of crime can affect older persons' patterns of leisure activity.

Obviously, one's interests are pivotal in determining leisure activity choices. One's interests may be influenced by: parents' and peers' attitudes toward work and leisure, as well as their recreation participation patterns; physical and mental abilities; activity skills; and knowledge of available leisure services.

Possibly the greatest influence on the leisure activities of elders is the amount of leisure time available to older persons. The leisure time available to persons age 65 and older might decrease or increase in the future, depending on numerous factors. In addition, today's older population greatly varies in terms of amount of leisure time available, due to numerous factors.

One factor affecting the leisure time of the aged is retirement. If laws and social norms dictate a rise in the retirement age, the leisure time of older persons would be reduced. On the other hand, if retirement at younger ages becomes more prevalent, then the leisure time of older persons would be increased.

In a related vein, future developments in social security and private pension systems will affect the leisure time of elders. The adequacy or inadequacy of social security and private retirement plans will influence whether or not more older persons seek full or part-time employment to supplement their incomes; this will in turn affect the amount of leisure time of elders. In fact, some government programs are presently in existence for the purpose of providing gainful employment for older persons in need of additional income (for example, Project Green Thumb).

Also related to the quantity of leisure time of elders is the amount of time spent performing household and personal care functions. For many older persons, household tasks are reduced because of children moving away from home. However, some elders experience an increase in responsibilities in old age because of an illness affecting their spouse or other relative. Some older persons have very little leisure time due to the large amount of time devoted to caring for a family member.

Thus, it might be inaccurate to say that *all* older persons have a great deal of leisure time. For many people, advanced age brings an increase in leisure time; for some, old age brings a reduction in leisure time. Due to the aforementioned factors, future aged populations might have more or less leisure time than our present-day older population.

Thus, in reading descriptive studies on the recreation participation patterns of elders, one should recognize that the interests of various groups of older persons differ due to differences in some of the previously described variables. Furthermore, it is likely that the recreation participation patterns of future aged populations will differ from those of today's elders, due to changes in the previously described factors.

Importance of Recreation for Elders

Numerous research studies have indicated that recreation activity is beneficial for older persons. Some of the hypothesized benefits of leisure activity for elders are: improved health; increased opportunity for social interaction; improved morale and life satisfaction; higher self-concept and improved body image; greater feelings of usefulness and self-worth; improved skills and better ability to function independently; and most of all, fun and enjoyment. The studies cited in this section lend support to the notion that higher levels of leisure activity among older persons are related to the aforementioned positive differences in quality of life variables.

Exercise is one type of leisure activity which is widely acclaimed to be beneficial for elders. A recent report in the *Journal of the American Medical Association* ("You're never too old for exercise, AMA study finds," 1984) states that exercise is as important for elders as it is for younger people. The report claims that exercise can help elders stay physically and mentally fit, and ward off crippling diseases. According to the report, many physical changes associated with aging are really due to inactivity, thus a lifetime program of physical activity can delay the onset of many of the degenerative changes associated with aging.

This view is supported by numerous studies on the effects of physically active recreation on elders. For example, Frekany and Leslie (1975) found that a seven month, twice a week, thirty minute exercise program produced significant improvements in ankle, hamstring, and lower back flexibility of fifteen women ages 71-90. Similarly, Kline (1973) describes an eleven year study of 135 persons ages 50-65 conducted by the National Institute on Mental Health (NIMH). The results of the study indicated that physical activity had a positive effect on physical and mental health of the subjects. In a related vein, Birren's (1972) study of 30 persons ages 60-75 indicated that participation in physically active sports is related to improved health.

Sidney and Shepherd (1977) also studied the relationship of participation in active recreation to health status. Sidney and Shepherd examined the activity patterns of 13 healthy men (average age 65.2 years) and 21 healthy women (average age 64.8 years) through the use of diaries, ECG tape recorders, and electro-chemical integrators. Although the subjects thought they were active relative to others their own age, initial assessments indicated that the subjects had an inactive lifestyle. Sidney and Shepherd (1977) introduced a one-hour physically active recreation class four times per week to the 34 subjects. The sessions were found to have increased the aerobic power of the subjects, induced favorable body composition changes, and initiated other favorable changes in lifestyle.

Several studies have also been conducted on the relationship of recreation participation patterns to life satisfaction. Graney (1975) conducted a four year longitudinal study of 60 women ages 62-89 (all in good health) on this topic. In Graney's study, the Affect Balance Scale was utilized as a happiness measure; social activity was measured through the use of nine measures of socially relevant activities. The results of the study lend support to the notion that leisure activity is related to life satisfaction; the subjects in this study with the highest activity levels also scored highest on measures of life satisfaction and happiness.

Ray (1979) also examined the relationship between life satisfaction and leisure activity. Ray interviewed 125 persons over age 65, using the Life Satisfaction Index, Adult Activities Inventory, and a demographic variables sheet. In this study, a significant relationship was found to exist between leisure activity and life satisfaction.

A similar study was conducted in England by Knapp (1977). Knapp examined the life satisfaction and activity levels of 51 persons ages 62 to 86. Knapp's findings concurred with those of Ray's study; a significant relationship was found to exist between life satisfaction and level of activity. Edwards' and Klemmack's (1973) study of 274 females and 233 males ages 45 and over produced results resembling those of Knapp's study. Similarly, studies by DeCarlo (1972), Adams and Groen (1975), Frekany and Leslie (1975), and Emes (1977) indicate that older persons derive various physical and social benefits from regular participation in leisure activities.

Owens (1982) examined the relationship of frequency and type of leisure activity to life satisfaction of a particular older population, the elderly deaf. Owens (1982) tested 42 deaf elders in New York City and concluded that informal leisure activity is significantly related to life satisfaction. Thus, this study also lends support to the need to develop and expand leisure services for elders which foster social interaction.

The importance of leisure in determining life satisfaction is further illustrated by Seleen's (1982) study in which the congruence between actual and desired use of time by 205 attendees of a senior citizens center in Rhode Island was examined as a predictor of life satisfaction. Seleen (1982) found that the degree of congruence between actual and desired time utilization was significantly correlated with life satisfaction. In this study, satisfaction with leisure was found to significantly contribute to life satisfaction.

In summary, the physical, mental, and emotional benefits of leisure activity for elders are well documented in the literature. Thus, recreation is clearly an important factor in the lives of elders, and the provision of leisure services for elders should be an important concern for our society.

BIBLIOGRAPHY

Adams, M., and Groen, R. Media habits and preferences of the elderly. *Leisurability*, 1975, *2*(2), pp. 25-30.

American Association of Retired Persons. *A profile of older Americans: 1984.* (PF3049 (1184)). Washington, D.C.: American Association of Retired Persons, 1984.

Babchuk, N., Peters, G.R., et al. The voluntary associations of the aged. *Journal of Gerontology*, 1979, *34*(4), pp. 579-587.

Birren, J.E. Time for active sports. *Retirement Living Magazine*, 1972, *8*(3), pp. 72-74.

Brightbill, C.K. *The challenge of leisure.* Englewood Cliffs, NJ: Prentice-Hall, Inc., 1960.

Creecy, R.F., Wright, R., and Berg, W.E. Correlates of loneliness among the black elderly. *Activities, Adaptation, and Aging*, 1982, *3*(2), pp. 9-16.

Cutler, S.J. Aging and voluntary association participation. *Journal of Gerontology*, 1977, *32*(4), pp. 470-479.

DeCarlo, T.J. *Recreation participation patterns and successful aging: A twin study.* Unpublished doctoral dissertation, Columbia University, 1972.

Edward, J.N., and Klemmack, D.L. Correlates of life satisfaction: A reexamination. *Journal of Gerontology*, 1973, *28*(4), pp. 497-502.

Emes, C.G. The aging process and its effects on activity selections for the elderly. *Leisurability*, 1979, *4*(1), pp. 14-17.

Frekany, G.A., and Leslie, D.K. Developing an exercise program for senior citizens. *Therapeutic Recreation Journal*, 1974, *8*(4), pp. 178-180.

Frekany, G.A., and Leslie, D.K. Effects of an exercise program on selected flexibility measurements of senior citizens. *Gerontologist*, 1975, *15*(2), pp. 182-183.

Gelfand, D.E. *The aging network: Programs and services* (2nd ed.). New York: Springer Publishing, 1984.

Ginsberg, B.R. Leisure patterns and leisure satisfaction attitudes of a select sample of urban retired male executives (Doctoral dissertation, Columbia University Teachers College, 1981). *Dissertation Abstracts International*, 1981, *42*, 2315A. (University Microfilms No. 8122946).

Gordon, Gaitz, Scott. Leisure and lives. In R.H. Binstock and E. Shanas (Eds.), *Handbook of aging and the social sciences.* 1976.

Graney, M.J. Happiness and social participation in aging. *Journal of Gerontology*, 1975, *30*, 701-706.

Guttman, D. Leisure-time activity interest of Jewish aged. *Gerontologist*, 1973, *13*(2), pp. 219-223.

Kaplan, M. *Leisure: Theory and policy.* New York: John Wiley and Sons, 1975.

Kaplan, M. *Leisure: Lifestyle and lifespan.* Philadelphia: W.B. Saunders, 1979.

Kline, J. Live it up and live longer. *Prevention Magazine,* 1973, *25*(10), pp. 107-108.

Knapp, M.R.J. The activity theory of aging: An examination in the English context. *Gerontologist,* 1977, *17*(6), pp. 553-559.

Lambing, M.L. Leisure time pursuits among retired blacks by social status. *Gerontologist,* 1972, *12*(4), pp. 363-367.

McArthur, J.D., and Fillmore, E.R. Access to forest recreation for urban senior citizens. *Leisurability,* 1978, *5*(4), pp. 30-37.

McAvoy, L.H. The leisure preferences problems and needs of the elderly. *Journal of Gerontology,* 1979, *11*(1), pp. 40-47.

McCullum, M. Outdoor recreation and the senior citizen. *Leisurability,* 1978, *5*(4), pp. 16-19.

Meyer, L.E. A view of therapeutic recreation: Its foundations, objectives, and challenges. In G. Zaso (Ed.), *Therapeutic recreation: Dialogues in development.* University of New Hampshire, 1977.

Moss, M.S., and Lawton, M.P. Time budgets of older people: Window on four lifestyles. *Journal of Gerontology,* 1982, *37*(1), pp. 115-123.

Murphy, J.R. *Recreation and leisure service.* Philadelphia, PA: Lea and Febiger, 1975.

National Recreation and Park Association. Editor's diary. *Dateline: NRPA,* 1983, *6*(1), pp. 2; 14; 16.

National Therapeutic Recreation Society (NTRS). *A philosophical statement of the National Therapeutic Recreation Society.* Arlington, VA: National Therapeutic Recreation Society, 1979.

Neulinger, J.M. *The psychology of leisure.* Springfield, IL: C.C. Thomas, 1974.

Owens, D.J. The relationship of frequency and types of activity to life satisfaction in elderly deaf people (Doctoral dissertation, New York University, 1981). *Dissertation Abstracts International,* 1982, *42,* 3110A. (University Microfilms No. 8128225).

Peppers, L.G. Patterns of leisure and adjustment to retirement. *Gerontologist,* 1976, *16*(5), pp. 441, 446.

Ray, R.O. Life satisfaction and activity involvement: Implications for leisure service. *Journal of Leisure Research,* 1979, *11*(2), pp. 112-119.

Scott, E.O., and Zoerink, D.A. Exploring leisure needs of the aged. *Leisurability,* 1977, *4*(4), pp. 25-31.

Seleen, D. The congruence between actual and desired use of time by older adults: A predictor of life satisfaction. *Gerontologist,* 1982, *22*(1), pp. 95-99.

Sidney, K.H., and Shepherd, R.J. Activity patterns of elderly men and women. *Journal of Gerontology,* 1977, *32,* pp. 25-32.

Spotlight on older Americans. *U.S. News and World Report,* January 2, 1984, p. 53.

U.S. Bureau of the Census. *Statistical Abstract of the United States: 1981.* Washington, D.C.: U.S. Government Printing Office, 1981.

Verhoven, P.J. Recreation and aging. In T.A. Stein and H.D. Sessoms (Eds.), *Recreation and special populations* (2nd ed.). Boston, MA: Holbrook Press, 1977.

Ward, R.A. The meaning of voluntary association participation to older people. *Journal of Gerontology,* 1979, *34*(3), pp. 438-445.

Weiskopf, D.C. *Recreation and leisure: Improving the quality of life* (2nd ed.). Boston, MA: Allyn and Bacon, 1982.

You're never too old for exercise, AMA study finds. *Chico Enterprise Record,* August 23, 1984.

Chapter 2

Recreation Leadership Principles

INTRODUCTION

The leadership and program planning competencies discussed in the next two chapters were identified through a multi-phased process (Leitner, 1978): (1) an exhaustive review of literature on the topic of recreation and aging; (2) a Nominal Group Technique Meeting of five experts in the area of recreation and aging; and (3) a survey of 42 personnel engaged in the provision of recreational services for elders in the Washington, D.C. Metropolitan area. Therefore, the competencies presented in these chapters reflect the concerns of practitioners as well as educators and researchers.

Leadership and program competencies specific to particular settings are discussed in the chapters on senior day care centers, nursing homes, and senior centers and clubs. The next two chapters focus on skills germaine to work in most settings for recreational programs for elders.

This chapter focuses on the acquisition of competencies or skills needed in order to effectively *lead* recreational activities with elders. Most of the leadership skills discussed in this chapter are presented in the following format: (1) a statement of the skill or competency; (2) a problem situation related to the skill; and (3) examples of solutions to the problem, incorporating knowledge related to the skill or competency. This problem-solving approach is utilized in order to facilitate skill acquisition.

The following is a list of learning objectives for this chapter:

LEARNING OBJECTIVES

1. Understand the basic principles of group work with elders.
1.1 Plan, construct, and maintain activity groups.
1.2 Demonstrate the ability to communicate accurately, effec-

tively, and concisely, both orally and in writing, to program participants and staff.

1.3 Provide the opportunity for social development among program participants.

1.4 Modify activities appropriately to facilitate the involvement of participants with a wide range of physical and mental abilities.

2. Effectively motivate older adults to participate in program activities.

2.1 Use of touch, and other non-verbal communication techniques to motivate the participants.

2.2 Use of verbal communication techniques to motivate the participants.

2.3 Ability to foster a positive self-image within the older adult.

2.4 Use of the remotivation technique.

3. Effectively implement the daily program or schedule.

3.1 Assistance in daily activities, such as lunch and transportation.

3.2 Ability to perform effectively in *leading* various activities.

3.3 Ability to perform effectively in *teaching* activity skills.

COMPETENCIES

I. Understand the Basic Principles of Group Work with Elders

1.1 Plan, Construct, and Maintain Activity Groups

In most settings for recreation services for elders, many activities are conducted on a group basis. Therefore, the recreation leader must know how to effectively initiate new activity groups and foster the success and continuation of a group over a period of time.

Situation. The supervisor has suggested a new activity to be initiated at the center, a singing group. A group must be initiated which will meet and rehearse at least once a week for twelve weeks. The objectives of the group are enjoyment and improved performance in singing. Describe how to approach planning, developing, and maintaining this singing group.

Solution. In planning the group, the concept or theme of the group should appeal to the needs and interests of the group. For instance, at a Veteran's Home or Hospital where patriotic feelings are more prevalent, the group could be called "Singing Patriots." The group could concentrate on singing patriotic standards such as "God Bless America." On the other hand, if the participant population is primarily Jewish then the group should focus on singing Yiddish or Hebrew songs. The key factor in initiating the group is to attract participants to the group by centering the group's activities to the needs and interests of the target population.

In developing the group, it is essential to have a leader of the group, someone who will see that cohesiveness in the group is maintained and progress in goal attainment (i.e., mastering songs) is achieved.

It is also important to consider the varying functioning or ability levels of group members. It is desirable to offer slower learners extra assistance or opportunity to practice, so that group progress is not inordinately slowed down. Also, lower ability participants can be matched with the highest functioning participants in order to receive assistance and also enhance the higher functioning participants' self-esteem by giving them a special role as "assistant." However, if the varying ability levels of participants is seriously straining the group, then it might be appropriate to divide the group into "beginning level" and "intermediate or advanced" level. Perhaps the two different groups can eventually sing together, with the beginners singing an easier harmony part to accompany the advanced singers who perform the more difficult lead part.

Positive reinforcement is an important consideration in maintaining activity groups. Participants should be praised for their efforts, and should be made aware of progress achieved in terms of goal attainment. Providing variety and challenge are also important considerations in ensuring that the group continues (e.g., new songs should frequently be presented, in addition to practicing and perfecting a small number of familiar songs).

In summary, some essential considerations in planning, developing, and maintaining activity groups are: (1) gear the group toward the interests and needs of the target population; (2) compensate for the varying ability levels of participants by either forming subgroups or developing a buddy system; (3) provide positive reinforcement to motivate group members to continue in the group; (4) present new challenges (e.g., new songs) often enough to prevent boredom from setting in; and (5) schedule the group to meet one or two times per week, often enough to maintain familiarity and interest, but not too often so as to become tiresome.

1.2 Demonstrate the Ability to Communicate Accurately, Effectively, and Concisely, Both Orally and in Writing, to Program Participants and Staff

Effective communication skills are vital in performing recreational work with any population. However, effective communication is especially challenging in working with elders, due to the prevalence of sensory deficits among elders.

Situation. A college class is scheduled to come to the center to lead a massage activity. Some of the program participants have considerable vision and/or hearing deficits. What methods of communicating this announcement can be utilized to compensate for the sensory impairments of the participants?

Solution. All of the following techniques should be utilized, as it is imperative to use a combination of verbal and written communication methods in order to compensate for the variety of sensory impairments of group members: (1) verbal announcement of the upcoming activity during lunch or some other large group activity; (2) posters prominently placed throughout the center, or announcements on a blackboard or display board; (3) verbal reminders to individual participants; and (4) personalized written invitations to participants.

In summary, it is important to use both written and verbal communication techniques, so as to combine the strengths and counteract the weaknesses inherent in each type of communication. Some helpful techniques to utilize to enhance the effectiveness of communication in working with elders are:

1. Whenever possible, determine if hearing is keener on one side than the other, and get as close to the better ear as possible when talking.
2. Maintain eye contact when talking and keep lips in plain view to facilitate lip reading.
3. Talk clearly, slowly, and loudly.
4. Keep explanations short and simple; whenever possible, provide an easily understood example. For instance, if one is trying to communicate that a massage activity will take place next week, perhaps briefly massage the person's hands so that the person understands what the activity will entail.
5. Write messages in large print.
6. Repeat both written and verbal messages numerous times. It is

especially important to repeat the message just before the activity.

7. Remember to ask for feedback, to ensure that the person really understood the message.

1.3 Provide the Opportunity for Social Development among Program Participants

A recreation program is often the only social outlet for an individual. Even non-verbal activities, such as dancing, can facilitate social development. Considerations such as the wearing of name tags and personal introductions of participants at the beginning of each activity can enhance the social aspects of activities.

Situation. Mr. X is one of the higher-functioning residents in his nursing home, yet he does not talk to other participants and tends to shy away from group activities, avoiding almost all social contact. How can this man's social interaction be improved?

Solution. First, it is important to understand the root causes of Mr. X's problem. Is he afraid of being embarrassed or looking foolish? Does he feel inadequate among others, or on the other hand, does he feel so superior to the others that he feels interacting with the other residents is "below his level?" Or, is it possible that none of the activities offered interest him? Action designed to foster Mr. X's social interaction should be based on the results of assessing the causes of the problem. This assessment can be accomplished by interviewing Mr. X and possibly also talking to his family. Nevertheless, there are some generally applicable techniques worth trying, regardless of the causes of the problem:

1. Encourage Mr. X to merely "try" an activity, stressing that he has the opportunity to leave the activity whenever he so desires.
2. Offer Mr. X some status which gives him higher self-esteem and encourages others to seek interaction with him. For example, ask Mr. X to be the leader's assistant for a particular activity.
3. Try to involve Mr. X in non-verbal activities which interest him, activities in which social interaction is *not* the main focus, but would be an important by-product. An example of such an activity is an exercise session.

In summary, remember that social interaction is as important for elders as people in any age group. Interaction should be encouraged in a gentle manner in order to avoid strong resistance by elders who tend to avoid social interaction.

1.4 Modify Activities Appropriately to Facilitate the Involvement of Participants With a Wide Range of Physical and Mental Abilities

In leading group activities, varying ability levels among participants can pose a special challenge.

Situation. A shuffleboard game is planned for ten participants. Four participants have no significant mental or physical impairments; two are blind; two are confused, but mobile; and two are wheelchair-bound and frail. Describe how to modify and conduct this activity to facilitate the involvement and enjoyment of all participants.

Solution. In a competitive game such as shuffleboard, the activity is most exciting and interesting to the participants when the players are of equal ability. When modifying a game the objective is to make the competition as even as possible. The activity leader and/or higher-functioning participants should help the lower-functioning participants as needed. For example, the blind participants should be guided to the starting line and be given a great deal of verbal feedback, but should push the disc independently. Meanwhile, the frail people should receive physical assistance in pushing the disc, or be allowed to begin from a closer position. The confused participants should receive a great deal of orientation to the game through demonstration.

Imagination is an important asset in appropriately modifying activities. Rules can be modified in a variety of ways. While it is desirable to make activities easier for lower-functioning participants, it is also important not to overly modify an activity, resulting in higher-functioning participants feeling frustrated.

2. Effectively Motivate Elders to Participate in Program Activities

2.1 Use of Touch and Other Non-Verbal Communication Techniques to Motivate the Participants

Although non-verbal techniques can be as effective as verbal motivational techniques, non-verbal techniques are oftentimes overlooked. The squeeze of a hand, a hug, or a kiss can be a great stimulant or reinforcer for a particular behavior. Also, smiles and laughter can provide a great deal of motivation.

Sincerity is essential in utilizing non-verbal techniques to motivate elders to participate in activities. Especially in working with impaired elders, one might play "favorites"—some confused elders might seem especially affectionate. However, it is important *not* to play favorites—even higher-functioning people crave attention. Also, remember that elders of different cultural/ethnic backgrounds respond differently to non-verbal techniques. Non-verbal techniques might *not* be appropriate in working with elders of certain cultural backgrounds, due to cultural norms in which physical contact is less accepted.

2.2 Use of Verbal Communication Techniques to Motivate the Participants

Elders who have experienced a loss of physical skills, the loss of a spouse, or have dealt with other difficult life changes can be especially difficult to motivate. These people can often potentially benefit the most from participating in activities. Another challenge the recreation leader often faces in attempting to motivate elders to participate in activities in their belief in the work ethic. Many elders view work as the most important life activity, and view recreational activity as meaningless. Thus, many elders do *not* wish to participate in recreational activities.

Do *not* coax, beg, threaten, or force an elder to participate in activity—treat elders with the respect they deserve. Emphasize the specific benefits of an activity related to the particular needs of an individual (e.g., in trying to convince an elder with back problems to participate in an exercise activity, emphasize the back flexibility improvements that can be gained from an exercise session). Personal invitations and providing leadership roles for people can help motivate them to participate in an activity. In addition, a brief demonstration of the activity or display of a finished product (e.g., for an art activity) can be a motivating factor. Another useful technique is to utilize peer influence to motivate participation. Determine who the "leaders" in a group are, and focus on obtaining the "leaders'" participation in the activity. Then, have the leaders attempt to motivate the others to join in.

Remember that lack of motivation is *not* the only reason for non-participation in an activity. Lack of interest can also be a major factor. It is important to distinguish between these two factors and determine the criteria necessary to induce participation for each individual.

2.3 Ability to Foster a Positive Self-Image Within the Older Adult

One's self-image is an important factor in motivation to participate in recreational activities. A low or negative self-image can lead a person to feel incompetent to participate in activities which in reality they could participate in and enjoy.

Situation. Mr. C is in excellent health, loves sports, but refuses to be involved in sports-related activities, claiming "I don't want to make a fool of myself." How should Mr. C be approached in attempting to get him involved in sports-related activities?

Solution.

1. Break-down the activity into component parts and sub-tasks. Allow Mr. C the opportunity to master each sub-task, and after feeling a sense of accomplishment in mastering the easier sub-tasks, encourage him to attempt the activity.
2. Involve Mr. C in the activity initially in a non-threatening, non-active role (e.g., scorekeeper) and focus on his expertise in the scorekeeper role.
3. Provide a great deal of sincere positive reinforcement for tasks performed well.
4. Allow Mr. C to reminisce about past sports accomplishments.
5. Try non-competitive sports in which all participants are winners.
6. Modify activities to ensure success (and a positive self-image).
7. Perhaps make the activity especially challenging. Have Mr. C "challenge the champ"—in this situation, there's nothing to lose, and simply playing against the best, win or lose, will enhance one's self-image.

In summary, enhancing self-image is not only important in attempting to motivate one to become involved in an activity, but is also an important by-product of participation in activities.

2.4 *Use of the Remotivation Technique* (Kohut, et al., 1979; Moran, 1979; Teaff, 1985)

Remotivation is a motivational technique appropriate for use in work with disoriented elders. The purposes of remotivation are to remotivate old interests, draw people out, and bring them closer in touch with reality. Remotivation helps to reduce feelings of isolation by providing opportunities for interaction with others.

The leader of a remotivation session is called the remotivator. The remotivator begins by choosing a topic to discuss. The range of topics is limitless (e.g., animals, seasons, baseball, desserts, flowers, dance, children, etc.). However, topic areas should not be sensitive ones which might arouse negative feelings (examples of inappropriate topics are politics, death and dying). The remotivator plays the role of the student by only asking questions concerning the topic and not supplying any answers to questions. The participants become the experts, supplying all the information. There are no right or wrong answers; all responses are accepted.

A remotivation session works well with a group of about eight persons. A session consists of five steps, each step lasting approximately ten minutes. Visual aids should be used whenever possible.

The five steps of a remotivation session are:

1. *Climate of acceptance.* The remotivator personally greets each member of the group, making everyone feel welcome. A warm, supportive atmosphere is created.

2. *Bridge to reality.* The remotivator begins by asking questions about a broad topic, then through questions and answers, narrows it down to the topic at hand. The remotivator then reads a relevant poem to the group (the poem can be original, already published, or taken from a song). The purpose of the poem is to create imagery and stimulate thought about the topic. The remotivator then asks questions about how the participants fit into the topic.

3. *Sharing the world we live in.* A bounce question can be asked (a question with no logical answer) to stimulate thought. An example of a bounce question is: How many drops of rain have ever fallen? The remotivator then asks the group members questions concerning personal experiences related to the topic.

4. *Appreciation of the world.* The remotivator asks questions

regarding the pros and cons of the topic. The participants are asked to relate the topic to other things in the world.

5. *Climate of appreciation.* The remotivator briefly reviews what has been said during the session, then personally thanks each person for attending.

The following are two sample remotivation sessions:

Sample Session #1
  I. *Topic:* Desserts
 II. *Props:* A bag of cookies or candy to share. Photographs of desserts from magazines.
III. *Steps:*
  A. *Climate of acceptance:* Personally greet all members of the group. Shake hands and talk briefly to each individual.
  B. *Bridge to reality:*
   1. *Broad questions:*
      a. What is your favorite part of a meal?
      b. Do you ever eat less food and try to save room for dessert?
      c. Which meal do you end with dessert?
   2. Pass around props to stimulate interest in the topic.
   3. *Poem:* "Savoy Truffle" by George Harrison
      Creme tangerine and montelimat,
      A ginger sling with a pineapple heart,
      A coffee dessert, yes you know it's good news,
      But you'll have to have them all pulled out after the savoy truffle.
      Cool cherry cream and a nice apple tart,
      I feel your taste all the time we're apart,
      Coconut fudge really blows down those blues,
      But you'll have to have them all pulled out after the savoy truffle.
      You might not feel it now
      But when the pain cuts through you're going to know and how,
      The sweat is gonna fill your head,
      When it becomes too much you'll shout aloud
      You know that what you eat you are,
      But what is sweet now turns so sour,
      We all know ob-la-di-bla-da,
      But can you show me where you are

4. *More specific questions:*
   a. What are your favorite desserts?
   b. Are there particular times of the day when you like to eat sweets?
   c. What beverage do you like to drink with dessert?
   d. What are the different types of desserts?
C. *Sharing the world we live in:*
   1. *Bounce question:* How many chocolate chips do you think you have ever eaten?
   2. *Personal experience questions:*
      a. Do you ever give sweets as a gift?
      b. Did you ever bake a birthday cake for someone?
      c. What is the most delicious dessert you make?
      d. What is your favorite kind of candy?
      e. What is your favorite flavor of ice cream?
      f. Are there any desserts you do not like?
D. *Appreciation of the world:*
   1. *Pros and cons:*
      a. How do you feel when you eat dessert?
      b. Do you ever eat dessert and wish you had not indulged?
      c. What are the good things about dessert?
      d. What are the bad things about dessert?
   2. *Relate the topic to other things in the world:*
      a. How do desserts affect your teeth?
      b. How do children feel when they eat desserts?
      c. How much money do you think is spent in the U.S. on sweets?
      d. How many people do you think are employed by companies and bakeries that make desserts?
E. *Climate of appreciation:* Review what has been said and thank each person for attending.

Sample Session #2
   I. *Topic:* Rain
   II. *Props:* A bucket of rain water.
            Umbrellas, rain jackets, and other rain apparel.
   III. *Steps:*
   A. *Climate of acceptance:* Personally greet all members of the group, shake hands and talk briefly to each individual.
   B. *Bridge to reality:*
      1. *Broad questions:*

    a. Did anyone have any trouble getting to the center today?
    b. What do you think of all the rain lately?
2. Pass around the bucket of rain water, and let everyone wet their hands in the water, in order to bring the participants closer in touch with the discussion topic. Also pass around the props as a visual aid.
3. *Poem:* "Rain" by John Lennon and Paul McCartney
    If the rain comes they run and hide their heads,
    They might as well be dead,
    If the rain comes.
    When the sun shines they slip into the shade,
    And sip their lemonade,
    When the sun shines,
    The weather's fine.
    I can show you that when it starts to rain,
    Everything's the same,
    I can show you.
    Can you hear me that when it rains and shines,
    It's just a state of mind,
    Can you hear me?
4. *More specific questions:*
    a. What other songs have been written about rain?
    b. What causes rain?
    c. Where are the rainiest places in the U.S.?
    d. What time of year does it rain the most?

C. *Sharing the world we live in:*
1. *Bounce question:* How many drops of rain fall in five minutes in an area of one square mile?
2. *Personal experience questions:*
    a. Has anyone ever had a flood in their house due to excessive rain?
    b. Do you enjoy going for a walk in the rain?
    c. Have you ever seen a rainbow?
    d. Do you ever wish the rain would turn to snow?
    e. When you stay indoors when it rains, what kinds of things do you like to do?
    f. Can you tell when it's going to rain?

D. *Appreciation of the world:*
1. *Pros and cons:*
    a. What are some of the good things about rain?
    b. What are some of the bad things about rain?

c. What activities are you prevented from doing when it rains?
d. How can rain be used productively?
e. How can rain be a destructive force?
2. *Relating the topic to other things in the world:*
a. How does the rain affect the traffic?
b. How do people dress when it's raining?
c. What happens to grassy fields when it doesn't rain for a long time?
d. How does rain affect football games and other outdoor sports events?
e. What happens to the reservoirs and dams when it rains a great deal?
E. *Climate of appreciation:* Review what has been said and thank each person for attending.

3. Effectively Implement the Daily Program or Schedule.

3.1 Assistance in Daily Activities, such as Lunch and Transportation

Regardless of the setting, most recreation programs for elders include the provision of lunch and/or other meals. In addition, transportation is an important consideration in conducting field trips. Therefore, assistance skills related to transportation and the provision of meals are very important in performing recreational work with elders.

Situation. A field trip has been planned to a museum which is located approximately thirty minutes away from the center. How can the travel time be utilized as "recreational" time?

Solution. There are numerous activities possible within the confines of a van. The following list identifies some feasible activities:

1. A sing-a-long, facilitated (if possible) by live musical accompaniment on a guitar or recorder flute, or taped music.
2. A musical jamboree, in which the riders play along on small rhythm instruments and kazoos.
3. A "name-that-tune" quiz game, which involves singing and guessing the names of songs.
4. Any type of verbal game, such as "license plate bingo", "20 questions", and trivia quizzes.
5. A discussion on a selected topic, perhaps current events, or a

review of the day's activities and discussion of upcoming activities.

6. An excellent activity for impaired elders is a remotivation session on a selected topic. Also appropriate might be a reality orientation activity, in which the riders are familiarized with their environment and oriented to time, place, and person.

7. A tape recording produced by the participants for a former staff member can be quite enjoyable, and the tape is usually greatly appreciated by the recipient.

8. Movement to music, utilizing taped or live music, and incorporating exercise which requires very little space, such as finger, hand, ankle, head, and neck exercises.

9. A music appreciation activity, requiring only taped music and closed windows.

In summary, many activities are possible while traveling. However, the opportunity to recreate during transit is often not utilized. The ride can be just as enjoyable as the field trip itself. Without recreation or stimulation in general, the riders might become so drowsy during the ride that they continue to be in a low energy state during the field trip.

Situation two. While observing the noontime meal, it is obvious that the program participants tend to eat quickly and do not interact. How can the mealtime be made more recreational?

Solution. Mealtime should be a very enjoyable time; some ideas for making meals more recreational are listed below:

1. Relaxing, pleasant music (live or recorded) will make the mealtime more enjoyable and relaxing.

2. A performance by staff, either dramatic or musical can transform the noon meal into a dinner theater.

3. A theme created for mealtime can stimulate the atmosphere of eating in a speciality cuisine restaurant. For example, Italian, Mexican, or French days can be simulated, in which the menu items are identified in both English and the foreign language, appropriate music is playing in the background, and props and decorations are placed in the dining area to create the desired atmosphere.

4. Discussion topics can be suggested or announced for the entire group, to encourage interaction among the "diners".

5. Assigned seating can be utilized as a mechanism for facilitating

conversation, seating elders together who might be most likely to engage in conversation. How frustrating it is to sit too far away from a friend to be able to converse during the meal!
6. An activity which requires group input, such as discussing possible topics or scripts to be utilized in an upcoming drama activity would not only be enjoyable but would also encourage interaction among the "diners".

Meals should not only be nutritional, but enjoyable too. As with transportation, mealtime is often not fully utilized as an opportunity for socialization and enjoyment, but can be a very recreational experience.

3.2 Ability to perform effectively in leading various activities

In order to effectively lead group activities, it is important to understand group dynamics and theories of leadership. These topics are described only briefly in this section; however, further reading on these topics is suggested (see the bibliography at the end of this chapter).

In terms of group dynamics and leadership theory, it is important to recognize the need for different leadership styles in different situations. For example, in leading a discussion group for high-functioning elders, the leader should be more laissez faire, allowing the participants to control or lead the activity themselves as much as possible. At the other extreme, the leader of a field trip for mentally impaired elders would need to be quite autocratic to ensure the safety of the participants. Although one might desire to be a "democratic" leader, maintaining a balance between exerting authority and allowing freedom, many situations might necessitate leadership which is either more laissez faire or autocratic.

In general, six steps should be followed in leading group activities:

1. The leader introduces herself and each person in the group.
2. Introduce the activity, using the introduction as an opportunity to arouse interest in the activity.
3. Explain the activity, providing clear step-by-step directions.
4. Demonstrate the activity with a few participants and ask for questions.
5. Conduct the activity.
6. End the activity *before* it becomes boring.

One additional consideration in leading group activities is the position of the leader in the group. A common mistake made by inexperienced recreation leaders is explaining an activity from the position of being in the center of a circle of participants. In this position, several participants will only see the leader's back. The activity leader should be a part of the circle, in a position from which the leader is facing all of the participants.

In summary, the quality of leadership in an activity is critical to the successfulness of an activity. Personality traits which are difficult to teach, such as genuine enthusiasm for the activity, and caring for group members are also important for a recreation leader to consider when leading a group activity.

3.3 Ability to perform effectively in teaching activity skills

Often in a recreational setting, a recreation worker not only leads activities, but also provides instruction in various recreational activity skills. In providing instruction, one must not lose sight of the "means" (the learning process) due to overly focusing on the end product (acquisition of activity skills). In other words, the method by which a person acquires skills can be just as enjoyable and rewarding as the actual acquisition of the skill(s) itself. Elders *can* and *do* learn new skills, although progress might sometimes be slower and more difficult to notice. Patience on the part of the recreation leader can greatly enhance the enjoyment of the learning process.

In order to enhance the learning process, the following considerations should be kept in mind:

1. Reassure participants who are having difficulty and give these people extra assistance.
2. Demonstrate techniques as much as possible, but try to keep explanations as brief as possible. Do *not* overload a person with verbal feedback.
3. Do not refer to written materials if possible, rather, try to focus attention on seeing how participants are progressing and assisting them as necessary.
4. If possible, post clearly visible directions or illustrations which are easy to refer to and can be helpful in trying to perfect a new skill.
5. Frequently ask for feedback and questions from participants.
6. Avoid frustration and fatigue from developing by taking periodic brief rest periods.

7. Discourage competitiveness; learning should be individualized. However, periodically observing other participants can be helpful in two ways and should be encouraged. First, observation of others also having difficulty learning the skill will prove reassuring to a struggling participant that they're not the only one having difficulty. Conversely, observing participants performing well can serve as motivation and an instructional aid for participants attempting to learn a new activity.

8. Volunteers can also be very helpful in teaching activity skills, especially with a large group with diverse abilities. Volunteers can be used to provide individual assistance to group members who are having greater difficulty with skill acquisition.

In summary, remember that elders can acquire new skills, and the acquisition of new skills can be very enjoyable and rewarding. Individualized goal-setting in teaching new skills is desirable and can help to compensate for variance in the ability levels of participants.

BIBLIOGRAPHY

American Alliance for Health, Physical Education, and Recreation (AAHPER). Leisure today: Leisure and aging: New perspectives. *Journal of Physical Education and Recreation,* 1977, *48*(8), pp. 25-56.

Berryman, D.C., et al. *A modular training program for therapeutic recreation technician 1: The NTRS 750 hour curriculum.* Arlington, VA: National Recreation and Park Association, 1975.

Barrett, S.L. *Parties with a purpose: A handbook for activity directors.* Springfield, IL: C.C. Thomas, 1980.

Burnside, I.M. Formation of a group. In I.M. Burnside (Ed.), *Nursing and the aged.* New York: McGraw-Hill, 1976.

Burnside, I.M. *Working with the elderly.* Belmont, CA: Wadsworth Publishing Company, 1978.

Chan, D.C. Using patients as group leaders in a VA hospital (Program Briefs). *Hospital and Community Psychiatry,* 1973, *24*(8), p. 531.

Deichman, E.S., and O'Kane, C.P. (Eds.). *Working with the elderly: A training manual.* Buffalo, NY: D.O.K. Publishing Co., 1975, pp. 12-14; 66-109.

Fish, H.U. *Activities program for senior citizens.* West Nyack, NY: Parker Publishing Co., 1971, pp. 47-58; 59-66; 77-197.

Forman, M. Conflict, controversy, and confrontation in group work with older adults. *Social Work,* 1967, *12*(1), pp. 80-85.

Harbin, E.O. *The fun encyclopedia.* Nashville, TN: Abingdon Press, 1940.

Jacobs, B. *Working with the impaired elderly.* Washington, D.C.: National Council on Aging, 1976.

Kohut, S., Kohut, J.J., and Fleishman, J.J. *Reality orientation for the elderly.* Oradell, NJ: Medical Economics Company, 1979.

Kraus, R. *Recreation today.* New York: Appleton-Century-Crofts, 1966, pp. 52-66; 72-73; 160-168; 172-174.

Kubie, S.H., and Landau, G. *Group work with the aged.* New York: Greenwood Press, 1971, pp. 63-190.

Leitner, M.J. A competency-based in-service training program for entry-level personnel in leisure services for the aged. Unpublished master's thesis, University of Maryland, 1978.

Lucas, C. *Recreation in gerontology.* Springfield, IL: C.C. Thomas, 1964, pp. 14-26; 121-172.

Merril, T. *Activities for the aged and infirm.* Springfield, IL: C.C. Thomas, 1967, pp. 7-10; 21-24; 192-260; 263-341.

Michelle, M. How to work with older people. *Geriatric Nursing,* January/February, 1966.

Moran, J.M. *Leisure activities for the mature adult.* Minneapolis, MN: Burgess Publishing Company, 1979.

National Remotivation Technique Organization
Research and Education Blvd.
Philadelphia State Hospital
1400 Roosevelt Blvd.
Philadelphia, PA 19114

Niepoth, E.W. *Leisure leadership: Working with people in recreation and park settings.* Englewood Cliffs, NJ: Prentice-Hall, 1983.

O'Morrow, G.S. *Therapeutic recreation: A helping profession.* Reston, VA: Prentice-Hall, 1976, pp. 152-156.

Perlman, B., Weinstein, A., and Compton, J. Group with the elderly in a community center. *Journal of Geriatric Psychiatry,* 1976, *9,* pp. 89-91.

Shivers, J.S., and Fait, H.F. *Recreational service for the aging.* Philadelphia: Lea and Febiger, 1980.

Teaff, J.D. *Leisure services with the elderly.* St. Louis, MO: C.V. Mosby Company, 1985.

Toepfer, C.T., Bicknell, A.T., and Shaw, D.O. Remotivation as behavior therapy. *Gerontologist,* 1974, *14*(5), pp. 451-453.

U.S. Department of Health, Education, and Welfare, (DHEW). *Working with older people* (volume 3). Washington, D.C.: U.S. Government Printing Office, 1970, pp. 3; 7-14.

Vickery, F.E. *Creative programming for older adults: A leadership training guide.* New York: Assoc. Press, 1972.

Wapner, E.B. *Recreation for the elderly.* Great Neck, NY: Todd and Honeywell, 1981.

Chapter 3

Program Planning Principles

INTRODUCTION

This chapter focuses on the acquisition of skills or competencies needed to effectively plan recreation programs for elders. The chapter begins with a list of competencies followed by a discussion of these competencies. Similar to the previous chapter, a problem-solving approach has been utilized in discussing many of the competencies.

LEARNING OBJECTIVES

1. Identify and understand the needs, abilities, and interests of program participants.
　1.1 Develop an awareness of recreational activities which can meet the need for recognition, achievement, and intellectual stimulation.
　1.2 Develop an awareness of the special needs and interests of various ethnic and racial groups.
　1.3 Develop an awareness of the effects of variation in social economic status on the needs and interests of program participants.
2. Effectively utilize resources which can enhance recreational activities and programs.
　2.1 Solicit contributory services from appropriate agencies (awareness of community resources).
　2.2 Solicit volunteer assistance for activities.
　2.3 Effectively supervise and coordinate a volunteer program.
3. Plan an appropriate program of recreational activities.
　3.1 Develop an awareness and understanding of program goals and objectives.

3.2 Solicit input from program participants in program planning.

3.3 Plan appropriate, stimulating field trips.

3.4 Devise daily, weekly, and/or monthly activity schedules.

COMPETENCIES

1. Identify and Understand the Needs, Abilities, and Interests of Program Participants

1.1 Develop an Awareness of Recreational Activities Which Can Meet the Need for Recognition, Achievement, and Intellectual Stimulation

Recognition, achievement, and intellectual stimulation are important needs for most people, including elders. These needs are fulfilled through work activities for many people. However, it is especially important to allow elders the opportunity to meet these needs through recreational activities, because most participants in a recreation program for senior citizens are likely to be retired. Feelings of achievement, recognition, and intellectual stimulation are benefits of a variety of recreational activities.

Situation. Many of the program participants are recently retired from prestigious jobs, and in order to compensate for this role loss, there exists a need to plan activities which will give these people feelings of achievement, recognition, and intellectual stimulation.

Solution. Some recreational activities which can generate feelings of *achievement* are:

1. Goal-oriented recreational activities, such as arts and crafts projects.
2. Skill acquisition recreational activities, such as learning a new sport, craft, musical instrument, or dance.
3. Recreational activities with long-range goals, such as a twenty mile/month walking club or a weight reduction program.

Some recreational activities which can generate feelings of *recognition* are:

1. A resident council or membership committee in which elected officers (president, vice president, etc.) receive recognition.

2. A monthly newsletter in which achievements of participants and their family members are announced.
3. Celebrate milestones such as birthdays and anniversaries.
4. A monthly awards ceremony in which participants receive recognition for accomplishments such as charitable donations, assistance with activities, and progress made in weight reduction or exercise programs. Be sure to give recognition in a meaningful way to *every* participant.

Some examples of *intellectually stimulating* activities are:

1. Foreign language classes.
2. Creative writing activities.
3. Current events discussions.
4. Intergenerational activities in which elders share knowledge with children or even tutor the children in subjects (e.g., history).
5. Creative drama activities.

In summary, achievement, recognition, and intellectual stimulation are important needs which can be met through recreational activities. The fulfillment of these needs will enhance the psychological well-being and overall life satisfaction of program participants.

1.2 Develop an Awareness of the Special Needs and Interests of Various Ethnic and Racial Groups

Situation. The program participants are quite ethnically and racially diverse. It is desirable to foster social interaction among all participants, but the problem of deep-rooted prejudices among the program participants exists.
Solution.

1. First, staff should not deny that the problem exists. Elders grew up in a different era in which prejudice was more prevalent and accepted, thus prejudice can often be more common among program participants than staff.
2. Coercion, or forced attitude change is *not* a solution. Such an approach will most likely cause resentment.
3. Staff should encourage interaction among participants in an unobtrusive manner. Cooperative activities, such as a large-

scale arts and crafts project, and group activities, such as singing or exercise can often be so involving and stimulating that
prejudices are temporarily forgotten, barriers are broken, and
interaction occurs among all participants of the activity, regardless of race or ethnic background.
4. Prejudicial remarks should be confronted immediately in order
   to discourage this type of behavior or attitude.
5. Plan activities which give recognition to various racial and ethnic groups and also help to educate participants about positive
   contributions of that group. For example, a discussion on
   famous Black Americans, a Latin music appreciation session,
   or an entertainment/comedy half hour featuring famous Jewish
   comedians would not only be enjoyable, but would also make
   the participants appreciate the special contributions of these
   ethnic, racial, and religious groups.

In summary, attitude change in the area of prejudice can be quite
difficult. The most effective approach for a recreation leader is to
plan enjoyable activities which include non-threatening interaction
among all participants, and also educate participants about different
groups through recreational activities.

*1.3 Develop an Awareness of the Effects of Variation in Social
Economic Status on the Needs and Interests of Program
Participants.*

Variation in social economic status is an important factor influ-
encing recreational needs and interests. The participants of recreation programs in nursing homes, adult day care centers, and senior
centers and clubs often vary greatly in terms of educational background and economic status.

Situation. Most of the program participants have never attended
college, in fact, many never completed high school. One of the new
participants is a retired lawyer. This new participant is *not* becoming involved in the activities offered or even socializing with other
program participants, because he feels "above" everyone else.

Solution.

1. Encourage the ex-lawyer to utilize his superior educational
   background constructively. This man could initiate and lead a
   new weekly or daily "legal advice" session, in which he

would help participants with legal questions or problems. Alternatively, he could prepare presentations or discussions on selected legal topics. Such activities would give recognition to and utilize the ex-lawyer's superior educational background and also involve the man in interaction with other participants. Hopefully, once the man has talked with other participants, barriers will be broken down, common interests will be discovered, and he will become more involved in program activities.

2. Provide other leadership roles for the ex-lawyer, such as involvement in planning program activities and assisting in leading discussion groups.

On the other hand, the special needs of participants with a very limited educational background must be considered. Confusion during activities due to an inability to understand written or verbal instructions should not be misinterpreted as disorientation or senility.

Similarly, variation in economic status of the participants needs to be considered, especially for field trip activities where there is a cost. A small amount of petty cash should be allocated in the budget to pay for field trips and other activities for which some participants would not be able to afford.

2. Effectively Utilize Resources Which can Enhance Recreational Activities and Programs

2.1 Solicit Contributory Services From Appropriate Agencies (Awareness of Community Resources)

Situation. The activity leader is trying to think of new activity ideas, but it seems as if all activity ideas have been exhausted. What community agencies or businesses could provide recreational activities for the program?

Solution. The following list identifies some community resources and ideas for recreational activities.

1. Local *florists* could present a flower show, or provide an activity on flower arranging.
2. The local *police* department could send a representative to make a presentation on crime prevention; the local *fire* de-

partment could send a representative to discuss fire prevention.

3. The local *humane society, pet stores,* and *dog fanciers clubs* could provide puppies, birds, or other animals for a pet show or pet grooming activity.
4. *Ministers* from local *churches* could lead bible reading or discussions on holidays and other topics.
5. *Arts and crafts* stores could provide demonstrations.
6. Local *dance studios* could schedule a performance (perhaps bring a children's class to perform).
7. Local *pharmacies* might be interested in leading discussions on drug use.
8. Local *clothing stores* could plan a fashion show.
9. The local *public library* can provide large print books for leisurely reading, films for free rental, and book discussions.
10. *Travel agencies* are often willing to present slide shows on travel to foreign countries.
11. Local *restaurants, bakeries,* or *bakers' supply stores* can present a cooking or baking demonstration or class.
12. Local *beauty supply stores* or *cosmetologists* can present a display or demonstration of beauty products.
13. Local *hospitals, doctors, dentists,* and *nurses* can lead discussions on health-related topics.
14. Youth organizations such as *boy scouts* and *campfire girls* might be interested in joining with the program participants for special holiday celebrations and other intergenerational activities.
15. Local *universities and community colleges* can be helpful in many areas.
    a . *Professors* in fields such as *history, political science,* and *health education* can lead discussions on topics of interest to program participants.
    b. *Students* from the *recreation* or *community services* department can plan and lead a variety of activities.
    c. Students from the *music* department could be invited to perform.
    d. *Art* students could lead an art activity, or demonstrate art techniques.
    e. *Students clubs and organizations* might be interested in doing a presentation or demonstration. For example, a *folk dance club* might be interested in performing, or a

foreign students organization might be interested in leading a discussion on life in foreign countries.

16. A *horticulture group or club* could conduct a gardening class.
17. An *agricultural organization* could present an informational
    discussion on farming.
18. *Ecological or environmental groups* could lead discussions
    on the environment or perhaps lead a nature walk.
19. Local *historical societies* or *clubs* could make presentations
    on a variety of topics.
20. *Hobby clubs* could be called on to present fascinating dis-
    plays. For example:
    a. An *antique collectors club* or *antique automobile collec-
       tors club* could bring a display of their collections.
    b. A *stamp* or *coin collectors club* could bring a display and
       present information on collecting stamps and/or coins.
    c. A *bridge club* might be interested in teaching a "bridge
       for beginners" class.
    d. A *photography club* could present a lecture on the art of
       photography and display some outstanding photographs.
    e. A *martial arts club* might be willing to schedule a demon-
       stration.
21. The local *Chamber of Commerce* will be able to provide in-
    formation on most of the aforementioned resources, as well
    as other potential program resources.

In summary, there are a large number of potential program
resources available in most communities. These resources should be
utilized fully in order to provide as diverse a program as possible.

2.2 Solicit Volunteer Assistance for Activities

Volunteer assistance is essential in order to conduct activities
such as field trips which require a great deal of supervision. Solicitation of volunteers should be an ongoing process, as volunteers tend
to have a high turnover rate. The following is a list of organizations
to contact for volunteers:

1. Local universities and community colleges, in particular,
   Departments of Recreation and Leisure Studies, Gerontology,
   Community Services, and Physical Education should be con-
   tacted. These departments might be able to offer volunteers

through regular classes, students required to accumulate field work experience hours, or internship students who are required to work full-time for one semester.

2. Local high schools might be able to provide some motivated student volunteers.

3. The state or area agency on aging can often refer elders who wish to do volunteer work.

4. Fraternities and sororities often seek to provide voluntary assistance for worthy community causes.

5. Local churches often provide some volunteers for programs.

6. Service groups such as Lions or Eagles might be able to provide some volunteers for the program.

7. A notice in local newspapers along with a brief description of volunteer opportunities available can be very helpful in attempting to recruit volunteers.

2.3 Effectively Supervise and Coordinate a Volunteer Program

During the initial interview with a volunteer, administer a questionnaire to determine interests and abilities, and subsequently direct the volunteer in those directions. Explain the goals and philosophy of the program and arrange a work schedule.

Expose the volunteer to all facets of the program, including field trips, staff meetings, program planning, and leading or co-leading diverse activities. Also establish a one-on-one relationship between the volunteer and one participant for the purpose of meeting on a regular basis to form a working relationship.

To maintain continuity in the program, keep in close contact with the volunteer by meeting on a regular basis to discuss concerns or problem areas. Another effective means of promoting a cohesive volunteer program is to organize meetings for all volunteers to meet as a group periodically (every two or three weeks) to share experiences. This group interchange can be both educational and motivational.

Volunteers should receive recognition for their work, both daily and also in special ways. For example, an annual or once a semester "awards banquet" for volunteers can be an excellent way to provide recognition to volunteers.

The volunteer coordinator should keep a record of each volunteer's time schedule for future reference. The coordinator should be cognizant of giving recognition and support to volunteers since they are working mainly for intrinsic purposes.

Situation. A volunteer, when not assigned to a specific activity, loafs around the center and does not get involved in activities.

Solution. First of all, volunteers should receive a job description when they begin work, in order to clarify in writing exactly what is expected of volunteers. However, some volunteers may have less initiative than others and require more direction from the staff. The volunteer coordinator should be prepared to direct the volunteer to specific tasks in the event that all activities are being led by other personnel.

Volunteers can experience a greater sense of commitment and responsibility if they have their own individual projects to work on during their free time at the center. Various projects assigned to each volunteer to be worked on during their unscheduled time can enhance the volunteers' feelings of achievement and creativity. Volunteer projects can include:

1. Planning a special field trip, including making phone calls, transportation arrangements, advertising, and visiting the site prior to the trip to ensure accessibility for the handicapped.
2. Working one-on-one with a participant writing a biography, letter, journal, etc.
3. Researching a specific area of interest (e.g., art, music, dance therapy for the elderly, etc.) and presenting an in-service training session to the staff.
4. Preparing a special event at the center and making the necessary arrangements (e.g., guest speakers, holiday celebrations, theme events such as a Mardi Gras or European Appreciation Day, etc.).
5. Creating a special bulletin board in honor of a particular participant and working with that individual and/or family members to gather memorabilia to present.
6. Write and/or collect articles from staff and/or participants for a monthly newsletter.

In summary, a volunteer program can be a great advantage to a facility. Keeping lines of communication open between coordinator and volunteer and allowing the volunteer a creative working environment can greatly enhance the volunteer's experience.

3. Plan an Appropriate Program of Recreational Activities

3.1 Develop an Awareness and Understanding of Program Goals and Objectives

It is important to understand the goals and objectives of the agency in general and the recreation program in particular in order to have a clear philosophy to guide program planning efforts. Careful attention should be paid to ensure that program activities are supportive of, and not in opposition to program goals and objectives.

Some goals which usually apply to most recreation programs for elders are:

1. Activities should be enjoyable and emotionally satisfying.
2. Activities should be participated in by free choice.
3. A varied program of activities should be presented.
4. Social interaction among participants should be encouraged.
5. Physical, mental, and emotional benefits of activities should be maximized. Recreational activities should facilitate improvements in or maintenance of physical and mental functioning and/or promote developmental growth.
6. Maximal involvement in activities should be encouraged.
7. Maintenance of activities of daily living (e.g., dressing, eating, etc.)

3.2 Solicit Input From Program Participants in Program Planning

Program participants can often offer very useful input in program planning. The following are some techniques which can be utilized for obtaining participants' input in program planning.

1. A resident council or participants executive committee can be formed. This body can meet on a regular basis, perhaps without the presence of staff to ensure the independence of this body. The president and vice president of this committee could then represent the participants at staff program planning meetings.
2. Ask participants for feedback on specific activities. For example, if a luncheon outing is being planned, ask for suggestions from all participants on what restaurant to patronize.
3. Hold a monthly or weekly activity in which past activities are reviewed and discussed, and participants have the opportunity

to vote for their "favorite activities" in order to give staff feedback on participants' enjoyment of activities. Such an activity will aid staff in deciding which activities to repeat in the next program period.

4. Ask participants for feedback individually, so that peer pressure does not influence their responses.
5. Written questionnaires could be administered to participants in order to obtain unbiased feedback. However, not all participants might be capable or inclined to complete a written questionnaire.

Regardless of the successfulness of efforts to solicit participant input in program planning, participants will appreciate the opportunity to provide input and will be likely to enjoy activities more, knowing that they were consulted in the program planning process. Therefore, efforts should be made to solicit participant input, even if these efforts seem frustrating at times.

3.3 Plan Appropriate, Stimulating Field Trips

Field trips are potentially the most enjoyable, memorable activities and yet can also be the most disastrous activities. Many elders (especially nursing home residents) rarely have the opportunity to travel to see new places or simply experience a change of environment, thus field trips can be especially rewarding. However, when working with more impaired elders, special precautions must be taken to avoid problems. Some suggested precautions are:

1. Try to enlist enough staff and volunteers on the trip so that each wheelchair bound, blind, and confused participant has their own individual assistant. If adequate staffing is not possible, but many of the participants are mobile and alert, pair those participants in need of assistance with a high functioning participant. If either option is not possible, the number of participants who go on the trip should be limited in order to ensure the safety of all who do go on the trip.
2. Bring extra wheelchairs if the trip involves substantial walking and/or standing. Some of the mobile participants might become tired and prefer to be in a wheelchair for at least part of the time.
3. Be sure to make the ride to the destination recreational to avoid

having a van full of drowsy people upon arrival at the destination.

4. Check in advance if the facility is accessible for the handicapped, and if parking close to the facility is available. Also, ask about senior citizens discounts.
5. Allow extra time at each end for loading and unloading the vehicle.
6. Encourage participants to wear identification/name plates. In the event confused participants stray from the group, they could be more readily identified and returned to the group. In addition, if all members of the group are wearing identification which includes the program name, people in the community will be made more aware of the program.

The following are some ideas for field trips:

1. A luncheon at a nearby restaurant.
2. A dinner theater.
3. A day at a race track.
4. A tour of a museum.
5. A tour of a local television station.
6. A picnic and walk in a nearby park.
7. A shopping trip to a nearby mall.
8. A trip to a nearby beauty shop.
9. A matinee at the movies.
10. A visit to a local elementary school or preschool, to either observe a performance, or participate in a joint activity.
11. A trip to a local festival or fair.
12. An afternoon at the bowling alley.
13. A trip to see a sporting event (professional or collegiate).
14. A home or hospital visit to an ill or recuperating program participant.
15. A trip to another senior center for a joint activity.
16. A trip to the library to borrow books for individuals and/or the center.
17. A trip to the voting polls to give the participants the opportunity to vote in elections.
18. A trip to a nearby historical site.

In summary, there are numerous appropriate, stimulating field trip options. If the necessary precautions are taken, field trips can be very rewarding activities.

3.4 Devise Daily, Weekly, and/or Monthly Activity Schedules

Because of advance notice often needed in order to arrange special events and field trips, it is advisable to plan activities on a monthly basis, with more detailed daily activity schedules (structured around the special events and field trips) printed either weekly or bi-weekly. Daily activity schedules should be posted throughout the center or nursing home, and a schedule of staff assignments should be posted prominently so that all staff and participants will know where to locate a particular staff member in case of emergency. Some guidelines to follow in devising daily activity schedules are:

1. Always offer more than one activity simultaneously in order to provide a distinct choice for participants (e.g., if the main activity is physically or mentally demanding then the alternate activity should be more passive).
2. Passive and active recreation should be interspersed. Do not plan more than two consecutive physically active or sedentary activities in order to prevent fatigue and drowsiness.
3. Physically active recreation should not immediately follow lunch.
4. Cognitively demanding activities should be scheduled in the morning, because people tend to be most alert before lunch.
5. Exercise sessions for impaired elders should last only thirty minutes or less in duration, and should be offered twice a day (once in the morning, and once in the afternoon).
6. The schedule should allow for transition time for staff between activities, to allow staff to adequately prepare for activities and clean-up after activities.
7. In general, activities should last for no longer than 45 minutes, due to the limited attention span of most people.
8. Try to schedule at least one special or main activity each day, something for participants to look forward to and talk about afterward.
9. Most importantly, activities should be scheduled which meet specific goals and objectives of the program.

In summary, activity schedules should follow the aforementioned guidelines and be posted in numerous places in order to remind participants and staff of the day's activities. Although flexibility is sometimes desirable, the schedule provides structure for each day which facilitates the smooth operation of the program.

BIBLIOGRAPHY

American Alliance for Health, Physical Education, and Recreation (AAHPER). Leisure today: Leisure and aging: New perspectives. *Journal of Physical Education and Recreation,* 1977, *48*(8), pp. 25-56.

Avedon, E.M. *Therapeutic recreation.* Englewood Cliffs, NJ: Prentice-Hall, 1974, pp. 106-109.

Babic, A.L. The older volunteer: Expectations and satisfactions. *Gerontologist,* 1973, *13*(52), pp. 87-90.

Barrett, S.L. Parties with a purpose: A handbook for activity directors. Springfield, IL: C.C. Thomas, 1980.

Beverly, E.V. Creative approaches to the fulfilling use of leisure time. *Geriatrics,* 1975, *30*(12), pp. 86; 90; 92-94.

Binstock, R.H., and Shanas, E. (Eds.). *Handbook of aging and the social sciences.* New York: Van Nostrand Reinhold Co., 1976.

Birren, J.E., and Schaie, K.W. (Eds.). *Handbook of the psychology of aging.* New York: Van Nostrand Reinhold Co., 1977.

Boyack, V.L. (Ed.). *Time on our hands.* Ethel Percy Andrus Gerontology Center, Los Angeles: University of Southern California, 1973.

Fish, H.U. *Activities program for senior citizens.* West Nyack, NY: Parker Publishing Co., 1971, pp. 19-31.

Ginsburg, I. Therapeutic recreation: A modality for rehabilitation of the aged. *Therapeutic Recreation Journal,* 1974, *8,* pp. 42-46.

Jacobs, B. *Senior centers: Options and actions.* Washington, D.C.: National Council on Aging (NCOA), 1975.

Leanse, J., Tiven, M., and Robb, T.B. *Senior center operation.* Washington, D.C.: NCOA, 1977.

Maynard, M. Achieving emotional well-being for the aged through leisure programs. *Therapeutic Recreation Journal,* 1974, *8,* pp. 64-71.

Merril, T. *Activities for the aged and infirm.* Springfield, IL: C.C. Thomas, 1967, pp. 15-21; 25-32.

National Council on Aging. *Program planning: A guide to accountability, credibility, and trust.* Washington, D.C.: NCOA, 1975.

Pierce C.H. Recreation for the elderly: Activity participation at a senior citizens center. *Gerontologist,* 1975, *15,* pp. 202-205.

Rowthorn, A.W. The American style of aging. *Therapeutic Recreation Journal,* 1974, *8,* pp. 34-37.

Shivers, J.S., and Fait, H.F. *Recreational service for the aging.* Philadelphia: Lea and Febiger, 1980.

Vickery, F.E. *Creative programming for older adults: A leadership training guide.* New York: Assoc. Press, 1972.

Wapner, E.B. *Recreation for the elderly.* Great Neck, NY: Todd and Honeywell, 1981.

Chapter 4

Program Evaluation

INTRODUCTION

The purpose of this chapter is to provide information which can be utilized to enhance program evaluation efforts. The chapter begins with a discussion of the purposes of evaluation and an overview of evaluation methods. The chapter then focuses on considerations and procedures in two particular evaluation methods, interviewing and behavior observation.

PURPOSES OF EVALUATION

According to Theobald (1979), evaluation of recreation programs is important for several reasons:

1. Evaluation data is needed to justify funding and allocation of resources for a program;
2. Evaluation data is needed to determine if program goals and objectives are being met;
3. Evaluation data can point to needed program changes;
4. Evaluation data can provide insight into the relative effectiveness of different types of recreational activities in meeting program goals and objectives; and
5. Evaluation can provide objective feedback for staff on the effectiveness of their programs.

EVALUATION METHODS

There are several different methods for collecting evaluation data:

1. Unobtrusive observation and notation of statistics such as: the number of participants in an activity; the percentage of residents or center attendees that choose to participate in an activity; the number of participants who arrive to an activity more than five minutes early, or leave the activity more than five minutes early; and the time duration and frequency of the activity.
2. Written questionnaires completed by program participants on their attitudes toward activities, as well as questionnaires to assess the impact of a program on variables such as life satisfaction and perceived health.
3. Oral interviews with program participants, in order to assess attitudes and the effects of a program on life satisfaction, perceived health, and other variables.
4. Behavior observation by independent, unbiased observers, in order to assess participants' enjoyment of activities or other variables.

Each of the aforementioned techniques has particular advantages and disadvantages. The questionnaires and interviews have the advantage of directly assessing variables whereas observational methods are less direct and more prone to inaccurate interpretations. However, observational methods have the advantage of being less obtrusive and less likely to generate biased responses from participants than interviews and questionnaires.

Written questionnaires have the advantage of being less costly, less time consuming, and therefore easier to administer to large numbers of people than the other methods. Unfortunately, when working with impaired elders, written questionnaires are often not feasible. Therefore, in order to evaluate recreation programs for impaired elders, interviews and behavior observation tend to be more effective. The remainder of this chapter will focus on considerations in interviewing impaired elders, and the use of behavior observation to assess elders' enjoyment of recreational activities.

Interviewing Impaired Elders

The JWK International Corporation (1978) discussed the problems of survey research methods with elders. One problem cited is the potential influence of others, particularly authority figures, on the results of a study.

Another problem cited by the JWK Corporation (1978) was short-term memory deficits commonly found among older adults. To compensate for this problem, the number of answer choices to questions should be limited, and an attempt should be made to ask questions which require recognition rather than recall. The authors also suggested that the use of technical language and elaborate scaling be avoided, and that although the interviewer should try to keep interviews on the topic of the questions, interviewees should *not* be interrupted excessively.

Faber and Leitner (1981) also discuss considerations in interviewing impaired elders, based on a study of the effects of an intergenerational music activities program on senior day care participants. The authors offer the following recommendations for interviewing impaired elders:

1. Questionnaires should be as short and simple as possible to compensate for deficiencies in cognitive functioning. A combination of closed-ended and open-ended questions seems to be most effective in that closed-ended questions are simple enough for most people to answer, while the open-ended questions allow more alert respondents an opportunity to fully express their feelings on a topic. Negative and positive statements should be interspersed in the closed-ended questions, in order to deter interviewees from simply answering yes (or no) to every question without really considering or understanding the meaning of each question.

2. Prior to initiating data collection, the interviewer should develop a rapport with the interviewees by engaging the interviewee in a conversation on any topic the interviewee feels comfortable discussing. Also, the interviewer should familiarize oneself with the interviewees by unobtrusively observing them during activities.

3. The interviewer should be an "outsider," not a staff member, in order to ensure that the results of the study are unbiased.

4. Interviews should be conducted in a quiet, isolated area. The interview setting should be free of sensory distractions and minimize the potential impact of peer influence on the interviewee's responses. As noted by Pastalan's Empathetic Model (1980), older adults expressed a marked inability to hear clearly in crowded areas where there is background noise. In fact, locating the source of various sounds was proven difficult in

that noise from across a room may seem to be coming from only a few feet away—the same distance from which the interviewer's voice originates. In addition, a secluded quiet area for interviews prevents peer pressure from affecting the interviewee's responses and also prevents interruptions from disturbing the interview.

5. The interviewer should have predetermined, standardized responses to requests for clarification of questions. Otherwise, variation in clarification of questions could cause the questions to be interpreted and answered in different ways. Thus, standardizing clarifications can further enhance the validity of the results.

6. The interviewer should introduce the purpose of the interview in vague terms, such as "we are seeking your input in attempting to improve the quality of recreation programs here" rather than specifically identifying what particular aspect of the program is being evaluated. If interviewees are informed of the specific objectives of the evaluation research, their responses might be biased, in an attempt to provide the interviewer with information the interviewee thinks the interviewer is seeking.

7. Periodically reorient interviewees to the subject of concern but do allow the interviewees to engage in some seemingly unrelated rambling and reminiscing. Occasionally, elders with impaired mental functioning are actually organizing their thoughts while engaging in apparently irrelevant discussion. Moen (1978) also noted that the expressed needs of older adults are often elicited during the course of conversation rather than in direct response to questions.

8. Do not dwell on negative comments such as "I wish I was dead," rather, acknowledge and gently accommodate such comments with a reassuring hand on the shoulder, sustained eye contact, and several concerned head nods. In order to renew interest in the topic of the interview, the interviewer might add: "I'm also interested to hear your responses to the questions on this survey. Would it be all right with you if we looked into some of these questions?" In this way, the needs of the interviewee are not ignored, but the interview is kept moving and eventually completed.

Although these suggestions will enhance data collection through interviewing, other data collection methods should be utilized in combination with interviews in order to obtain more valid data. The following section discusses the use of behavior observation in examining the effectiveness of recreation programs for elders.

Behavior Observation

There are several important considerations in using behavior observation in evaluating recreation programs for elders: the variable(s) to be examined; development of a behavior observation instrument; selection and training of behavior observers; establishment of inter-rater reliability among behavior observers; and procedures to follow in behavior observation.

Variable(s) to Be Examined

The variable(s) to be studied through behavior observation are determined by the criteria for evaluating the effectiveness of a program. For example, enjoyment of activities is typically an important criterion in evaluating a recreation program, in that enjoyment is a very essential goal of recreation. Therefore, observing and comparing enjoyment levels during different types of activities is one means of comparing the effectiveness of different types of recreation programs.

Instrument Development

Once the variable to be studied has been identified, behavioral indices for measuring the variable must be identified. The behavioral indices for a variable such as enjoyment will be different for different types of activities (e.g., musical activities versus art activities). A behavior rating form used in behavior observation should list the behavioral indices with space to note the frequency of occurrence of each behavior. Space should be left for comments and a numerical rating. Explicit instructions should be given for assigning numerical ratings based on the frequency of occurrence of the behavioral indices listed. Please refer to the behavior observation forms at the end of this chapter (Appendix A).

Selection and Training of Behavior Observers

As much as possible, behavior observers should have equal familiarity with the population to be observed before commencing data collection. Staff or others very familiar with the target population could use their knowledge to produce more accurate ratings, but are also prone to be more biased in their ratings than observers who are less familiar with the people to be observed. An effective alternative is to use observers who are unfamiliar with the population, because such observers will probably be less biased in their ratings. To compensate for their lack of familiarity with the people to be observed, the observers should undergo a thorough training period which not only involves practice behavior rating sessions, but also informal interaction with the population, not only to familiarize the observers with the people to be observed, but also to help make the people to be observed more at ease with the presence of the behavior observers. The training of the behavior observers should culminate in the establishment of a high rate (.75 or above) of inter-rater reliability before beginning data collection.

Inter-Rater Reliability

Inter-rater reliability refers to the percentage of agreement among behavior observers rating a particular individual or group (e.g. .75 reliability means that three of four raters obtained the same rating for a particular observation). During the training period for behavior observers, the trainees should observe the same individuals simultaneously, and then compare ratings. At least a .75 level of inter-rater reliability should be established before commencing data collection of an evaluation study.

Inter-rater reliability should be checked periodically throughout an evaluation study, in order to ensure that the behavior observers are still consistent in their rating procedures and interpretation of the rating scale. If the behavior observers are observing different people during the observation sessions, then the raters should also assign a numerical rating for the entire group. The data on group ratings could then be compared in order to examine inter-rater reliability. If inter-rater reliability is lower than .75 on two consecutive trials, then data collection should be suspended until the raters receive additional training and a .75 level of inter-rater reliability is reestablished.

Behavior Observation Procedures

When working with elders with some short-term memory loss, it is advisable to periodically remind the group of the *general* purpose of the observers' presence, in order to allay any fears or suspicions regarding the purpose of the observers' presence. However, the group being observed should *not* be informed of the specific hypotheses of the evaluation study, in order to prevent the elders being observed from biasing the results by attempting to provide the observers with hypothesis-confirming (or hypothesis-disconfirming) results. For example, if behavior observation is being conducted in order to evaluate if intergenerational music activities are more enjoyable than musical activities without children, the group can simply be told that the observers are observing activities in order to examine ways to improve the recreational activities program.

Behavior observers should be seated as part of or slightly outside of the activity formation (e.g., a circle) and perform minor tasks to facilitate their acceptance as a natural part of the activity setting. The observers should be interspersed throughout the group and *not* confer with each other during the activities being observed. The observers should be inconspicuous and avoid peering at the elders being observed. Paraphernalia such as clipboards which attract attention to the fact that observations are being conducted should not be used.

A critical factor in maintaining unbiased ratings is to ensure the observers' status of nonparticipant in activities. In addition, it should be stressed that the observer's own enjoyment of an activity should *not* influence their ratings. The ratings should reflect the observer's perception of an individual's or group's reaction to an activity.

A Research Example

In order to further clarify the aforementioned behavior observation considerations, an example of the use of behavior observation in an evaluation study will be discussed in-depth. Leitner (1981) utilized behavior observation in addition to interviewing in examining the effects of the presence of elementary school children on senior day care participants' enjoyment of musical activities. Thus, the variable examined in this study was enjoyment of activities. One group of senior day care participants were observed during activities with children for six weeks, and during activities without children for six weeks. Another group was observed for twelve weeks during activities without children. The behavior ratings for activities with children were compared to those for activities without children in order to assess the effects of the presence of children on the participants' enjoyment of activities.

Leitner (1981) developed a behavior rating form to be used by the observers in this study through a multi-phased process. First, a review of literature on behavior observation was conducted in order to gather information on behavioral indices of enjoyment. Senior day care personnel were also consulted in order to gain further insight into behavioral indices of enjoyment during musical activities. A draft version of the behavior rating form was then developed and sent to fifteen senior day care centers in Maryland for review by full-time personnel. Changes in the form were made based on the feedback from the senior day care personnel. Next, a panel of five researchers with expertise in behavior observation were consulted for further refinement of the form. Thus, the behavior-rating form was developed through a multi-phased process.

This particular study utilized four behavior observers, all of whom were students in either gerontology or recreation. The observers were oriented to methods and techniques of behavior observation, and to the physical, psychological, and social characteristics of senior day care participants.

A .75 level of inter-rater reliability was established on two consecutive practice trials before commencing data collection. Nine practice trials were conducted in which all four observers rated the same participant during an activity. Inter-rater reliability was checked throughout the study by noting the percentage of agreement on ratings of group enjoyment of activities. In this study, inter-rater reliability never fell below .75 on two consecutive trials.

Leitner (1981) noted that the involvement of observers in one of the activities biased the results of one session. The observers were unable to refuse participants' requests to dance with them during one activity, and the observers' participation in the activity appeared to affect the participants' enjoyment of the activity. The observation data for that particular session was not used in the data analysis because of this problem.

The behavior rating form and accompanying instructions used in this study are included at the end of this chapter in order to further clarify the development of behavior observation instruments. In addition, sample behavior observation forms for other types of activities are presented in order to illustrate how behavioral indices for a variable (enjoyment) should vary depending on the nature of the activity being observed. These additional behavior observation forms were developed by a graduate class in recreation for special populations at California State University, Chico.

In summary, the use of behavior observation techniques in evaluating the effectiveness of recreation programs for elders is recommended, because combining behavior observation with survey research methods can help provide a clearer picture of how to improve recreation programs for elders and also provide clearer evidence of the benefits of recreation programs, an especially important concern in times of budget cuts and the need to justify the existence of programs.

BIBLIOGRAPHY

Faber, M., and Leitner, M.J. Considerations in interviewing the impaired elderly. Unpublished Manuscript, 1981.

JWK International Corporation. *Data collection problems and the elderly: Survey research methods.* Washington, D.C.: Administration on Aging, 1978.

Leitner, M.J. The effects of intergenerational music activities on senior day care participants and elementary school children. (Doctoral dissertation, University of Maryland, 1981). *Dissertation Abstracts International,* 1981, *42*(08), p. 3752A.

Moen, E. The reluctance of the elderly to accept help. *Social Problems,* 1978, *25*(3), pp.293-294.

Pastalan, L. The distorted world of old age. *Human Behavior,* December, 1978.

Theobald, W.F. *Evaluation of recreation and park programs.* New York: Wiley and Sons, 1979.

APPENDIX A

BEHAVIOR RATING FORM

Observer # _____ Participant # _____ Observation # _____

Activity Observed _____ Date _____

Number of Participants in the Activity _____

Note the frequency of the following behaviors:

Laughter _____

Smiles _____

Eyes Closed _____

Unhappy Facial Expressions _____

Affectionate Touching Behavior _____

Withdrawal Behavior _____

Rhythmical Movements _____

Singing, Humming, and/or Whistling _____

Verbal Requests for Music Selections _____

APPENDIX A continued

Exclamations of Annoyance or Anger _____

Statements of Affection or Liking _____

Verbal Exclamations of Enjoyment and/or Happiness _____

1	2	3	4	5
Very low, Dislike	Low	Moderate	High	Very High

_____ Rating of participant's enjoyment of the activity

_____ Overall rating of all participants enjoyment of the activity

Comments:

APPENDIX B

INSTRUCTION SHEET FOR BEHAVIOR RATING FORM

1. For all of the behaviors listed on the rating form, note the number of times each behavior is elicited by using slashes (e.g. ////). Comments may also be written in the space provided next to each item. If the participant exhibits a particular behavior throughout an activity session, write "present throughout" in the space next to that item.

2. Laughter includes a range of behavior, from loud outbursts of violent laughter, to slight giggles.

3. Smiles includes a range of behavior, from wide, full smiles, to slight half-smiles.

4. Eyes Closed -- Note the number of times the participant's eyes close and remain closed for at least ten seconds. If the participant's eyes remain closed for more than one minute, note the length of time for which the participant's eyes were closed. If a participant's eyes are closed and appears to be sleeping, it does not necessarily mean that this person is drowsy due to boredom with the activity. Senior day care participants have a wide range of ailments and impairments; many of the people are under medication which may cause drowsiness.

5. Unhappy Facial Expressions -- This includes frowns, cry of sadness, pursed lips, and horizontal head shaking. Caution should be taken in noting the frequency of these behaviors, particularly frowns. Many of the older participants might appear to have drooping mouths due to sadness, but these drooping mouths may be due to facial muscles which have lost their tightness.

6. Affectionate Touching Behavior -- This includes hugs, kisses, hand squeezes, hand pats on another person's head or back, a child sitting on a participant's lap, and other touching behavior as well.

7. Withdrawal Behavior includes a wide range of behavior: non-participation in an activity; non-response to verbal and non-verbal cues; movement to sit farther away from coparticipants; and avoidance of contact with a coparticipant.

APPENDIX B continued

8. Rhythmical Movements includes: swaying; dancing; foot stomping or tapping; head swaying or nodding; hand clapping; snapping of fingers; and other whole body and/or finer extremity rhythmical movements.

9. The items "Singing, Humming, and/or Whistling" and "Verbal Requests for Music Selections" are self-explanatory.

10. Exclamations of Annoyance or Anger includes both verbal and nonverbal behaviors. Nonverbal behavior such as a wave of hand or the shake of a head in disgust should be noted. Statements such as "Leave me alone" and "I don't like this" should also be noted.

11. Statements of Affection or Liking is focused on participant's verbal behavior toward coparticipants in the activity. Examples of such behavior would be: "I like you," "You're so cute," and "It's nice to see you here today."

12. Verbal Exclamations of Enjoyment and/or Happiness is focused on participants' comments related to the activity. Comments such as "This is wonderful," and "Wasn't this fun" should be moted. In addition, statements of happiness such as "I feel great!" should be noted. Participants' requests for prolongation or repetition of the activity should also be noted (e.g., "Let's do this again!" or "I wish they didn't have to leave so soon!").

13. The following scale should be used in completing the ratings of activity enjoyment:

1	2	3	4	5
Very low, Dislike	Low	Moderate	High	Very High

The following is an explanation of the different ratings:

(1) Very Low, Dislike -- This rating is to be used in instances where the participant outwardly displays displeasure with the activity. The rater should be able to point out specific behaviors elicited during the activity which are indicative of the participant's dislike for the activity.

(2) Low -- A rating of "2" indicates below average of enjoyment; a rating of "2" does not mean that the participant disliked the activity. A participant that displays a low or below average frequency of behaviors indicative of enjoyment would be rated a "2".

(3) Moderate -- A rating of "3" is indicative of an average level of activity enjoyment. A participant rated "3" should be one that outwardly displays enjoyment, but only at a moderate (average) level.

(4) High -- If a participant displays above average enjoyment of an activity, a "4" rating should be given. A "4" rating should be supported by notations of above average incidence of behavior indicative of enjoyment.

(5) Very High -- When an activity appears to be truly special to a participant, a "5" rating should be given. A rating of "5" must be supported by observations which indicate a very high level of enjoyment. It is possible for a participant to obtain a "5" rating on numerous successive trials; however, the rater must indicate specific observations which support a rating of "5".

APPENDIX B continued

Before completing the rating of activity enjoyment for the participant observed, reflect on your observations for this participant. Review the notes you took on the behavior of the participant during the activity session. Remember that the participant's overall enjoyment of the activity just observed takes into account both the participant's reaction to the activity itself, as well as the participant's interaction with other people involved in the activity.

14. The second rating, of all participants, is an estimation of the entire group's level of enjoyment of the activity.

15. Comments -- Please include the following in your comments:

    a. Criteria for your rating of the participant's level of enjoyment; provide justification for the rating you gave.

    b. Criteria for your rating of all participants' level of enjoyment.

    c. Unusual circumstances which might have influenced participants' enjoyment of the activity (e.g., inclement weather, illnesses, background noise, etc.).

    d. Incidents which you felt were most significant or indicative of participants' level of enjoyment.

APPENDIX C

BEHAVIOR RATING FORM
Art Activity

Observer #_____

Activity Observed_____ Date_____

Number of Participants in the Activity_____

Note the frequency of the following behaviors:

Withdrawal_____

Ignoring_____

Being Sloppy_____

Frowning_____

Leaving Early_____

Verbal Expression_____

Yawning_____

Sighing_____

Talking to Neighbor (unrelated)_____

Checking the Clock/Watch_____

Impatient_____

Talking to Neighbor (related, e.g. Asst.)_____

APPENDIX C continued

Helping Others_____

Asking Questions_____

Investigate_____

Creative_____

Looking at Someone Else's Work_____

Smiling_____

Displaying Work_____

Reminiscing (Related to Art)_____

Asking for Repetition_____

Asking How to Get More Involved_____

High Concentration_____

Verbal Expression_____

1	2	3	4	5
Very Low, Dislike	Low	Moderate	High	Very High

Overall rating of <u>all</u> <u>participants'</u> enjoyment of the activity
_____

Comments:

APPENDIX D

BEHAVIOR RATING FORM
Stress Management

Observer #_____

Activity Observed_____   Date_____

Number of Participants in the Activity_____

Note the frequency of the following behaviors:

Withdrawal_____

Verbal Expression_____

Leaving Early_____

Disruptive Noise: comments, laughing_____

Fidgety Behavior_____

Unrelated Talking_____

Checking the Time_____

Missing an Instruction/Not Following Directions_____

Wandering Eyes_____

APPENDIX D continued

Doing Activity_____

Following Instructions_____

Asking for Clarification_____

Smiling_____

Asking for Repetition_____

Reduced Energy Level_____

Flowing with Music_____

1	2	3	4	5
Very Low, Dislike	Low	Moderate	High	Very High

Overall rating of <u>all</u> <u>participant's</u> enjoyment of the activity
_____

<u>Comments</u>:

Section II:
Settings for Recreation
Services for Elders

Chapter 5

Senior Day Care Centers

INTRODUCTION

The purpose of this chapter is to provide the reader with an understanding of senior day care services. More specifically, this chapter focuses on the role of recreational services in day care. Topics covered include: history and background of senior day care; goals and objectives of senior day care programs; a rationale for recreation as a component of senior day care services; research in senior day care; population served; description of the setting for day care programs; considerations in provision of services; and funding sources.

HISTORY AND BACKGROUND

Senior day care is fairly new in the United States, although it is a well established program in many European countries. Padula (1983) traces the beginning of senior day care programs to the establishment of the first psychiatric day hospital for the emotionally disburbed in 1942. England initiated day hospitals for physically impaired adults; by 1969, there were 90 geriatric day hospitals in Great Britain (Matlack, 1975).

On the other hand, senior day care services did not really become widespread in the United States until the 1970's. According to the U.S. Department of Health, Education and Welfare (1978) there were nearly 300 adult day care programs in the United States in 1978, although fewer than fifteen of these programs existed prior to 1973. In a 1980 Directory of Senior Day Care Centers (U.S. Department of Health and Human Services, 1980), the total number of existing day care centers more than doubled to 618 centers, serving 13,500 participants daily. According to Gelfand (1984), most centers serve 15 to 25 participants per day.

A distinction needs to be made between geriatric day hospitals and senior day care. According to Matlack (1975) geriatric day hospitals are hospital-based health-related programs which serve ill and impaired older persons. Emphasis is placed on remedial services such as physical therapy, occupational therapy, and psychotherapy, although social and recreational activity are components of such programs. Some of the purposes of geriatric day hospitals are: to help maintain frail elderly persons in the community; to discharge patients into the community earlier than would otherwise be possible; and to reduce recidivism of clients discharged into the community.

In a different light, Padula (1983) defines senior day care as a primarily social program for frail and handicapped older persons. According to Matlack (1975), senior day care programs place more emphasis on providing physical and mental stimulation for patients and respite for their families, whereas geriatric day hospitals focus more on remedial services. Many senior day care centers offer occupational therapy, physical therapy, therapeutic recreation, transportation, meals, educational programs, crafts, and counseling (Gelfand, 1984).

Senior day care is the primary concern of this chapter; its goals and objectives are described in detail in the following section.

GOALS AND OBJECTIVES OF DAY CARE

Day care promotes the social, psychological, emotional, and physical well being of the impaired elderly. The objective of day care is to restore and/or maintain individuals at their optimal functioning level. Activity programs afford participants the opportunity to become motivated to increase their competence in the skills of daily living (e.g., grooming and eating). Day care assists individuals in dealing with the environment.

Another important objective of day care is to provide respite for families. Day care affords families the opportunity to continue in their day to day lives and yet feel comfort in knowing that their elderly family member is spending the day in a caring environment.

In addition, day care attempts to increase physical independence. Through a program of exercise and physically active activities, seniors are able to strengthen or relearn skills and gain confidence in their own mobility.

An additional objective of day care is to maintain the "at risk" elderly in the community. Senior day care serves as an alternative to nursing home care and without day care services many seniors would have no choice but to enter a nursing home.

Social interaction is another goal of day care services. Programming attempts to foster socialization among the participants through a variety of activities. Many seniors enter the program due to social isolation.

Day care programs also offer diversion for the seniors. Activities attempt to alleviate boredom and help participants make better use of leisure time.

RECREATION IN SENIOR DAY CARE: A RATIONALE

Based on the aforementioned goals and objectives of senior day care programs, it is apparent that recreation services should be a major component of such programs. In particular, some of the goals of therapeutic recreation which coincide with those of senior day care programs are: provision of enjoyable leisure activities; promotion of individual growth on a continuum of dependence—independence; provision of opportunities for social contact and formation of friendships; and maintenance and/or improvement of physical and/or mental capabilities. The provision of social contact opportunities is especially important in light of statistics which indicate that approximately 30% of senior day care participants live alone (Gelfand, 1984).

Indeed, recreation activity in senior day care programs play a major role in facilitating the happiness and well-being of its participants. As described later in the chapter, participants of senior day care centers are retired and usually do not have major household responsibilities; senior day care attempts to help impaired older persons make beneficial use of their vast amount of leisure time. The research studies cited in the next section further illustrate the value of recreation programs in senior day care centers, and the value of senior day care centers in general.

RESEARCH IN DAY CARE

Several articles support the notion that senior day care services are beneficial for the aged (Gustofson, 1974; Kistin and Morris, 1972; Koff, 1974; Kostick, 1972; Kostick, 1974; Lurie and Kolish, 1976; Rathbone-McCuan, 1976; Rathbone-McCuan and Levenson, 1975; Singer, 1980; Turbow, 1975; and Wan, Weissart, and Livieratos, 1980). Many of these articles describe successful senior day care programs and explain the benefits of day care services for impaired older persons. Turbow's (1975) study examined the effects of senior day care services on forty-five persons over a six month period. The results of Turbow's study indicated reduced anxiety, improvement of interpersonal relationships, and maintenance of independent living for the forty-five persons studied.

The study by Wan, Weissart, and Livieratos (1980) is of particular interest because of the large sample size and sophisticated research methodology used. The researchers examined the physical, psychological and social functioning of over 1,000 older persons receiving day care and/or homemaker services (experimental group) and of a control group of over 1,000 aged persons. Subjects in this study were randomly assigned to control and experimental groups, thus establishing initial equivalency of the two groups.

The results of this study indicated that persons receiving day care and homemaker services were significantly better off in terms of physical, psychological and social functioning than the control group. This study provides scientific evidence that day care services can help make significant improvements in the lives of the elderly. Naturally, it is not always feasible to study problems in a controlled, experimental fashion similar to the Wan, Weissart and Livieratos (1980) study (comparison groups, random assignment of subjects to control and experimental groups and control of variables). However, similar types of research efforts on the effects of different kinds of recreation services in senior day care settings will yield further insight on how to improve recreation opportunities for senior day care participants, as well as provide information which can help justify the existence of recreation programs in senior day care settings.

TARGET POPULATION

Senior day care centers serve impaired and/or homebound persons generally age 60 and older. Most day care participants are at risk of institutionalization and day care plays a major role in allowing these individuals to remain in the community. Participants with a broad range of impairments are represented in the day care population. All of the persons enrolled in a senior day care program are in some way mentally and/or physically impaired. Mental impairments include: depression, senile dementia; and emotional disturbances. Physical impairments include: stroke disabilities; vision impairment; arthritis; amputees; heart disease; and pulmonary disease. The severity of the handicap differs with each person, but all are given individualized and meaningful activity to assist in adjusting to disabling conditions.

Senior day care centers serve people of a wide age range; participant ages may range from 60 to over 100. Thus, it is possible for three generations to exist at a day care center. This is a major consideration in programming in that people of different age groups may have different activity interests.

A majority of the seniors are women; most are widowed. A common complaint for many of the seniors is the feeling of loneliness. Many of the participants live with a family member (children or other relative), some live either alone or with a spouse, while others live in personal care or foster homes. Family tension often exists for those seniors living with families. The causes of family tension are usually two-fold: threat of loss of independence on the part of the elder; and resentment on the part of the care-taker because of the added responsibilities in caring for an older family member.

Some other characteristics that generally apply to day care recipients are:

1. They are not engaged in gainful employment or in child-rearing responsibilities, and thus have a good deal of leisure time.
2. They have limited means of transportation resulting in isolation from most community resources. For many persons, the day care center provides the only social contacts in their lives.
3. Many people initially feel threatened by the concept of day care. For the majority, it is their first exposure to such a facility and the idea of a leisure-oriented program is unfamiliar. Many are committed to the work ethic and view any recreational programs as a waste of time. Also, some elders feel threatened by exposure to other handicapped adults and many deny any identification with this group.

Although most day care participants reside in the community, most are not eligible to attend a senior center, because senior center participation would require a higher functioning level than they possess. Day care offers a structured program of activities, while senior centers offer a more elective program of activities. Day care participants would not be capable of attending a senior center on their own initiative.

Another source of participants are nursing home residents. Some institutionalized persons may attend day care in preparation for re-entry to the community. Other nursing home residents attend day care as an off premises activity several days per week, but continue to reside in the nursing home. As with populations found in other activity settings for the aged, the main characteristic of the participant population in day care centers is great diversity in terms of needs, interests and abilities.

THE SETTING

One important characteristic of senior day care centers is that they must be accessible to the handicapped. There should be as few steps as possible; a chair lift should be present at staircases because many of the participants are unable to negotiate steps. Restrooms should be nearby and also be accessible for the handicapped. The restrooms should have grab bars; high toilet seats; and be large enough for wheelchairs. Doors should be easy to open, not pressurized. There should be ramps and railings at all stairways. Another safety hazard to be avoided is scatter rugs. There should be curtains at the windows in order to minimize glare. Centers should provide good lighting, good ventilation, and proper temperature maintenance. (Older persons usually prefer warm room temperatures.) Low lounge chairs or sofas should be avoided as this type of furniture may be difficult for seniors to get in and out of. All centers should have fire and health regulations. There should always be at least two exits. Telephones should be readily available. Another desirable feature is a canopy at the entrance in the event of inclement weather.

The interior of the center usually reflects four major themes: comfort and enjoyment; maximal mobility; facilitation of social interaction; and orientation to time and place. Comfortable chairs (all chairs should have arms), music, and aesthetically pleasing decoration help to maximize the comfort and enjoyment of the participant. Arrangement of furniture and equipment is usually such that the participant can move about freely and safely with minimal chance of accident. A large clock and posters and signs in large print should be present to help orient the participant to time and place. The daily schedule and a calendar should be within easy view for all to see. A bulletin board where participant art work can be displayed and/or announcements can be posted is highly recommended for the benefit of the more confused participants. The reality orientation board can be made out of a large piece of tag board. In large print it lists the date, weather, upcoming holidays, and the name of the facility.

The arrangement and complexity of the facility varies greatly from center to center. Most centers have a dining room where lunch and snacks are served daily. It is desirable to have a "quiet" room for rest and/or solitude. There is also usually a separate office area for staff. In addition, it is advantageous to utilize more than one partitioned or separate activity room so that more than one activity may occur simultaneously without interference. Some centers have separate rooms for crafts, exercise, games, discussions, media center (books, magazines, talking books for the blind, etc.), and sitting rooms (for small group discussions and impromptu conversations), while some centers simply have one large room where all activities take place. In addition, an area for smoking should be provided. Storage areas and an area for participant personal belongings are also desirable.

CONSIDERATIONS IN THE PROVISION OF SERVICES

Leading Activities

In this section, leadership skills which are different from those needed by workers in other settings for recreation for the aged are highlighted.

Safety and health considerations must be taken into account when leading activities for impaired senior citizens at a day care center. Since many of the seniors are taking some kind of medication, the activity leader must be aware of the effects of drug use on program involvement and interaction (for example, if a person is administered a medication which causes a side effect of drowsiness, allow that person to engage in a passive activity, or provide an opportunity to just sit and rest).

Not all day care centers are equipped with medical staff, therefore it is desirable that the activity leader be able to respond effectively to medical emergencies (for example, administer aid to a person who is choking). It is advantageous to have training in both first aid and cardiopulmonary resuscitation.

In senior day care centers, the staff may find themselves assuming various roles while carrying out different responsibilities. The participant may see the staff in varying positions, changing with each activity. It is not uncommon for participants to view staff as teachers, counselors, nurses or doctors, secretaries, or personal confidants. Although the roles may shift, the relationship between staff and participant should always remain professional. Participants' responses to activity leaders may be influenced by their perceptions of the leader's role at that moment.

In general, the leader of recreational activities in a senior day care center needs to be more autocratic in leadership style than a recreation leader working with higher functioning populations. For example, in senior centers, the participants are more capable of being involved in program planning. On the other hand, the staff at senior day care centers are responsible for more of the planning. The participants enrolled in a day care center tend to be not as mentally competent as attendees of senior centers and clubs. Thus, day care personnel should be more autocratic in both leading and planning activities. However, senior day care staff should attempt to solicit input from program participants regardless of what level it is.

Senior centers and day care differ in another aspect of leadership. There is a greater staff/participant ratio in day care, thus affording more individualized programming. Also, participant evaluation is more of an objective in day care than senior centers; consequently, there is a greater extent of individualized goal setting.

In a related vein, the format of activities may differ in a senior center as opposed to a day care center. Because of the large handicapped population that exists at a day care center, leadership techniques will vary accordingly. Modification of activities is an important component in day care. Activities must be adjusted to suit each individual's abilities. For example, activities should be slow paced, simple in complexity and contain few steps. In contrast, in senior centers, there would be less structure and modification of activities needed to accommodate the more healthy and vital population attending senior centers.

Day care centers also differ from nursing homes with regard to leadership style. Most day care centers operate five days per week, and within this framework, each participant has their own individual attendance schedule. Some attend two days per week while others attend four days per week. This is unlike nursing homes, which operate seven days per week. This has several implications for program planning: (1) senior day care cannot take advantage of community resources which are only available evenings and weekends, whereas nursing homes can; (2) not all participants are present on any specified day of the week to attend a particular activity. Thus, one must be sure to afford participants scheduled for all days the opportunity to participate in special events. For example, Tuesday participants might become disturbed if all field trips were scheduled for Wednesdays. This would not be a concern for nursing homes but it would be for day care programs.

Day care center participants tend to be less independent than seniors attending a senior center. One objective of day care is to foster independence and to attain this, activities tend to be more therapeutic in nature. On the other hand, senior centers incorporate more ''pure recreation'' activities rather than therapeutic recreation activities.

Field trips may entail more planning, coordination, and supervision for day care centers than senior centers. Because of the impaired population that exists at a day care center, more special provisions for field trips are needed than would be required for a senior center population.

Attracting Participants

Several techniques are involved in the process of attracting participants. One publicity technique is to issue brochures in the mail and in person to the general public. Eligibility criteria and vital information about the program should be included in these brochures. Also, an article should appear in each issue of the local senior citizen's newspaper (if one exists). Special events can be publicized through the mass media (television, radio, newspaper). In addition, county and state social service agencies should be well informed of the program so they can refer potential applicants to the program. Naturally, each participant has the potential to attract other seniors by word of mouth.

Community involvement in various activities can be an effective tool in letting people know about the program. As an example, bazaars and pot luck dinners keep the community aware of the program and help the day care center to keep in touch with potential enrollees. It is also helpful to display a large sign outside of the facility so that the community is aware of its existence.

Referrals should be kept up to date. Any applicant who has not yet committed him/herself to the program should be contacted periodically. Letters and/or phone calls should be made to these applicants to determine their eligibility.

Once a prospective participant is identified, a home visit should be made by a staff member to assess eligibility status. Information about the program is disseminated to the applicant at this time. Bringing photographs of activities that occur at the center to the home visit can give the applicant a better idea of what the program offers. Also, it may be beneficial for another participant to accompany the staff member on the home visit. The participant who has been enrolled in the program for a good length of time may be able to offer insight into the program and relate well to the potential enrollee's apprehensions about joining the program.

Transportation

Another vital concern for day care centers is getting the participants to and from the center each day. For most handicapped senior citizens, transportation is a serious problem; most are unable to provide their own transportation. In order to have high attendance, most senior day care centers will find it necessary to provide their own transportation. Money should be allotted in the budget to purchase and maintain a transportation vehicle. This vehicle must be designed for the handicapped since many senior day care participants have some degree of physical impairment.

The center should establish a transportation area within which they can transport people to and from the center. Anyone living within this radius (for example five miles) will have transportation provided. Those living outside the boundary will have to provide their own transportation (usually a family member or some other community resource). In addition, car pools should be encouraged. In this way, the bus routes can be held to a minimum and restricted to a reasonable time frame. (It would be inconvenient if the bus route was so long that people had to ride for excessive amounts of time.) It should be remembered that the upkeep of a vehicle can be quite costly; therefore, sufficient funds should be allocated for vehicle maintenance.

Assessment

A thorough assessment of needs, interests, and abilities should be conducted before a participant is involved in a program of activities. Needs, interests, and abilities may change once a person has been enrolled in the program for a period of time, in that old skills are relearned, new skills may be acquired, and interests may expand. During the initial home visit, a basic overview of the applicant is obtained. A mental status questionnaire is administered to the prospective participant and the physician is asked to complete a medical form which lists any physical limitations, medications, physical and psychological ailments, and any other comments or recommendations. An environmental assessment can also be completed during the home visit to better understand the person's living environment.

The following are some questions that could be asked during a home visit:

1. What do you do around the house every day?
2. What kinds of things are you interested in?
3. Do you have any social contacts? How often do you talk on the phone, and to who?
4. What are your hobbies and interests?
5. Why would you like to come to the day care center?
6. Do you have any health problems?
7. Do you take any medications?
8. Do you have any health insurance coverage?
9. Who would we contact in case of an emergency?
10. Should we know of any special considerations (medical, meals, or religious)?
11. Have you had any recent hospitalizations?
12. Are you involved with any other social service agency?
13. Are you able to take care of your own personal care needs (bathing, eating, grooming)? If the answer is no, who does these things for you?
14. Do you do the housekeeping, laundry, and meal preparation?
15. When is your birthday?
16. What is your total income?
17. What was your previous career?
18. What is your marital status?
19. Do you need transportation to the center?
20. Which days would you like to attend the center each week?

Special Events

Special events are very important in that they give the seniors a special activity to look forward to and involve the efforts of many people (staff and participants) in planning the event. Special events usually generate a great deal of enthusiasm and involve the coordination of the entire staff. Outstanding events are usually talked about among members for weeks after; participants frequently suggest engagements for future events as a result of involvement in a stimulating special event.

The following are some interesting examples of special events which handicapped senior citizens can enjoy: a picnic at a nearby park; a trip to a local racetrack; trips to various cultural sites (museums, theater); or attending the circus. Dining out is another favorite activity (allow the participants to choose the restaurant). Stimulating activities that can take place right at the center are: Las Vegas Day; theme days (such as Mardi Gras or International Day); musical performance; talent shows; parties; senior olympics, holiday celebrations; and yoga.

Family Contact

For a more effective program, it is important that staff maintain close contact with participants' families. Phone calls should be made periodically to assess how the person is doing at home and discuss any problems the staff should be made aware of. Families should be encouraged to contact the center to ask questions or make suggestions. Families should be mailed copies of monthly schedules, announcements, and any other relevant information, and they should be invited to special events. Family dinners can be held periodically at the center (annually or bi-annually) so that family involvement can be maintained.

Another function of family contact is to involve family members in the assessment of participant programs; this can be achieved at a family conference with family members and staff. Equally beneficial are support groups formed for families so that people with similar concerns can get together and discuss their aged family members.

FUNDING

It is important to be able to demonstrate clear-cut, objective program evaluations in seeking funds. Also, some funding agencies require that the recipient of funds periodically administer program and participant evaluation procedures specified by the funding agency.

Senior day care programs receive financial support from a wide variety of sources; many programs have several different funding sources. Local, state, and federal governments provide funds under numerous different programs, such as: revenue sharing; Title III, IV, V, & VII of the Older Americans Act; and Title XVIII, XIX, and XX of the Social Security Act (U.S. DHEW, 1978). In addition, state and county offices on aging or Departments of Health and Human Services sponsor programs. According to Gelfand (1984), the cost of the provision of senior day care services is $11 to $33 per day per participant.

One source of private funds is direct payment by participants. Philanthropic contributions by individuals and organizations is another source of funds. In addition, local churches and synagogues are a frequent source of support (in terms of money and/or providing space for facilities). As indicated earlier in the chapter, research in the area of senior day care services lends support to devoting increased resources for senior day care programs.

SUMMARY

In summary, senior day care is a rapidly growing form of service which serves the social and recreational needs of non-institutionalized handicapped older adults. Day care is a critical service in enabling handicapped older persons to maintain an independent, non-institutional life style; recreation is a vital component of day care services.

BIBLIOGRAPHY

Gelfand, D.E. *The aging network: Programs and services* (2nd ed.). New York: Springer Publishing, 1984.

Grieff, S.A., and McDonald, R.D. Roles of staff in a psycho-geriatric day care center. *Gerontologist,* 1973, *13*(1), pp. 39-44.

Gustafson, E. Day care for the elderly. *Gerontologist,* 1974, *14*(1), pp. 46-49.

Holmes, M.B., and Holmes, D. *Handbook of human services for older persons.* New York: Human Sciences Press, 1979.

Kistin, H., and Morris, R. Alternatives to institutional care for the elderly and disabled. *Gerontologist,* 1972, *12*(2), pp. 139-42.

Koff, T.H. Rationale for services: Day care, allied care, and coordination. *Gerontologist,* 1974, *14*(1), pp. 26-29.

Kostich, A. A day care program for the physically and emotionally disabled. *Gerontologist,* 1972, *12*(2), pp. 134-138.

Kostich, A. Levindale day care program. *Gerontologist,* 1974, *14*(1), pp. 31-32.

Leitner, M.J., and Merenbloom, S. Senior day care centers ensure fun for the elderly. *Parks and Recreation Magazine,* 1979, *14*(11), pp. 58-61; 84-89.

Lurie, E., and Kalish, R. On Lok senior day health center. *Gerontologist,* 1976, *16*(1), pp. 39-46.

Matlack, D.R. The case for geriatric day hospitals. *Gerontologist,* 1975, *15*(2), pp. 109-113.

O'Brien, C.L. *Adult day care: A practical guide.* Monterey, CA: Wadsworth Health Sciences Division, 1982.

Padula, H. *Developing adult day care: An approach to maintaining independence for older persons.* Washington, D.C.: National Institute on Adult Day Care, 1983.

Rathbone-McCuan, E. Geriatric day care—A family perspective. *Gerontologist,* 1976, *16* (6), pp. 517-21.

Rathbone-McCuan, E., and Levinson, J. Impact of socialization therapy in a geriatric day care setting. *Gerontologist,* 1975, *15*(4), pp. 338-42.

Snyder, M.A. The differential usage of services by impaired elderly. *Journal of Gerontology,* 1980, *35*(2), pp. 249-55.

Trans Century Corporation. *Adult day care in the U.S. A comparative study.* Washington, D.C.: Trans Century Corporation, 1975.

Turbow, S.R. Geriatric group day care and its effects on independent living. *Gerontologist,* 1975, *15*(6), pp. 508-510.

United States Department of Health, Education, and Welfare. *Directory of adult day care centers.* Rockville, MD: United States Department of Health, Education, and Welfare, 1978.

Wan, T.H., Weissart, W.G., and Livieratos, B.B. Geriatric day care and homemaker services: An experimental study. *Journal of Gerontology,* 1980, *35*(2), pp. 256-74.

Chapter 6

Senior Centers and Clubs

INTRODUCTION

The purpose of this chapter is to provide information on senior centers and clubs, more specifically, the role of recreation in senior centers and clubs. Topics discussed in this chapter include: history and background of senior centers and clubs; goals and objectives of senior centers; a rationale for recreation as a component of senior center programs; the population served; description of the senior center setting; considerations in recreation program planning in senior centers; and funding sources for senior centers.

HISTORY AND BACKGROUND

For the purposes of this book, a senior center is defined as a focal point in the community where elders can come for services and activities which heighten their dignity, encourage their independence, and support their involvement with the community (Ralston, 1983). Senior centers are a relatively new concept in the United States, with the greatest growth occurring after 1965 (Gelfand, 1984). The first senior club was established in Boston in 1870, and more than 70 years later the first senior center was established in New York City in 1943. Since that time there has been a tremendous growth in the number of senior centers: in 1966 there were 340 senior centers; by 1970, there were 1,200 senior centers; and by 1978, approximately 6,000 centers were in operation (Gelfand, 1984).

A distinction needs to be made between senior centers and senior clubs. A senior center operates in a permanent facility and provides a central location for services, whereas a senior club may have no regular meeting place (Ralston, 1983). A senior center is usually more available to elders than clubs and may be open three or more days per week whereas a senior club may be open only one day per week or less, but depending on the individual club, it may stay open five days per week. The personnel working in a senior center and club usually differ: senior centers commonly employ a full-time administrator, full and part-time activity leaders, volunteers, and a secretary. On the other hand, many senior clubs have no paid staff. In addition, according to Ralston (1983), senior centers have diverse funding sources and implement a variety of activities. Senior clubs typically are supported by dues and contributions and programming usually emphasizes social and recreational activities. In general, senior centers are more concerned with serving as a bridge to the community and as a focal point for common interests and concerns than are senior clubs (Gelfand, 1984).

Senior centers are the primary concern of the next section: their goals and objectives are described in detail.

GOALS AND OBJECTIVES

Senior centers are non-institutional, community based, non-commercial, non-profit organizations for fairly high functioning older adults over 60 (Leanse, Tiven, and Robb, 1977). A primary goal of senior centers is to attract elders coming from a diverse range of backgrounds, abilities, and interests (Holmes and Holmes, 1979). This is accomplished by offering the following programs: (1) Socialization programs to develop communication skills, offer appreciation and acknowledgement to elders, and develop a sense of status outside of the family unit; (2) Educational/Cultural programs to promote problem solving and learning skills; (3) Health services; (4) Nutritional services; (5) Entitlement services (e.g., Medicaid, Medicare, food stamps, rent reductions, etc.); (6) Legal and income counseling; (7) Homemaker assistance; and (8) Transportation. A current trend is the expansion of senior centers into multi-purpose centers where all services for elders are offered at one convenient location. A diverse range of programs are provided at multi-purpose centers, including all of the aforementioned programs.

Generally, senior centers provide an informal support system (Ralston, 1983) and should try to meet the needs of the older adults in the community it serves. In addition, senior centers serve as a resource for information on community affairs and senior citizens' services, as well as a training center (Gelfand, 1984).

An important objective of a senior center is to encourage input from the elders it serves and maintain their support (Gelfand, 1984).

According to Gelfand (1984), another important objective is to provide activities which are relevant to the target population. The elders' needs should be assessed, then subsequently, programs should be planned according to their needs, interests, and abilities.

RECREATION IN SENIOR CENTERS: A RATIONALE

Recreation is an important service offered by senior centers, and contributes greatly to the effectiveness of senior centers in enhancing the well-being of attendees. In a study of senior centers (Gelfand, 1984), the data indicated that attendees of senior centers viewed themselves as being more healthy than elders who do not attend senior centers. In addition, attendees had higher life satisfaction than non-attendees.

In a related survey of senior centers (Kaplan, 1979), it was determined that 39% of the total hours senior centers are open for operation are devoted to leisure programs. In *Senior Centers: A Report of Senior Group Programs in America* by the National Council on Aging (NCOA, 1975), a survey was conducted to determine which senior center activities have the highest levels of participation. The highest ranked activity was meals, followed by sedentary recreational activities, then creative recreation activities. Lower ranked activities were educational programs, counseling, health and employment services. Clearly, recreational activities are an important component of senior center programs.

TARGET POPULATION

More than five million older adults in the United States age 60 and older are members of a senior center (Gelfand, 1984). In any two week period, six percent of all elders in the U.S. attend a senior center and 18% have attended one recently (Gelfand, 1984). The majority of senior center members are between the ages of 65 and 74. One fourth of the total senior center population are between the ages of 75 and 84. The majority are women (75%) and white (85%). The majority of attendees live alone (59%) as opposed to living with another family member or congregate housing situation. Most attendees are retired blue-collar workers (47%); the remaining are retired white collar workers (16%) and retired professionals (16%) (Gelfand, 1984).

Just 10% of the senior center attendees are physically impaired and 10% are deaf. According to Kaplan (1979), loneliness and a desire to meet others were the prominent reasons for attending a senior center.

The National Council on Aging (NCOA, 1975) administered questionnaires to all senior group programs listed in the 1974 directory of senior group programs in the U.S. to determine attendees' reasons for senior center participation. At least half of those surveyed suggested they attended for social reasons, almost half replied that they attended a senior center to just fill their leisure time, and several others mentioned that loneliness was their primary motive for attendance. Another finding of this study was that elders who join a senior center tend to be people who were members of organizations and clubs throughout their lifetime. Individuals who were not involved in group programs earlier in their life tend to not join senior centers.

THE SETTING

A senior center should be located in an area in the community that is attractive and where elders feel comfortable and want to come to (Gelfand, 1984). Gelfand (1984) also notes that the area should be convenient and accessible to the target population. The facility itself should be accessible to the handicapped, contain a variety of rooms of different sizes, and provide private areas for counseling (Gelfand, 1984).

In a study surveying senior center programs (Gelfand, 1984), 20% of those programs surveyed were in new buildings, 42% were in old renovated buildings, and 37% were in old buildings not renovated.

Ideally, a large multi-purpose senior center with an attendance of over 200 older adults should be spacious and provide a variety of rooms. According to Murrin and Bilezikjian (1975), a large multi-purpose senior center should be based on the following model:

Spaces offered	*Square Feet Recommended*

1. *Outdoor space:* parking
   lot, patio, game courts, landscaped areas,
   pickup and drop-off zone.

Spaces offered	Square Feet Recommended
2. Indoor space:	
a. Administration area/office space	250
b. Conference space	200
c. Classroom and crafts room	650 & 550
d. Arts and crafts room	1,000
e. Library, quiet lounge	500
f. Game room, noisy lounge	800
g. Kitchen	500
h. Restrooms	400
i. Coatroom	50
j. Janitor/Custodian space	50
k. Storage	225
l. Large assembly room	5,000
m. Circulation space	475
Total square footage	10,500

The large assembly room should be the focal point of the facility. This can be established by allowing the assembly room to be in the middle of the center with all adjoining rooms leading to the assembly room forming a circle around it. As a general guideline, there should be thirty square feet of space per person (Mirrin and Bilezikjian, 1975).

Of the programs surveyed in the National Council on Aging's 1975 survey of senior group programs in America (NCOA, 1975, 26% owned the building, 17% met in a church, 15% met in a recreation center, 15% met in a local government facility, 10% met in a community center of a voluntary organization, and 10% met in a housing authority building. Other possible locations for programs are libraries, universities, and apartment house recreation rooms.

RECREATION PROGRAM PLANNING
IN SENIOR CENTERS

Senior centers offer a wide range of challenging and diverse activities to accommodate the needs of the high functioning elders it serves. Unlike day care centers, senior centers serve elders with little or no impairment, and successful program planning must take this into account.

Another important consideration of program planning is the high elder/staff ratio. Activities with a very high attendance (e.g., 50 to 100 attendees) can occur with only one or two staff members available to oversee the activity. Because of the great number of participants for every staff member, the type of recreational services provided tend to be more diversionary or educational in nature, as opposed to programming in senior day care centers, where therapeutic activities are more appropriate. Thus, in senior centers, recreational programming often does not include individual goal setting and charting of progress, as opposed to therapeutic recreation services in senior day care centers.

According to Gelfand (1984), programming should be under the direction and support of the elders it serves. In this way, senior center attendees have direct input into programming activities related to their specific interests, abilities, and needs.

For a well-balanced program, senior centers should incorporate the following program ideas (Leanse, Tiven, and Robb, 1977): recreational activities; educational activities; trips and special events; and work opportunities (e.g., produce hand-made crafts for sale). The provision of work-like roles in a senior center program can help many elders justify or rationalize their attending the center (Yearwood, 1983). The work experience can help to make leisure time purposeful, create a sales outlet for crafts, yet still preserve the retirement lifestyle (Schreter and Hudson, 1981).

The NCOA (1975) developed a philosophy of the senior center movement which should be utilized as a philosophical basis for program planning:

1. Aging should be viewed as a normal developmental process;
2. People need peers for interaction, encouragement, and support;
3. Adults have the right to have input in matters affecting them;
4. Elders have ambitions, capabilities, and creative capacities;
5. Elders have basic needs;
6. Elders are capable of continued growth and development;
7. Elders need access to information to solve problems; and
8. Elders need a climate of trust and support.

If the philosophical principles listed above are incorporated into the program planning process, recreational activities and services will enhance attendees' morale.

According to the NCOA (1975), program planning should follow the following steps:

1. Assess individual needs;
2. Identify criteria and indicators of need fulfillment;
3. Identify barriers to need fulfillment;
4. State objectives and action steps to attain these needs;
5. Monitor and assess the objectives; and
6. Examine the impact, measure the data, and evaluate the program.

Recreation programs in senior centers should cover a very wide range of activities since the high functioning population usually attending senior centers allows limitless possibilities. Sincere attempts to understand elders' needs, and allowing senior center attendees the opportunity to have input in program planning will greatly enhance the effectiveness of the recreation program.

FUNDING

Rarely is there a single source of funding for a senior center (Gelfand, 1984). Funding is usually determined by the auspices under which the center is operated. There are many sources available for funding for senior centers (Gelfand, 1984):

1. *The Older American's Act*
   a . Title III provides support for construction, operation, nutrition, and special programming.
   b. Title IV provides support for training and research, and model projects.
   c. Title V provides support for senior community service employment programs.
2. *Other federal funding*
   a. Block grants from the Department of Housing and Community Development for developing and coordinating senior center programs.
   b. General Revenue Sharing.
   c. Social Services block grants.
   d. Title I of the Higher Educational Act for educationally-oriented activities.

3. *State and local funding*
4. *Civic and religious organizations*
5. *Private philanthropists and non-profit organizations*
6. *The senior center itself*
   a. Membership dues.
   b. Fund-raisers.
   c. Sale of hand-made products.

According to Holmes and Holmes (1979) the Administration on Aging is the only government agency at the federal level specifically authorized to promote the development of multi-purpose senior centers. Some senior centers have as many as ten different funding sources. In the NCOA's (1975) report of senior programs, it was concluded that 47% of the senior centers surveyed received funding from public sources, 18% of the centers received funding from private sources, and the remaining 34% received both public and private support.

SUMMARY

In summary, senior centers are a rapidly growing form of service for high functioning elders. Senior centers serve as a community focal point, a resource center for information and health services, and a center for recreational, social, and educational activities.

BIBLIOGRAPHY

Gelfand, D.E. *The aging network: Programs and services* (2nd ed.). New York: Springer Publishing, 1984.
Holmes, M.B., and Holmes, D. *Handbook of human services for older persons.* New York: Human Sciences Press, 1979.
Kaplan, M. *Leisure: Lifestyle and lifespan.* Philadelphia: W.B. Saunders Company, 1979.
Leanse, J., Tiven, M., and Robb, T.B. *Senior center operation.* Washington, D.C.: National Council on Aging, 1977.
Maeda, D. Growth of old people's clubs in Japan. *Gerontologist,* 1975, *15*(3), pp. 254-256.
Murrin, R., and Bilezikjian, E. *Architectural programming for a senior center: Spatial allocation, organization, and recommendations.* Washington, D.C.: National Council on Aging, 1975.
National Council on Aging (NCOA). *Senior group programs in America.* Washington, D.C.: National Council on Aging, 1975.
Ralston, P.A. Levels of senior centers: A broadened view of group-based programs for the elderly. *Activities, Adaptation, and Aging,* 1983, *3*(2), pp. 79-92.
Schreter, C.A., and Hudson, N. Investing in elder craftsmen. *Gerontologist,* 1981, *21*(6), pp. 655-661.

Taietz, P. Two conceptual models of the senior center. *Journal of Gerontology,* 1976, *31*(2), pp. 219-222.

Williams, S. A victory for seniors: A center under one roof. *Parks and Recreation Magazine,* October 1983, pp. 35-37.

Woolf, L.M., and Sterne, R. Synthesizing hospital care with a senior center program. *Gerontologist,* 1973, *13*(2), pp. 197-203.

Yearwood, A.W., and Dressel, P.L. Interracial dynamics in a southern senior center. *Gerontologist,* 1983, *3*(5), pp. 512-517.

Chapter 7

Nursing Homes

INTRODUCTION

The purposes of this chapter are to present general information on nursing homes, discuss the role of recreation in nursing homes, and examine special considerations in the provision of recreation in nursing homes. Topics discussed in this chapter include: background information on recreation in nursing homes; considerations in the provision of recreation for nursing home residents; an overview of the characteristics of nursing home residents; and a humanistic perspective of recreation in nursing homes.

RECREATION IN NURSING HOMES: AN OVERVIEW

Nursing Homes in the U.S.

In 1983 there were over one million elders in nursing homes (Goodman, 1983). There were nearly 19,000 nursing homes in 1979 in the United States, an increase from 15,700 nursing homes in 1973. The number of beds in nursing homes has increased 7.2% from 1954 to 1976 (Jones, 1982).

Recreation in Nursing Homes

Recreation programs in nursing homes are growing, thus creating an increasing need for recreation personnel. According to the Department of Health, Education, and Welfare (1979), there were 10,200 full-time activity directors employed in nursing homes across the country, and a total of 4,500 part-time activity directors in 1979. Women have tended to dominate this field of employment: almost 9,600 of the full-time activity directors were females, and less than 700 were males. It is important to note that there were 1,300 vacant staff positions for activity directors. By 1985, nursing homes are expected to employ 1,431,000 persons, an increase of 73% from 1976 (Gelfand, 1984). Although only 5% of the older population is institutionalized, a prime area of employment for recreation therapists desiring to work with elders is nursing homes.

Studies investigating the recreation participation patterns of nursing home residents indicate a need for increased resident involvement. According to the Department of Health, Education, and Welfare (1979), for activities occurring inside the facility, 65% of all residents nationwide attend at least one activity per month, while 35% do not attend. Activities outside the facility were not as well attended; only 31% of all residents nationwide attended one activity outside of the facility during the course of a month. Of this total, 20% visited with family and friends, 10% went on shopping trips, and 8% participated in a group walk. There were additional small figures for attending movies, libraries, parks, etc. Of the 68% that did not attend programs outside of the institution, 36% of the residents indicated that they did not attend the activities due to illness. The reasons why the remaining 32% who were physically able to attend activities but did not were confusion, fright, or a refusal to attend (United States Department of Health, Education, and Welfare, 1979).

CONSIDERATIONS IN PROVIDING RECREATION SERVICES

Providing recreation for nursing home residents requires an understanding of the rationale for recreation for elders. Refer to Chapter One for information on this topic, including an overview of research documenting the value and benefits of recreation for elders. Another area of knowledge necessary in providing recreation to nursing home residents is recreation program planning and leadership principles. Information on program planning and leadership principles can be found in Chapters Two and Three. In providing a recreational program in a nursing home, evaluation of the program must occur to determine the recreational program's effectiveness. Refer to the chapter on evaluative techniques for information on this topic. It is also desirable to have the knowledge to plan and lead recreational exercise and adapted dance in order to provide a well-balanced recreational program to nursing home residents. The chapters on these topics emphasize modification of activities for low functioning populations commonly found in nursing homes.

Other recreational techniques such as massage, music, art, pet therapy, drama, and others are also important components in the provision of recreation in nursing homes. This information is included in other chapters in the book, and adaptations for low functioning elders are discussed in these chapters.

Being familiar with the traits and characteristics of the nursing home population is essential in providing an optimum recreation program. The following section describes the characteristics of nursing home residents, and how these characteristics affect the type of recreational services provided.

CHARACTERISTICS OF NURSING HOME RESIDENTS AND THEIR IMPLICATIONS FOR RECREATION SERVICES

Resident Characteristics

Five out of every 100 persons aged 65 and over live in nursing homes (Kaplan, 1979). In 1983, over one million persons were residents of nursing homes (Goodman, 1983). The median age of nursing home residents is 82 years old: 90% are 65 and over; 17% are 65 to 74 years old; 40% are 75 to 84 years old; and 43% are at least 85 years old (Pepper, 1982). According to Pepper (1982), the major physical impairments affecting nursing home residents are: circulatory disorders, including heart problems (36%); arthritis (33%); digestive problems (20%); speech disorders (14%); stroke disabilities (11%); and other problems (42%). Also, according to Gelfand (1984), 33% of the residents are incontinent, and less than 50% are ambulatory. In addition to physical impairments, many of the residents suffer from mental impairments as well, including: advanced senility (34%); moderate senility (27%); and disorientation (17%).

There is a relatively high turnover rate among nursing home residents (Gelfand, 1984), with the average length of stay totalling approximately two years. The turnover rate is due to: (1) residents returning home after a temporary stay (20%); (2) residents transferring to other nursing homes (13%); and (3) residents dying (e.g., in

Alabama, 44% of patient deaths occurred within a few months of admission).

According to Gelfand (1984), most nursing home residents have no family support system to encourage their staying in the community. Only 10% of the residents have a living spouse, with 63% widowed and 22% never married. Many of the residents are socially isolated and more than 50% have no close living relative. In addition, at least 60% have no visitors at all. The majority of nursing home residents are indigent: 68% of the residents have an annual income of less than $3,000, and 22% receive no income at all (Goodman, 1983).

According to Kaplan (1979), out of every 100 nursing home residents, 96 are white, 70 are female, and 85 will never leave the nursing home and die there. At any one time, there are more people staying in nursing homes than hospitals, although 33% of the nursing home residents are admitted directly from hospitals (Gelfand, 1984).

Implications for Recreation Services

The statistics on the degree of impairments found among nursing home residents indicate that recreational activities must be geared toward a low functioning population. A great deal of adaptation of activity should be implemented into the program to facilitate successful resident participation. Activity modification can include: a large degree of repetition; reducing the number of steps required to accomplish specific tasks or goals; a great deal of demonstration; and activities which utilize long-term memory skills, rather than short-term memory.

The institutional nature of the nursing home has several implications for recreation. Since the facility is open 24 hours per day, seven days per week, activities can be scheduled for evenings and weekends, unlike most senior centers and senior day care centers. This is helpful, in that it enables the scheduling of performers and speakers who are available only during evening hours or weekends.

Due to the large numbers of residents living in any one facility and the typically limited recreation personnel, a low staff/resident ratio is a common concern for many facilities. With relatively few recreational staff, an activity program in a nursing home commonly offers only one activity at a time. In addition, recreational activities may not be offered continuously all day. Another implication of the low staff/resident ratio is that individual attention on the part of the activity leaders may be quite limited.

Yet another important factor affecting recreation programming in nursing homes is government regulations. The federal government and state governments have various regulations and requirements regarding activity programs in nursing homes.

A HUMANISTIC PERSPECTIVE

This last section of the chapter is intended to be a humanistic perspective of recreational work in nursing homes. The author is presently performing volunteer work in a nursing home, and would like to share some insights gained through this experience.

I have had many years of experience as a professor of recreation with a specialization in gerontology, and extensive experience as a recreation specialist in nursing homes, day care centers, senior centers, and community/private enterprise recreation programs for elders. Nevertheless, my current volunteer work has reinforced my feelings of how rewarding it is to be involved in the provision of recreation services for nursing home residents. Residents are exceptionally expressive of their gratitude for efforts to provide them with recreational experiences. Elders in general are great to work with because they tend to appreciate services provided to them; in particular, elders in nursing homes tend to be very appreciative.

At first, working in a nursing home might seem to be a very unenjoyable, almost dreaded job. Quite honestly, I was a bit unenthusiastic during the first few days of my current volunteer stint in a nursing home. The environment seemed so unpleasant, and many of the residents appeared to be severely mentally impaired.

However, after the first few days, my attitude changed. Now, after having worked several weeks, I have developed enjoyable, meaningful relationships with many of the residents. These relationships as well as the successes I have enjoyed in planning and leading well-received recreational activities have been instrumental in changing my attitude. I honestly now *enjoy* the time I spend in the nursing home, look forward to going there every day, and have pleasant experiences to think about when I've finished my work for the day. Thus, my advice is: if you don't enjoy working in a nursing home initially, stick with it for awhile! Your attitude will probably change.

As a staff member or volunteer, one's perception of residents changes drastically over time. Initially, one might perceive the residents as a mass of very old people, impaired both mentally and physically. However, that perception is almost totally destroyed after awhile. One begins to relate to the residents as people—unique individuals each with their own special personality and characteristics. One realizes what a mistake it is to lump all nursing home residents into the category of very old and impaired. Nursing home residents are as far from being a homogeneous population as a crowd at a baseball game! However, you must take the time to carefully listen to them in order to find this out!

However, there is one statement which applies to almost all nursing home residents: the provision of recreational services is absolutely vital to their well-being! Recreation can help to compensate for some of the negative aspects of the nursing home environment. It can take a person's mind off their troubles or illnesses and cheer them up for awhile. Recreational activities give residents something to look forward to, and something to discuss besides illnesses and complaints. Recreational activities not only make the residents happy, but they also brighten the atmosphere of the entire nursing home and have a positive effect on staff as well. Recreational activities can give staff an opportunity to see residents in new roles, possibly helping non-recreation staff to gain insight into their work with the residents.

In particular, recreational activities involving volunteer groups or presentations by individuals or organizations in the community are exceptionally well-received. Guest presenters often can generate a special kind of excitement. New experiences are important for all people, and nursing home residents are no exception.

Another basic need of human beings which applies to nursing home residents as well is the need to experience new environments, and experience new places. Field trips are excellent recreational activities for this reason. In addition to being enjoyable, field trips give residents a much needed opportunity to be outside of the nursing home environment for a while.

However, it is wrong to assume that all residents necessarily dislike being in the nursing home. One high functioning woman mentioned to me that she had been living in the nursing home for twelve years. I expected her to continue the conversation by complaining about her long stay in the home, and hoping she could live at home or with her children. Instead, she said: "This is really like home. When I stay with my children for a weekend, I can't wait to get back here.'' Although this woman didn't claim the home to be a utopian environment, she is clearly content with her living situation in the home. Nursing homes are not necessarily desperately depressing places, and activity directors can make sure that the environment is not depressing by planning and effectively leading an extensive and varied recreation program.

Don't permit stereotypes of nursing homes to prevent you from working in a nursing home. Nursing homes will continue to be a major employer of geriatric recreation specialists. If you do become an activity director in a nursing home, do *not* limit the recreation program to what has been done in the past. Recreation for nursing home residents is a relatively new field, in terms of both research and practice. There are constantly new developments in the field. An activity director needs to keep abreast of these developments, try new programs, use imagination, and try to continuously improve and expand the recreation program to make it better than ever.

Try to think what it would be like to live in a nursing home, and how much effort you would desire the nursing home to put into recreational programs. Keep this thought in mind, and try to contribute all you can to the provision of recreation services—display the effort you would desire as a resident. Elders in nursing homes are more in need of recreation than any other segment of the older population. Let's be sure to provide them with the enjoyable, meaningful recreational experiences that they so desperately need and can benefit from.

BIBLIOGRAPHY

Byrd, M. Letting the inmates run the asylum: The effects of control and choice on the institutional lives of older adults. *Activities, Adaptation, and Aging,* 1983, *3*(3), pp. 3-11.

Curley, J.S. Letting the inmates run the asylum: Another point of view. *Activities, Adaptation, and Aging,* 1983, *3*(3), pp. 13-16.

Gelfand, D.E. *The aging network: Programs and services* (2nd ed.). New York: Springer Publishing, 1984.

Goodman, M. I came here to die: A look at the function of therapeutic recreation in nursing homes. *Therapeutic Recreation Journal,* 1983, *17*(3), pp. 14-19.

Hunter, H.C. The activity director in a nursing care facility: How does she fit in? *Activities, Adaptation, and Aging,* 1984, *4*(4), pp. 13-44.

Incani, A.G., Seward, B.L., and Sigler, J.E. *Coordinated activity programs for the aged: A how-to-do-it manual.* Chicago: American Hospital Association, 1975.

Jones, C.C. *Caring for the aged: An appraisal of nursing homes and alternatives.* Chicago: Nelson-Hall, 1982.

Kaplan, M. *Leisure: Lifestyle and lifespan.* Philadelphia: W.B. Saunders Company, 1979.

Kelly, G.R., McNally, E., and Chamblis, L. Therapeutic recreation for long-term care patients. *Therapeutic Recreation Journal,* 1983, *17*(1), pp. 33-41.

Pepper, N.H. *Fundamentals of care of the aging, disabled, and handicapped in the nursing home.* Springfield, IL: Charles C. Thomas, 1982.

U.S. Department of Health, Education, and Welfare. *Activities coordinator's guide* (series three). Washington, D.C.: U.S. Government Printing Office, 1978.

U.S. Department of Health, Education, and Welfare. *The national nursing home survey* (DHEW Publication No. 79-1794). Washington, D.C.: U.S. Government Printing Office, 1979.

Chapter 8

Retirement Communities and Age-Segregated Housing

INTRODUCTION

The purposes of this chapter are to explore the status and desirability of age-segregated living arrangements, in particular, the desirability of age-segregation in terms of the provision of leisure services to elders. Many different types of age-segregated living arrangements are discussed in this chapter, but the primary focus of this chapter is on recreation in retirement communities. For the purposes of this book, a retirement community is defined as a small community which is relatively independent, age-segregated, and noninstitutionalized, whose residents are elderly, and are separated from their career occupation in paid or non-paid employment (Magnum, 1973).

In the first section of this chapter, the current status of age-segregation in the U.S. is described, including information on retirement communities, and age-segregation within residential areas of metropolitan areas. In the second section of the chapter, research on elders' preferences for age-segregation is presented. In the third section of the chapter, the desirability of age-segregated living arrangements is examined. Issues and questions for discussion are raised throughout this chapter.

CURRENT STATUS OF AGE-SEGREGATION

The degree of age-segregation in the U.S. has increased over the past few decades, and is projected to continue to increase. The trend toward increasing age-segregation of our society is caused by several factors: the growth of planned retirement communities; the growth of other retirement housing, such as sheltered housing and senior citizen's public housing; the migration of middle class families to the suburbs, leaving areas within metropolitan areas with a high concentration of elders; and as discussed in chapter one, the significant increase in the proportion of noninstitutionalized elders living alone. These factors are discussed more in-depth in this section of the chapter.

Retirement Communities

Planned retirement communities are a recent phenomena. The country's first retirement community was established in 1954 in Youngstown, Arizona (Gelfand, 1984). Many elders have moved to retirement communities in Arizona and other "Sunbelt" areas. According to Golant (1975), over 500,000 elders moved to Florida, Arizona, and California between 1960 and 1970. However, retirement communities in the "Sunbelt" states are not the only retirement communities experiencing growth. Golant (1975) projects a continued growth in planned retirement communities in the fringes of urban areas in the eastern and mid-western states. Thus, planned retirement communities in most areas of the country seem to be experiencing significant growth.

Other Retirement Housing

In addition to planned retirement communities, other prominent types of age-segregated housing are public housing for senior citizens, sheltered and congregate housing, foster care, retirement hotels, and mobile home parks. Public housing for senior citizens has increased significantly, with elders occupying nearly 50% of the over one million units of public housing that had been constructed by 1980 (Gelfand, 1984).

Sheltered and congregate housing are recent developments designed to meet the needs of elders not able to maintain full independent living and yet are not in need of institutional care. According to Gelfand (1984), congregate housing provides housekeeping, dining, emergency health, and recreational services, whereas sheltered housing offers more extensive services, with an emphasis placed on meals and personal care.

A specialized form of sheltered housing is foster care, in which elders not able to maintain full independence are placed in a setting with a family support system (Gelfand, 1984). Foster care first became available to elders in the 1970s, and according to Gelfand (1984), although foster care's effectiveness with older mental patients has been documented, it remains an underutilized resource.

Another type of age-segregated living arrangement is the single-room occupancy hotel. According to Gelfand (1984), approximately 600,000 elders live in hotels and rooming houses, most of which are located in commercial areas adjacent to downtown business districts. According to Gelfand (1984) residents tend to live in isolation and deep friendships rarely develop.

In contrast to the single-room occupancy hotels are mobile home parks. Mobile home parks are more similar to retirement communities than the previously discussed types of housing, but differ from retirement communities in that the developments tend to be smaller; recreational facilities are not as extensive, and housing costs are lower. However, it can sometimes be difficult to distinguish between a retirement community and a mobile home park for elders, especially some of the larger mobile home parks.

Age-Segregation Within Metropolitan Areas

Several recent studies have examined the extent of age-segregation within metropolitan areas in the U.S. One of the most extensive studies in this area was conducted by Cowgill (1978). Cowgill measured the extent of dissimilarity of residential distribution between the population of persons over age sixty-five, and persons under age sixty-five for 241 Standard Metropolitan Statistical Areas (SMSAs) in 1970. Cowgill also computed the extent of age segregation in those 241 SMSAs for the years 1940, 1950, and 1960. Cowgill found that a high degree of age-segregation existed in 1970, and that the extent of age-segregation had greatly increased since 1940. The greatest amount of age-segregation was found to exist in the more rapidly growing SMSAs (especially in the West and South), and in areas with major military or educational institutions (such institutions create age-homogeneous population clusters within an area). According to Cowgill, the main factor related to age-segregation is the growth and differentiation of the SMSA (the faster a SMSA is growing, the greater the extent of its age-segregation). Another factor related to age-segregation cited by Cowgill is the size of the non-white population, and the size of the aged population. Greatest age-segregation was found in the SMSAs where the non-white population was relatively large, and the aged population was relatively small. Such circumstances are most conducive to whites moving to the suburbs. The result of the migration of whites to the suburbs is a high concentration of younger white families in the suburbs; a high concentration of younger non-white families in certain sections of the central city; and a high concentration of white aged persons in other sections of the central city.

Similarly, Riley, Johnson, and Foner (1972) state that many of the newly formed suburbs (surrounding growing SMSAs) are characterized by a high degree of age homogeneity. The authors also state that age-segregation is partially caused by the presence of poor elderly persons in the inner cities who are economically incapable of moving out of these often slum-like areas.

Another study concerned with the segregation of aged persons in urban areas was conducted by Pampel and Choldin (1978). Pampel and Choldin conducted a block-level analysis of Cleveland, Ohio, and San Diego, California, in order to determine the mixture of over sixty-five and under sixty-five persons residing on each block within those cities. According to the authors, the extent of age-segregation was found to be higher through utilization of the block analysis technique, as opposed to merely examining the districts, or areas within those cities. The authors found that a high level of age-segregation existed in both Cleveland and San Diego.

In summary, a high level of age-segregation exists within metropolitan areas of the U.S. According to research on this topic, the degree of age-segregation in metropolitan areas of the U.S. seems to be increasing.

More Elders Living Alone

One very significant factor contributing to the increasing age-segregation of our society is the great increase in the proportion of noninstitutionalized elders living alone (only 1/6 lived alone in 1950, while approximately 1/3 lived alone in 1980 according to the U.S. Bureau of the Census (1981)). According to Golant (1975), the percentage of elders living in the household of an adult child dropped from 16% in 1950 to 9% in 1970. Thus, there are fewer intergenerational households, as well as fewer intergenerational areas within metropolitan areas.

ELDERS' PREFERENCES

The growth of age-segregated housing for elders has been well-documented, but one needs to ask if the trend toward age-segregated housing is desirable. Specifically, do elders prefer age-segregated housing, or intergenerational living arrangements? Numerous research studies on this topic have been conducted, several of which are discussed in this section in order to better understand the preferences of elders regarding age-segregation.

Swartout conducted an interesting study on this topic with residents of a Leisure World retirement community (Magnum, 1973). Thirty intensive, and thirty casual interviews were conducted, in which none of the interviewees cited age-segregation as a motive for residency in the community, nor as a desirable quality. However, community residents almost unanimously disapproved a proposed lowering of the minimum residency age from 52 to 42. This behavior somewhat contradicts their expressed attitudes regarding age-segregation. The residents stated that they opposed the proposed lowered minimum age because they didn't want children in the community; also, they felt that the younger people would have different interests than the older residents, which might cause conflicts (e.g., loud parties). Swartout concluded that the sample population actually viewed age-segregation as being desirable, and was a motive for their moving to the community. A similar view was expressed by Whitman (1961). Although most older people supposedly resent age-segregation, Whitman found that most people interviewed at Sun City (a planned retirement community in Arizona) enjoyed the fact that all residents were over age fifty, and that no children lived in the community.

Similarly, 83% of the subjects in Teaff's et al. (1978) study of 1,875 aged persons stated a preference for age-segregated, as opposed to age-integrated housing. However, Teaff et al. cited a 1975 study conducted by Lawton, in which only 37% of the subjects stated a preference for age-segregation.

The data on preferences of the aged with regard to age-segregation are somewhat inconclusive. In relation to this question, is it possible that it is racial segregation, rather than age-segregation which many elders desire when they seek planned retirement housing? Except for Messer's (1967) study, all of the literature cited in this chapter describes age-homogeneous environments which are also virtually homogeneous with respect to race and socio-economic status. Indeed, although Messer's study subjects were composed of an even mixture of white and non-white residents (51% and 49%), the reason for this balance was that the subjects in this study had not chosen their place of residence; it was assigned to them by the public housing authority!

This issue has great implications for leisure services for elders. Is it desirable to provide age (and race) segregated programs? Can older persons benefit more from age (and race) segregated programs even though service providers might believe otherwise? Should leisure service professionals provide services for elders which they think are most beneficial, or should the preferences of elders be the prime determinant of the type of services to be provided?

DESIRABILITY OF AGE-SEGREGATED LIVING ARRANGEMENTS

One area of emphasis in examining the desirability of age-segregation is that of life satisfaction and morale. Several studies on this topic are described in this section of the chapter.

Poulin (1984) examined the relationships of age-segregation, interpersonal involvement, morale, and life satisfaction of 232 elders. Data collected from 78 residents of senior citizens housing were compared to that of 154 residents of natural community housing. Poulin found that the senior housing residents had slightly larger and more supportive interpersonal networks, but had less contact with their friends than the community residents. No significant differences were found in the life satisfaction of the two groups. Similarly, Deimling et al. (1979) and Gubrium (1970) found no significant relationship between residential age concentration and life satisfaction.

Atchley (1975) cited a study conducted by Rosow involving 1,200 aged residents of aged-dense (comprised of 50% or more elders), aged-concentrated (33-49%), and normal aged-density (1-15%) housing. Subjects were screened for occupational status, and whether or not they were residing in public housing, in order to have a range of social classes represented in the sample.

Three successive interviews (25% drop-out rate) were conducted with the subjects. Rosow found that the greater the aged-density of the housing, the greater the morale of its socially unstable aged residents; the lower the morale of its socially isolated aged residents; and that the morale of the sociable aged residents remained the same. Rosow concluded that high aged-density is more conducive to the development of friendships among older persons, these friendships coming disproportionately from among their aged neighbors. Rosow concluded that this increased opportunity for social contact improved the social life for the socially unstable aged (and improved their morale); had little effect on the highly sociable aged (they already had many friends); but made the socially isolated aged more depressed, due to their continued inability to acquire friendships, even in the face of an increased opportunity to do so. Rosow concluded that the results of this study should not be interpreted to mean that age-segregation is a cure-all; some elders simply do not care to socialize.

Messer (1967) studied the activity levels and life satisfaction of aged residents of age-homogeneous (N = 88) and age-integrated (N = 155) public housing in Chicago. In this study, the problem of subject self-selection was minimized, in that residents of the age-homogeneous housing were not there by choice; in Chicago, aged persons that apply for public housing are not asked whether they would prefer to live in age-segregated, or age-integrated housing. Messer concluded that the age-segregated environment helped to ease the transition of its residents to the leisure-oriented role of later life. He also concluded that successful adjustment to old age is facilitated by the maintenance of high activity levels.

Hampe and Blevins (1975) examined the interaction patterns and life satisfaction of aged residents (N = 63) of a retirement hotel. Hampe's sample consisted of mostly female (75%), single, Caucasian, and low-income persons. Hampe and Blevins found that a high level of housing satisfaction existed among the residents. Hampe and Blevins concluded that the age-segregated environment provided a greater opportunity to create friendships and to interact with others. However, it was also concluded that age-segregation can contribute to feelings of uselessness—that one is no longer part of the mainstream of society.

Teaff et al. (1978) also examined the impact of age-segregation on the well-being of the aged. The researchers conducted interviews of aged persons (N = 1,875) in 753 public housing sites, based on a national probability sample. The authors found that age-segregation was significantly related to greater activity participation, morale, and general well-being. Teaff et al. attempted to explain this finding in terms of the reduced crime, and a more relaxed, less competitive atmosphere which existed in the age-segregated environments. Similarly, Carp's (1972) study of aged residents of San Antonio, Texas also demonstrated the positive aspects of age-segregated living.

Poorkaj (1972) also studied the relationship of age-segregation to life satisfaction. Poorkaj interviewed 52 elders with regard to life satisfaction, leisure activities, and health status. Three groups of subjects were studied: (1) residents of an age-integrated community, and participants at a senior center; (2) residents of an age-integrated community, and non-participants in social activities; and (3) residents of a planned age-segregated retirement community. The three groups of subjects were matched for age, sex, marital status, and religion. The researchers found that the morale of groups one and two were not significantly different, but that the morale of group three was significantly lower. Poorkaj concluded that possibly age-segregation is not really as beneficial as we might be led to believe.

In summary, it is difficult to draw clear-cut conclusions as to the relationship of age-segregation to life satisfaction. Sherman appropriately sums up this issue: "Either age-segregation or age-integration can be satisfactory, provided that the person has made the choice according to his own needs and preferences." (Gelfand, 1984).

Recreational Advantages of Retirement Communities

Although it is not clear whether age-segregation has a positive effect on life satisfaction, it is clear that there are great advantages to retirement communities with respect to recreation, in particular, the availability of recreational facilities. According to Gelfand (1984), the retirement community in Youngstown, Arizona has $2 million in recreation facilities, while nearby in Sun City, there is a retirement community with $12 million in recreation facilities. Gelfand (1984) describes the impressive recreational facilities of Leisure World in Laguna Hills, California. Their facilities include five clubhouses, swimming pools, a golf course, horseback riding, and theaters. Over 150 clubs and organizations serve the leisure needs of Leisure World's approximately 19,000 residents.

Similarly, Osgood (1982) describes the extensive recreational facilities and programs of Hidden Valley, a retirement community in Arizona with approximately 6,000 residents. Recreational facilities at Hidden Valley include theaters, golf courses, tennis courts, numerous swimming pools, meeting areas, arts and crafts facilities, shuffleboard courts, Jacuzzis, and card and game rooms. According to Osgood (1982), residents are very active, and the extensive facilities receive a great deal of use. Nearly 80% of the community residents are involved in one or more clubs or organizations. Some of the more notable groups are: the Aquabelles, which is a women's water ballet and water show team; the Garden Club, which directs an annual community-wide clean-up and beautification project; and the Community Choir, which gives two concerts a year for fellow residents. According to Osgood (1982), most Hidden Valley residents value leisure and enjoy participating in a great variety of recreational activities.

Aside from extensive recreational facilities and programs, retirement communities offer numerous other recreation-related advantages. One advantage of retirement community life is that it validates the retirement role. According to Dr. Maurice Hemovitch of the University of Southern California, the "guilt" of not working is eliminated in a retirement community, because one is surrounded by peers at play (Kaplan, 1979). Thus, retirement community life can have a positive effect on leisure attitudes, enabling greater participation in recreation, without feelings of guilt. Furthermore, the retirement community promotes and creates a leisurely atmosphere, conducive to recreation (Bultena and Wood, 1969).

Another recreation-related advantage of retirement communities is the clustering of age peers with similar interests. This clustering makes the provision of extensive recreation facilities and programs economically feasible (Sherman, 1975). In addition, the clustering of age peers with similar interests promotes higher levels of social interaction and the formation of friendships, as documented by numerous case studies of various retirement communities (Osgood, 1982).

Yet another recreational advantage of retirement communities is the easier lifestyle because of the services usually provided (e.g., building and grounds maintenance, and transportation). The provision of these services enables residents to have more leisure time, time which can be used for recreational pursuits. Also, the easier lifestyle promotes greater independence, and a feeling of freedom, which is a very desirable component of the recreation experience.

Also related to feelings of freedom, retirement community residents tend to be less restricted by crime and the fear of crime, due to the extensive security arrangements offered by many retirement communities. The reduced crime and fear of crime enables residents to feel free to enjoy a much greater range of night time recreational activities.

SUMMARY

Certainly, the recreational advantages of retirement communities are impressive. However, do these advantages outweigh the potential negative feelings of being in a closed-in environment, with constant reminders of death and aging all around? Is the segregation of elders from younger generations so harmful to our society that the growth of retirement communities should be discouraged? Finally, even if retirement communities are preferred by elders, is it any more ethical to allow age-segregation in housing than it is to permit racial segregation?

These are important, but difficult questions to answer. Meanwhile, retirement communities and other age-segregated living arrangements for elders seem likely to continue to grow in the near future. As these housing developments continue to grow, they will take on increasing importance as focal points for the delivery of leisure services to elders.

BIBLIOGRAPHY

Atchley, R.C. *The sociology of retirement.* New York: Schenkman, 1975.

Bley, N., Goodman, M., Dye, D., and Harel, B. Characteristics of aged participants and non-participants in age-segregated leisure programs. *Gerontologist,* 1972, *12,* pp. 368-70.

Brody, E.M. Community housing for the elderly: The program, the people, the decision-making process, and the research. *Gerontologist,* 1978, *18*(2), pp. 121-28.

Bultena, G.L. Age-grading in the social interaction of an elderly male population. *Journal of Gerontology,* 1968, *23*(4), pp. 539-43.

Bultena, G.L. The relationship of occupational status to friendship ties in three planned retirement communities. *Journal of Gerontology,* 1969, *24*(4), pp. 461-64.

Bultena, G.L., and Wood, V. The American retirement community: Bane or blessing? *Journal of Gerontology,* 1969, *24,* pp. 209-17.

Carp, F.M. Mobility among members of an established retirement community. *Gerontologist,* 1972, *12*(1), pp. 48-56.

Carson, G. Odyssey at eighty. *Blair and Ketchum's Country Journal,* August 1983, pp. 54-60.

Cowgill, D.O. Residential segregation by age in American metropolitan areas. *Journal of Gerontology,* 1978, *33*(3), pp. 446-53.

Deimling, G.T., Noelker, L.S., and Beckman, A.C. *The impact of race on the resources and well-being of aged public housing residents.* Paper presented at 32nd Annual Scientific Meeting of the Gerontological Society, Washington, D.C., November 1979.

Dickinson, P.A. *Sunbelt Retirement.* New York: E.P. Dutton, 1978.

Ehrlick, I.F. Lifestyles among persons 70 years and older in age-segregated housing. *Gerontologist,* 1972, *12*(1), pp. 27-31.

Erickson, R., and Eckert, K. The elderly poor in downtown San Diego hotels. *Gerontologist,* 1977, *17*(5), pp. 440-46.

Fitzgerald, F. A reporter at large (Sun City Center). *New Yorker,* April 1983, pp. 54-109.

Fry, C.L. Community as a commodity: The age graded case. *Human Organization,* 1977, *36,* pp. 115-23.

Gelfand, D.E. *The aging network: Programs and services* (2nd ed.). New York: Springer Publishing, 1984.

Golant, S.M. Residential concentrations of the future elderly. *Gerontologist,* 1975, *15*(1), pp. 16-23.

Graney, M.J. Happiness and social participation in aging. *Journal of Gerontology,* 1975, *30,* pp. 701-06.

Gubrium, J.P. Environmental effects on morale in old age and the resources of health and solvency. *Gerontologist,* 1970, *10,* pp. 294-297.

Hampe, G.D., and Blevins, A.L. Primary group interaction of residents in a retirement hotel. *International Journal of Aging and Human Development,* 1975, *6*(4), pp. 309-320.

Haynie, W.E. Cypen tower: A design for retirement living. *Aging,* Jan./Feb. 1983, pp. 18-25.

Kaplan, M. *Leisure: Lifestyle and lifespan.* Philadelphia: W.B. Saunders, 1979.

Kiester, E. Back to main street. *Fifty Plus,* October 1982, pp. 14-23.

Kleemeir, R.W. Leisure and disengagement in retirement. *Gerontologist,* 1964, *4*(4), pp. 180-84.

Klein, D. Retiring to a college town. *Fifty Plus,* December 1982, pp. 38-40.

Lemon, B.W., Bengtson, V.L., and Peterson, J.A. An exploration of the activity theory of aging: Activity types and life satisfaction among in-movers to a retirement community. *Journal of Gerontology,* 1972, *27*(4), pp. 511-23.

Magnum, W.P. Retirement villages. In R.R. Boyd and C.G. Oakes (Eds.), *Foundations of practical gerontology* (2nd ed.). Columbia, SC: University of South Carolina Press, 1973.

Marshall, V.W. Organizational features of terminal status passage in residential facilities for the aged. *Urban Life,* 1975, *4,* pp. 349-68.

Marshall, V.W. Socialization for impending death in a retirement village. *American Journal of Sociology,* 1975, *8,* pp. 124-44.

Martin, W.C. Activity and disengagement: Life satisfaction of in-movers into a retirement community. *Gerontologist,* 1975, *13*(2), pp. 224-27.

Messer, M. The possibility of an age-concentrated environment becoming a normative system. *Gerontologist,* 1967, *7,* pp. 247-51.

Osgood, N.J. *Senior settlers, social integration in retirement communities.* Praeger Publishing, 1983.

Pampel, F.C., and Choldin, H.M. Urban location and segregation of the aged: A block level analysis. *Social Forces,* 1978, *56*(4), pp. 1121-39.

Peterson, J.A., Hadwin, T., and Larson, A.E. *A time for work, a time for leisure: A study of retirement community in-movers.* Los Angeles: University of Southern California, 1969.

Pierce, C.H. Recreation for the elderly: Activity participation at a senior center. *Gerontologist,* 1975, *15*(3), pp. 202-05.

Poorkaj, H. Sociological-Psychological factors and successful aging. *Sociology and Social Research,* 1972, *56,* pp. 289-300.

Poulin, J.E. Age segregation and interpersonal involvement and morale of the aged. *Gerontologist,* 1984, *24*(3), pp. 266-269.

Riley, M.W., Johnson, M., and Foner, A. *Aging and society.* New York: Russel Sage Foundation, 1972.

Ross, J.K. *Old people, new lives.* Chicago: University of Chicago Press, 1977.

Sachs, M. Cooperative services, inc. *Aging,* March/April 1983, pp. 14-18.

Seguin, M.M. Opportunity for peer socialization in a retirement community. *Gerontologist,* 1973, *13*(2), pp. 208-14.

Sheley, J.F. Mutuality and retirement community success: An interactionist perspective in gerontological research. *International Journal of Aging and Human Development,* 1974, *5*(1), pp. 71-80.

Sherman, S.R. Mutual assistance and support in retirement housing. *Journal of Gerontology,* 1975, *30,* pp. 479-83.

Sherman, S.R. Provision of on-site services in retirement housing. *International Journal of Aging and Human Development,* 1975, *6*(3), pp. 229-247.

Sherman, S.R. Satisfaction with retirement housing: Attitudes, recommendations, and moves. *International Journal of Aging and Human Development,* 1972, *3*(4), pp. 339-66.

Sherman, S.R. The choice of retirement housing among the well elderly. *International Journal of Aging and Human Development,* 1971, 2(2), pp. 118-39.

Struyk, R.J. The housing situation of elderly Americans. *Gerontologist,* 1977, *17*(2), pp. 130-39.

Teaff, J.D., Lawton, M.P., Nahemon, L., Carlson, D. Impact of age-integration on the well-being of elderly tenants in public housing. *Journal of Gerontology,* 1978, *33*(1), pp. 126-33.

U.S. Bureau of the Census. *Statistical Abstract of the United States: 1981.* Washington, D.C.: U.S. Government Printing Office, 1981.

Wan, T.T. *Promoting the well-being of the elderly.* New York: Haworth Press, 1982, pp. 21-26.

Whitman, H. *A brighter later life.* Englewood Cliffs, NJ: Prentice-Hall Inc., 1961.

Williams, M.L. One of the best retirement centers as seen by one of the residents. *Gerontologist,* 1972, *12* (1), pp. 38-42.

Wilner, D.M., Sherman, S.R., Walkley, R.P., Dodds, S., and Magnum, W.P., Jr. Demographic characteristics of residents of planned retirement housing sites. *Gerontologist,* 1968, *8,* 164-69.

Winiecke, L. The appeal of age-segregated housing to the elderly poor. *International Journal of Aging and Human Development,* 1973, *4*(4), pp. 293-306.

Wolk, S., and Telleen, S. Psychological and social correlates of life satisfaction as a function of residential constraint. *Journal of Gerontology,* 1976, *31*(1), pp. 89-98.

Section III:
Resources
for Recreation
Programs for Elders

Chapter 9

Intergenerational Activities

INTRODUCTION

Improved intergenerational relations has been a topic of increasing concern in recent years, for several reasons: (1) people age 65 and over represent one of the fastest growing segments in American society; (2) phenomena such as the growth of retirement communities has increased the degree of segregation of the older population from younger age groups in society; and (3) research findings and theoretical assumptions indicate that intergenerational relations can be improved through increased opportunities for intergenerational interaction.

The purpose of this chapter is to examine intergenerational recreational activity as a means of improving intergenerational relations. In this regard, the primary focus of the chapter is to provide practical information on how to plan and lead successful intergenerational recreation activities. The chapter begins with a presentation of literature and research findings related to intergenerational recreation, followed by an explanation of guidelines to follow in planning intergenerational recreational activity programs.

RESEARCH ON INTERGENERATIONAL RECREATION

Several statements in the literature on the topic of intergenerational activity express the value of such activity for the aged, children, and society as a whole (Bronfenbrenner, 1970; Powell and Arquitt, 1978; Leviton and Santa Maria, 1979; Seefeldt, Jantz, Serock, and Bredekamp, 1979; and Weinberger, 1979).

The results of several research studies indicate that older persons desire intergenerational interaction. Daum and Getzel (1980) report that 74.3% of the respondents to the *Myth and Reality of Aging* survey (Harris, 1975) aged 65 and over expressed a preference for interaction with people of all ages as opposed to interaction with people their own age. Daum and Getzel recommend that greater opportunity for intergenerational interaction be provided, in that both young and old respondents to the Harris survey expressed a desire for interacting with people of all ages.

In a related vein, Seefeldt, Jantz, Serock, and Bredekamp (1979) examined the attitudes toward children of a nationwide sample of 542 persons aged 50 and over through the use of a self-report questionnaire. The results indicated that older persons feel that children are fun to be with, that children make good friends for the elderly, and that older persons prefer contact with children ages eight to twelve as opposed to children four to eight. The researchers also state the importance of intergenerational activity to children, as well as to the aged.

Furthermore, Powell and Arquitt (1978) state that children's attitudes toward the aged are a major influence on how older persons will be treated in the future society. Bronfenbrenner (1970) and Weinberger (1979) express the concern that future society will experience severe problems if intergenerational relations are not improved. According to Seefeldt, et al., increased intergenerational contact can improve the attitudes of the elderly and children toward each other.

The assertion by Seefeldt, et al. is supported by the success of an intergenerational interaction program involving older persons and Girl Scouts (Girl Scouts of the United States of America, no date). Other successful intergenerational interaction programs are described by Meier (1980) and Leviton and Santa Maria (1979).

A study conducted by Leitner (1981) on the effects of a six-week intergenerational music activities program on senior day care participants and twelve-year-old children indicated that the presence of children in the activity setting caused senior day care participants' enjoyment of musical activities to be significantly greater. Another finding of the study was that the children's attitudes toward older persons became more positive after participation in the intergenerational music activities program. The recommendations which follow are based on the results of this study.

RECOMMENDATIONS FOR PROGRAM PLANNING

(1) Eleven and twelve year-old children are excellent candidates for an intergenerational activities program, because they are attentive and mature enough to enable participation in a wide range of ac-

tivities with elders. Older children and adolescents could also work well with elders, perhaps even doing service projects for impaired elders. Conversely, with younger children, the range of activity possibilities would be more limited, due to their shorter attention span and less developed oral and written communication skills. However, higher functioning elders could work well as instructors for younger children in diverse areas such as crafts skills, spelling, and history. Even very young children (three and four year-olds) can provide enjoyment for elders on an occasional basis. For example, some nursing homes have had success with a once or twice a month "cuddling" hour, with young children providing a much-needed outlet for affectionate behavior.

(2) A variety of musical activities can work well on an intergenerational basis. Elders and children often find that they can learn about different types of music from each other, and that they share a common knowledge of music such as patriotic songs and religious songs. Some examples of musical activities which can be successful on an intergenerational basis are: Sing-a-longs; talent show; musical jamboree (elders and children play instruments such as woodblocks, kazoos, etc.); musical charades game (elders and children work together to compose a song about a famous person *without* using the famous person's name in the song); and a variation of "Name-That-Tune" musical quiz game, where children and elders work in intergenerational teams to guess the names of songs.

(3) An intergenerational music activities program conducted on a regular basis should involve activities on a twice a month basis. Twice a month activities would foster the formation of intergenerational friendships and yet would not be so frequent that such activities would become boring or tiring to the participants.

(4) The number of children participating in an intergenerational activities program should be limited so that a one-to-one ratio of elders to children is maintained. A one-to-one ratio of elders to children can best facilitate intergenerational interaction and ensure that activities are adequately adapted for elders. If children outnumber elders, activities tend to become more child-oriented and subsequently not as enjoyable for elders. In senior day care centers, absenteeism due to illness is a significant factor affecting participation in activities, especially in inclement weather, while in retirement communities, attendance for activities can fluctuate depending on outside commitments of residents. Therefore, particularly in senior day care centers and retirement communities, the number of children selected for an intergenerational recreation program should

be less than the number of potential elderly participants in the program, due to factors which restrict elders' attendance in activities.

(5) As a mechanism for facilitating the formation of intergenerational ties, a buddy system should be enacted for intergenerational programs whereby certain seniors and children are assigned as partners or teammates for activities.

(6) In a related vein, seating arrangements for activities should be such that seniors and children are sitting next to one another, not clustered in an age-segregated arrangement. The seating arrangement for an activity is an important factor in determining the extent of intergenerational interaction during an activity. The clustering together of seniors and children can severely restrict the amount of intergenerational contact that takes place during an activity. Unless seating arrangements are structured, elders will tend to cluster together, and children will also tend to cluster together. The following procedure can be very effective in ensuring that an intergenerational seating pattern is formed:

a. Have the residents or center attendees seated in an area *other* than the activity area where the activity is to be held before the children arrive;

b. When the children arrive, they are asked to wait in the lobby rather than enter all at once;

c. One or two children at a time are escorted in and introduced to their "host" or "hostess" for the activity;

d. The elder/children pairs then escort each other to the activity area;

e. One staff member remains in the lobby with the children until all children have entered.

(7) Another means of facilitating interaction among activity participants is to organize the larger group into several smaller groups of four or five persons each. Both the seniors and the children feel less inhibited in a small group than in a large group situation. Also, there is often times more opportunity for interaction in small group situations. In devising small groups, more alert seniors should be paired with the more confused seniors so as to facilitate interaction in groups where confused seniors are members.

(8) Before commencing activities, ample time should be allotted for the seniors and children to get acquainted with one another.

Tasks such as choosing a group leader can be helpful in initiating communication among the activity participants. Another aid in getting elders and children acquainted is wearing name tags. In fact, making name tags can be an appropriate icebreaker activity.

(9) Activities which require a great deal of cognitive functioning should be avoided. Many senior day care participants and nursing home residents are at least slightly impaired with regard to cognitive functioning and are thus at a disadvantage in activities with children that require a great deal of cognitive functioning. Thus, it becomes difficult to lead activities involving a great deal of cognitive functioning because of the disparity in the abilities of the children and the seniors. Furthermore, some senior citizens might feel embarrassed as not being able to "keep pace" with children. Therefore it is more desirable to conduct activities which do not rely heavily on short-term memory or the ability to think of an answer to a question while under the constraint of time limits.

(10) Conversely, activities which draw upon the past experiences of senior citizens are recommended. Older persons can share a great deal of knowledge from their past with children, such as anecdotes about historical events and living conditions of the past as compared to that of the present. In order to ensure the success of such activities, staff should prepare seniors for the activities so that each participant will be able to contribute to the activities.

(11) Senior citizens should be given specific roles in intergenerational activities which can enhance their self-esteem and encourage the children to seek their assistance in performing tasks related to the activity. For example, the role of host or hostess is one which many older persons probably enjoy, but rarely are able to experience in their later years. In addition, roles such as team or group leader can help give the seniors greater status in the activities and encourage children to consult with senior day care participants during activities.

(12) Activities which involve some degreee of competition seem to effectively motivate children. However, competitiveness should be kept at a moderate level, otherwise the competitive aspect of the activity will dominate and hinder interaction among participants.

(13) Before commencing an intergenerational activities program, the children should be thoroughly oriented to the purpose of the program. Children should be made to understand that the primary focus of activities is to interact with the senior citizens and learn from each other, not to win whatever games are played.

SUMMARY

Intergenerational activities can be the most successful and enjoyable activities for elders and children if planned and led properly. However, intergenerational activities can be disastrous if *not* properly planned, given the great differences in needs, interests, and abilities of elders and children. The implementation of the recommendations discussed in this chapter can help to ensure the successfulness of an intergenerational recreation program.

BIBLIOGRAPHY

Azadi, L. *The effects of instruction and recreation interaction on children's attitudes toward the elderly.* Unpublished master's thesis, California State University, Chico, 1983.

Bronfenbrenner, U. *Two worlds of childhood: The U.S. and the U.S.S.R.* New York: Russel Sage Foundation, 1970.

Daum, M., and Getzel, G. *Preference for age-homogeneous versus age-heterogeneous social interaction.* Paper presented at the 33rd Annual Scientific Meeting of the Gerontological Society, 1980.

Girl Scouts of the United States of America. *Hand-in-hand: Cross-age interactions* (Administration on Aging Grant 90-A-326). Washington, D.C.: Administration on Aging, n.d.

Harris, L., and Associates. *The myth and reality of aging in America.* Washington, D.C.: National Council on Aging, 1975.

Leitner, M.J. The effects of intergenerational music activities on senior day care participants and elementary school children. *Dissertation Abstracts International,* 1981, *42*(08), p. 3752A.

Leviton, D., and Santa Maria, L. The adults health and developmental program: Descriptive and evaluative data. *Gerontologist,* 1979, *19*(6), pp. 534-543.

Meier, P. Toddlers, elderly share quarters at day-care center. *Senior Citizens Day Care News,* 1980, *1*(1), p. 5.

National Council on Aging (NCOA). *Strategies for linking the generations: Report of the 1981 White House conference on aging mini-conference on intergenerational cooperation and exchange.* Washington, D.C.: National Council on Aging, 1981.

Powell, J.A., and Arquitt, G.E. Getting the generations back together: A rationale for the development of community based intergenerational activity programs. *The Family Coordinator,* 1978, *3,* p. 421-426.

Seefeldt, C., Jantz, R.D., Serock, K., and Bredekamp, S. *Elderly persons' attitudes toward children.* College Park, MD: University of Maryland, 1979.

Weinberger, A. Stereotyping the elderly: Elementary school children's responses. *Research on Aging,* 1979, *1*(1), pp. 113-136.

Chapter 10

Leisure Counseling

INTRODUCTION

The main purposes of this chapter are to help the reader to understand leisure counseling, and how to use leisure counseling with elders. The chapter has been organized as follows: an explanation of key leisure counseling concepts and terminology; an overview of the history, background, and rationale for leisure counseling; a discussion of how to use leisure counseling with elders, including a detailed explanation of procedures to follow in conducting leisure counseling with elders; and a discussion of special considerations and concerns in counseling elders.

CONCEPTS AND DEFINITIONS

For the purposes of this chapter, leisure counseling is defined as a helping process designed to facilitate maximal leisure well-being. Leisure education is also a process designed to facilitate maximal leisure well-being. However, leisure education is more of a self-help process, whereas leisure counseling is an individualized or small group helping process guided by a leisure counselor. This chapter focuses specifically on leisure counseling.

Although four different types of leisure counseling are identified in the literature (McDowell, 1980), this chapter will examine only the *three* different types or approaches to leisure counseling discussed by McDowell (1976): (1) the leisure resource guidance approach; (2) the developmental-educational approach; and (3) the therapeutic-remedial approach. The step-by-step procedures of each of these different types of leisure counseling are discussed later in the chapter.

BACKGROUND AND RATIONALE

The first documented leisure counseling program was initiated at the Kansas City Veteran's Administration Hospital psychiatric ward in 1957 (Olson and McCormick, 1957). The rationale for the early leisure counseling programs was that leisure counseling could be used to help reduce recidivism by orienting patients to better use their leisure time after discharge from the institutional setting. It was hypothesized that a prominent cause of recidivism was the inability of patients to effectively deal with the vast increase in unstructured leisure time after discharge from the institution. Therefore, it was hoped that leisure counseling could help reduce recidivism by preparing patients to more effectively deal with the increased leisure time they would face after discharge.

Overs and his associates (Overs, 1970) developed the first leisure counseling service for elders in the early 1970s. Overs' "Milwaukee Avocational Guidance Leisure Counseling Model" was not designed to be exclusively for elders, but rather sought to meet three human needs: (1) to help ease the transition from institution to community; (2) to facilitate developmental growth; and (3) to facilitate involvement in appropriate activity, especially for persons isolated from the mainstream of society. The Milwaukee Model was modeled after vocational counseling. Emphasis was placed on identification of recreational activity interests and awareness of available recreation resources. Attitudes and values related to leisure were not emphasized as strongly. (Humphrey, Kelley, and Hamilton, 1980).

McDowell (1976) tested the effectiveness of a leisure counseling model in an experimental study which examined the effects of a leisure counseling program on the leisure attitudes, work attitudes, leisure self-concept, work self-concept, and leisure satisfaction of forty adult mental health outpatients. The forty subjects were randomly assigned to control and experimental groups, and were studied over a nine-month period. The major findings of the study were that the leisure counseling program had a positive effect on leisure attitudes, leisure self-concept, and work self-concept.

McDowell's study is significant for several reasons. First, the study provides concrete evidence of the positive impact leisure counseling can have. It should be noted that McDowell used a powerful Solomon Four-Group design in this study, which lends even greater validity to the findings of the study. The study is also very significant in that it provides a clear rationale for leisure counseling services, especially if research on leisure and mental health is considered. According to Fromm (1968), Martin (1969), Neulinger (1971), and Gray and Greben (1974), leisure attitudes and self-concept are very important factors in determining psychological well-being. Keeping this statement in mind, and recognizing that McDowell's study indicated that leisure counseling had a positive effect on leisure attitudes and self-concept, it appears that leisure counseling has great potential to have a positive impact on mental health. The potential of leisure counseling to positively effect mental health provides a clear rationale for the existence and growth of leisure counseling programs for elders and other populations as well.

Leisure counseling has expanded rapidly through the 1970s and 1980s, as indicated by the extensive research and publications on this subject (see bibliography). Leisure counseling can be especially beneficial for elders in several ways: (1) to help elders adjust to the increased leisure which retirement usually brings; (2) to help senior center or adult day care attendees to most effectively use their leisure time away from the center; (3) to help nursing home residents to most effectively utilize their unstructured leisure time in the institution, and also prepare residents about to be discharged to make the best use of their leisure after discharge (so as to reduce recidivism); and (4) to help elders adjust to the changes in their life (and leisure) caused by death of a spouse.

USING LEISURE COUNSELING WITH ELDERS

The Leisure Resource Guidance Approach

The leisure resource guidance approach is most appropriate in working with healthy elders who have a variety of leisure interests and merely wish to learn of programs available related to their interests. The resource guidance approach is most appropriate for clients who do *not* seek to expand their leisure horizons, but rather are seeking information on recreational opportunities available to them. The procedures of the leisure resource guidance approach are outlined below (based on McDowell, 1976):

1. Initial interview to get acquainted with the client.
2. Administration of leisure-interest inventories and collection of

demographic data. Refer to the bibliography of leisure interest inventories at the end of this chapter.

3. Analysis of data collected (preferably computer-assisted).
4. Matching of client's leisure interests and demographic characteristics with appropriate recreation programs.
5. Discussion of the results of data analysis with the client, and referral to appropriate programs.
6. A follow-up meeting with the client to examine the client's satisfaction with the programs to which the client was referred.
7. The counseling process is terminated once one has satisfactorily been matched with appropriate programs and is participating in one's desired recreational activities.

In order to further clarify the leisure resource guidance approach to leisure counseling, a practical example is presented:

Example. Mrs. B has recently moved to Phoenix, Arizona to retire. She is very satisfied with the variety of her recreational pursuits: tennis; swimming; square dancing; folk dancing; and theatergoing. However, being new to Phoenix, she is not aware of all of the recreational opportunities available to her related to the aforementioned interests. Mrs. B wishes to facilitate her adjustment to life in Phoenix by becoming involved in her favorite activities as soon as possible. Therefore, she has sought out a professional leisure counselor to help her learn of and become involved in appropriate programs. Mrs. B does *not* wish to become involved in a long process to examine and expand her leisure interests but rather merely wishes to discover what programs are available to her in Phoenix.

The counselor meets with Mrs. B and explains the leisure counseling procedure to her. Mrs. B then completes several leisure interest inventories in order to clarify the nature and scope of her leisure pursuits. In addition, demographic data is collected such as: income; transportation availability; residence location; educational background; marital status; and religion and ethnic background. This information, along with information gathered informally in the interview are fed into a computer. The leisure counselor's computer has an up-to-date data base of recreational programs in the Phoenix area (including tennis, swimming, folk dancing, square dancing, and theater programs). The demographic data and leisure interests of Mrs. B are matched against the data base, and a referral of appropriate programs is produced. The referral includes a list of appropriate programs, including phone numbers, names, times available, cost and accessibility. The referral is then presented to and discussed with Mrs. B. An appointment with Mrs. B is set for two weeks later, to discuss Mrs. B's satisfaction with her involvement in the programs to which she was referred. The counseling process is terminated once Mrs. B is satisfactorily involved in her desired recreational activities. However, the client is encouraged to periodically contact the counselor after terminating the process if the client has any questions or problems.

In summary, the leisure resource guidance approach to leisure counseling focuses on the dissemination of information on leisure resources. This approach is most appropriate for high-functioning elders with well-defined leisure interests. This type of counseling can be extremely helpful for elders who have recently moved to a big city, or have recently retired and have inadequate knowledge of leisure resources available.

The Developmental-Educational Approach

The developmental-educational approach to leisure counseling is also suitable for high-functioning elders, but it is a more involving process than leisure resource guidance leisure counseling. In the developmental-educational approach, the counselor works closely with the client to discover new leisure interests and activities, in an attempt to broaden the client's leisure horizons. An important objective of developmental-educational leisure counseling is to help the client identify an "ideal" leisure lifestyle, and then assist the client to bridge the gap between their real leisure lifestyle and their ideal leisure lifestyle through goal setting.

Some of the other objectives of developmental-educational leisure counseling are:

1. To help one understand the importance of leisure in one's life.
2. To help one understand the effects of aging and social change on leisure.
3. To help one identify one's attitudes and values toward leisure which serve as barriers to leisure fulfillment.

Developmental-educational leisure counseling efforts with elders should include the following steps (adapted from McDowell's (1976) suggested leisure counseling process):

(1) *Pre-counseling assessment.* In this step, the client completes leisure interest inventories and other relevant questionnaires which can be analyzed by the counselor prior to the first counseling session in order to expedite understanding the client's leisure attitudes and behavior.

(2) *Establishing rapport.* In this step, the counselor should attempt to develop a warm trusting relationship with the client. In order for meaningful interaction to occur in which the client self-discloses a great deal, a trusting relationship is imperative. Thus, this stage of the counseling process should continue until the counselor feels assured that the client feels comfortable confiding in the counselor. If the counseling process skips to the next step before rapport has adequately been established, discussions are likely to be shallow and not very beneficial for the client.

(3) *Defining concepts.* Some of the more important concepts to discuss and define in this step include: leisure; recreation; work; and ideal leisure. Very often, counselors and clients define these terms differently. If these concepts are not defined and discussed at the beginning of the counseling process, discussions in the latter stages would be quite confusing. A counselor and client could talk about leisure and yet be talking about entirely different concepts (e.g., leisure as free time vs. leisure as a state of mind). Therefore, it is important to reach mutual understanding of key concepts with the client before proceeding further.

(4) *Identifying leisure needs.* In this step, the counselor helps the client identify the relationship of basic human needs (e.g., the need for physical activity, social interaction, new experiences, etc.) to leisure. First, the counselor must be assured that the client understands that the term "need" is being used to refer to a desirable component of one's life, *not* an urgent want or lack of something desired.

Next, the counselor should help the client to identify and understand basic human needs most relevant to their life. Recreational activities in which the client is currently involved which meet these needs should be identified. The counselor should also help the client explore "ideal" means of meeting these basic human needs, identifying desirable recreational activities the client is *not* currently engaged in (or not performed as frequently as desired) that would meet the needs identified.

It is useful for the counselor to chart notes related to this stage as follows:

Example

Need & Description	How Met (Real)	How Met Ideally
Physical Activity (doing enjoyable activity which improves flexibility, strength, or endurance)	Walking (30 min/day) Tennis (weekends only) Dancing (twice/year)	Walking (one hour/day) Tennis (90 min/day) Swim (20 min/day) Golf (3x weekly, 4 hours each time) Dancing (2x weekly, 2 hours each time)

Each need should be treated in-depth, with real and ideal means of fulfilling the need listed in columns. Occasionally, clients claim that they are meeting their needs ideally and that they cannot think of any other ways to achieve their needs. In these situations, the counselor should use resource materials to stimulate the client's thought on the topic. For example, some resources for ideas on how to meet the physical activity need are: the local college's physical education department course listings and descriptions in the college catalog; a sporting goods catalog; literature from the National Senior Sports Association; listing of clubs in the local phone directory; and listings of sporting events in the local newspaper.

Thus, this step helps the client to more fully understand the value and benefits of recreational activities. This step also prepares the client for the next step, goal-setting. Once real and ideal means of satisfying needs have been identified, goals designed to bridge the gap between real and ideal leisure lifestyles are more apparent.

(5) *Identifying leisure goals.* The purpose of the goal-setting phase is for the client to set realistic goals for improving one's leisure, both in the short-range (within the year), and long-term (beyond one year). Notes taken during the needs phase should be referred to in order to facilitate the goal-setting process. Goals should be set for each need identified, based on the discrepancies between the how met vs. ideally how met columns. Goals should focus on bringing one's real leisure lifestyle and fulfillment of needs closer to their ideal leisure lifestyle and ideal means of fulfilling needs. In order to encourage clients to set goals, emphasize that there are no risks in goal-setting, that the goals are *not* set in concrete, and can be changed.

(6) *Obstacles to goal attainment.* In this phase, the counselor helps the client to identify potential obstacles to attaining the goals identified in the previous phase. The counselor and client also discuss how the obstacles can be overcome.

The purpose of this phase is to ensure that goals set are realistic. If goals are not feasible or challenging enough, they should be revised. Discussion on obstacles should focus more on internal obstacles (e.g., guilt, procrastination, motivation, etc.) which the client can act on to overcome, as opposed to discussing external obstacles which the client has little control over (e.g., weather, cost, etc.).

(7) *Identifying performance criteria.* In this stage, goals are further refined so that each goal has clearly identifiable behavioral indicators which will serve as criteria for success in goal attainment. The key concern in this phase is to be sure that goals are stated in terms of observable, measurable behaviors, and that the desired direction of change is stated.

For example, suppose a client identifies "to ski more" as a goal. After clarification of what is meant by "skiing more," a clearer way to state the goal might be: "to increase time spent skiing from ten hours per month to twenty hours per month." Similarly, performance criteria for the successful attainment of each goal should be identified, and each goal should be stated in measurable terms.

(8) *Leisure alternatives and consequences.* In this step, alternative ways to approach meeting each goal are explored and evaluated. After examining the consequences of alternative means of meeting a goal, the most feasible alternative should be selected as an action plan for meeting the goal.

For example, if the goal is to increase time spent skiing from ten hours per month to twenty hours per month, the alternative ways of accomplishing this objective should be examined. Some alternatives might be: (1) make one three-day skiing trip per month, and ski six to seven hours each day; (2) go on four weekend ski trips each month, and try to ski approximately five hours each weekend; (3) go on five one-day ski outings, attempting to ski approximately four hours each day. The feasibility of each alternative should be examined, considering cost, travel time, physical conditioning and other factors. Finally, the best alternative for meeting the goal should be selected.

(9) *Disseminate information.* The purpose of this phase is for the counselor to provide the client with useful information on leisure re-

sources which will enable the client to enact their chosen alternatives for meeting their goals. The counselor should provide the client with agency names, phone numbers, program information, and other relevant information.

(10) *Participation and evaluation.* The purposes of this phase are to ensure that the client does become involved in the recreational programs and activities identified during the previous phases and to evaluate the client's progress in terms of goal attainment. As necessary, goals should be revised, or alternative means of meeting goals should be reexamined.

(11) *Termination and follow-up.* Once satisfactory progress toward goal attainment has been achieved, the counseling process should be terminated. The last session should summarize the counseling process in a manner which leaves the client with a clear direction for continuing to work to improve their leisure. Follow-up contacts should be made with the client after terminating the process in order to check on the client's progress.

Thus, the developmental-educational approach to leisure counseling is an in-depth approach which attempts to help clients to expand their leisure horizons and improve their leisure well-being. This approach is most appropriate with high-functioning elders who do not have specific leisure-related problems but wish to enhance their leisure.

The Therapeutic-Remedial Approach

In contrast to the developmental-educational and leisure resource guidance approaches to leisure counseling, the therapeutic-remedial approach is most appropriate for lower-functioning elders or elders with specific leisure-related behavioral problems. Some examples of behavioral problems which can be related to misuse of leisure time are boredom, chronic television watching, social isolation, depression, and alcoholism. Therapeutic-remedial leisure counseling necessitates a close, empathetic relationship with the client. Topics such as leisure attitudes and self-concept, coping skills, behavioral problems and impairments, and support systems should be carefully examined. The therapeutic-remedial approach is similar to the developmental-educational approach in that it is an in-depth approach and should cover the eleven steps described in the previous section of this chapter. However, the therapeutic-remedial approach differs from the developmental-educational approach in that the counselor is more directive, and focuses more on the remediation of specific problems rather than the exploration of broadening leisure horizons.

Some important objectives of therapeutic-remedial leisure counseling are (McDowell, 1976):

1. Identification of leisure-related behavioral problems and their causes.
2. Identification of desired changes in leisure attitudes and behavior to alleviate the behavioral problems.
3. Development of an individualized program of recreational activities that will facilitate integration into leisure living in the community.
4. Initiation of involvement in activities, with supervision.
5. Development of a positive self-image and positive attitudes toward community living (if the client is being prepared for discharge from an institutional setting).
6. Development of community contacts that will enable the client to participate in community activities without supervision.

In summary, the therapeutic-remedial approach is a more directive approach which attempts to alleviate specific behavioral problems. Although it has several objectives which the developmental-educational approach does not share, therapeutic-remedial leisure counseling would still follow the same eleven steps of the developmental-educational approach.

SPECIAL CONSIDERATIONS IN COUNSELING ELDERS

Leisure counseling with elders is different from leisure counseling with younger age groups in several respects. One consideration is the prevalence of the work ethic among elders. For some elders, the word leisure has a negative connotation. Strong negative attitudes toward leisure can sometimes be an obstacle to making progress. One approach to counteracting this problem is to give the client an exposure to the breadth and scope of recreation available to elders, possibly by showing slides, a videotape, or movie on this topic during one of the first few sessions. Doing so will give the client a more positive impression of leisure and recreation. Another suggestion is to strongly emphasize the specific benefits of various recreation activities, in order to help the client understand the potential benefits of leisure activity.

Another common problem encountered is short-term memory deficits. One way to alleviate this problem is for the counselor and client to take notes during the session, and also tape record the session. The notes and tapes can serve as useful reference materials for the counselor and client during each session, as well as between sessions.

Encouraging elders to participate in leisure counseling can be an especially perplexing problem. A helpful suggestion is to avoid labeling the process as leisure counseling, but rather name the program "leisure planning" or some other non-threatening title. Another useful motivational technique is to play excerpts of a video or audio tape which demonstrates what leisure counseling is like, and how it can benefit people.

The first step in beginning a leisure counseling program with an individual is to collect background information and conduct an initial interview. Based on the interview and data collected, one must choose the most appropriate orientation (leisure resource guidance, developmental-educational, or therapeutic-remedial) to use. Although one will expect to utilize the therapeutic-remedial approach more in nursing homes and adult day care centers and the leisure resource guidance and developmental-educational approaches more with higher-functioning elders in the community, there will be situations where a nursing home resident preparing for discharge needs nothing more than leisure resource guidance, whereas a healthy elder living in the community might need therapeutic-remedial leisure counseling.

The following is a list of suggested techniques and procedures to follow in counseling elders:

1. Plan sessions to last between 30 and 45 minutes. Allow at least twenty minutes after the session for taking additional notes on the session.
2. Conduct sessions a minimum of once a week, hopefully two or three times a week.
3. Every session should have a clearly defined purpose which is clearly stated at the beginning of the session in order to orient both the counselor and client to the topic at hand.
4. Note-taking and tape recording are helpful sources of information and are encouraged.

5. Select a style of counseling most suitable to the situation. Be flexible enough to change styles (e.g., become more confrontive) if the original method chosen becomes ineffective.

For further information on counseling techniques, leisure counseling theory and practice, and leisure interest inventories, refer to the bibliography at the end of this chapter.

SUMMARY

The aims of this chapter were to help the reader to develop a greater understanding of leisure counseling and how to use leisure counseling with elders. Realistically, it is quite difficult to conduct leisure counseling with elders, based solely on the information presented in this chapter. It is suggested that students attempt each of the three types of leisure counseling with fellow students, following the procedures and considerations discussed in this chapter. After some experience with fellow students, further training in counseling techniques, and using this chapter as a guide, one should well be able to conduct leisure counseling with elders.

Leisure counseling is a very important and useful skill in performing recreational work with elders. In almost all settings for recreational services for elders, leisure counseling has become a vital component of the program. Therefore, workers entering the field of recreational services for elders should be well-informed and well-trained in leisure counseling theory, procedures, and techniques.

BIBLIOGRAPHY

Brightbill, C.K. *Educating for leisure-centered living* (2nd ed.). New York: Wiley, 1977.

Chase, D.R. Leisure counseling and leisure behavior research. *Therapeutic Recreation Journal,* 1977, *11*(3), pp. 94-101.

Dowd, T. (Ed.). *Leisure counseling.* Springfield, IL: C.C. Thomas, 1984.

Edwards, P.B. Practice makes perfect. *Journal of Physical Education and Recreation,* 1977, *27*(4), pp. 40-42.

Edwards, P.B. *Leisure counseling techniques: Individual and group counseling, step by step* (3rd ed.). Los Angeles: Constructive Leisure, 1980.

Epperson, A., Witt, P., and Hitzhusen, G. *Leisure counseling: An aspect of leisure education.* Springfield, IL: C.C. Thomas, 1977.

Epperson, A. Educating recreators for leisure counseling. *Journal of Physical Education and Recreation,* 1977, *27*(4), pp. 39-40.

Fain, G.S. Leisure counseling: Translating needs into action. *Therapeutic Recreation Journal,* 1973, *7*(2), pp. 4-9.

Goldstein, J.E., and Compton, D.M. (Eds.). *Perspectives of leisure counseling.* Arlington, VA: National Recreation and Parks Association, 1977.

Gunn, S.L. Leisure counseling using techniques of assertive training and values clarification. *Expanding Horizons in Therapeutic Recreation,* 1976, *4.* Champaigne, IL: University of Illinois.

Gunn, S.L. A systems approach to leisure counseling. *Journal of Physical Education and Recreation,* 1977, *27*(4), pp. 32-35.

Gunn, S.L., and Peterson, C.A. Leisure counseling: An aspect of leisure education. *Journal of Physical Education and Recreation,* 1977, *27*(4), pp. 29-30.

Gunn, S.L., and Peterson, C.A. Therapy and leisure education. *Parks and Recreation,* 1977, *12*(11), p. 22.

Hartlage, L. Leisure counseling from personality profiles. *Journal of Physical Education and Recreation,* 1977, *27*(4), p. 43.

Hayes, G.A. Professional preparation and leisure counseling. *Journal of Physical Education and Recreation,* 1977, *27*(4), pp. 36-38.

Howe, C.Z. Leisure assessment instrumentation in therapeutic recreation. *Therapeutic Recreation Journal,* 1984, *18*(2), pp. 14-24.

Humphrey, F., Kelley, J.D., and Hamilton, E.J. (Eds.). *Facilitating leisure counseling for the disabled: A status report on leisure counseling.* College Park, MD: University of Maryland, 1980.

Joswiak, K.F. *Leisure counseling program materials for the developmentally disabled.* Washington, D.C.: Hawkins and Associates, 1979.

Keller, J.F., and Hughston, G.A. *Counseling the elderly: A systems approach.* New York: Harper and Row, 1981.

Land, C. Recreation counseling for psychiatric patients in a day treatment setting. *Therapeutic Recreation Journal,* 1974, *8*(4), pp. 156-159.

Langford, N. Leisure counseling: Lessons my clients taught me. *Journal of Leisurability,* 1980, *5*(3), pp. 52-59.

Loersch, L.C., and Wheeler, P.T. *Principles of leisure counseling.* Minneapolis: Educational Media Corp., 1982.

Mazulski, M., Faull, V.H., and Ruthowski, B. The Milwaukee leisure counseling model. *Journal of Physical Education and Recreation,* 1977, *27*(4), pp. 49-50.

McDowell, C.F., Jr. Toward a healthy leisure mode: Leisure counseling. *Therapeutic Recreation Journal,* 1974, *8*(3), pp. 96-104.

McDowell, C.F., Jr. Emerging leisure counseling concepts and orientations. *Leisurability,* 1975, *2*(4), pp. 19-25.

McDowell, C.F., Jr. Leisure counseling: Selected lifestyle processes. Center of Leisure Studies: University of Oregon, 1976.

McDowell, C.F., Jr. Integrating theory and practice in leisure counseling. *Journal of Physical Education and Recreation,* 1977, *27*(4), pp. 51-54.

McDowell, C.F., Jr. Leisure counseling issues: Reviews, overviews, and previews. In F. Humphrey, J.D. Kelley, and E.J. Hamilton (Eds.), *Facilitating leisure counseling for the disabled: A status report on leisure counseling.* College Park, MD: University of Maryland, 1980.

McLaughlin, L.T. Leisure counseling with drug dependent individuals and alcoholics. *Leisurability,* 1980, *5*(1), pp. 9-16.

McLellan, R.W. Valuing: A necessary phase in leisure counseling. *Journal of Physical Education and Recreation,* 1977, *27*(4), pp. 31-32.

Mundy, J., and Odum, L. *Leisure education: Theory and practice.* New York: Wiley, 1979.

Neulinger, J. Leisure counseling: A plea for complexity. *Journal of Physical Education and Recreation,* 1977, *27*(4), pp. 27-28.

Olson, W.E., and McCormick, J.B. Recreational counseling in the psychiatric service of a general hospital. *The Journal of Nervous and Mental Disease,* 1957, *25*(2), pp. 237-239.

Overs, R.P., Taylor, S., and Adkins, C. *Avocational counseling manual: A complete guide to leisure guidance.* Washington, D.C.: Hawkins and Associates, 1977.

Overs, R.P., Taylor, S., and Adkins, C. Avocational counseling for the elderly. *Journal of Physical Education and Recreation*, 1977, *27*(4), pp. 44-45.

Rule, W.R., and Jarrell, G.R. Time dimensions in leisure counseling. *Leisurability*, 1980, *5*(1), pp. 3-8.

Smith, D.A., and Reynolds, R.P. Integrating leisure counseling and psychological services. *Therapeutic Recreation Journal*, 1980, *13*(3), pp. 25-30.

Veda, B., Brown, R.I., Mulvihill, S., and Rolf, C. A systematic approach to leisure education in community based recreation facilities. *Leisurability*, 1980, *5*(1), pp. 60-69.

Ward, V.E. Transition through leisure counseling. *Journal of Physical Education and Recreation*, 1981, *31*(4), pp. 36-37.

Weiner, A., and Gilley, W. The instructional status of leisure counseling within the community of higher education. *Therapeutic Recreation Journal*, 1978, *11*(2), pp. 148-155.

Weiss, C.R. Leisure education as an aspect of gerontological staff development. *Leisurability*, 1980, *5*(1), pp. 9-16.

SELECTED BIBLIOGRAPHY FOR LEISURE INTEREST INVENTORIES

Anastasi, A. 1976. *Psychological Testing (fourth ed.)*. New York: Macmillan.

McDowell, C.F. 1978. *Leisure Well-Being Inventory*. Leisure Lifestyle Consultants, Eugene.

McDowell, C.F. 1978. *So You Think You Know How To Leisure? A Guide To Leisure Well-Being In Your Lifestyle*. Leisure Lifestyle Consultants, Eugene.

McKechnie, G.B. 1975. *Manual For The Leisure Activities Blank*. Palo Alto, Cal.: Consulting Psychologists Press, Inc.

McKechnie, G.B. 1974. *The Structure Of Leisure Activities*. Institute of Personality Assessment and Research: University of California.

McKechnie, G.B. 1974. *The Leisure Activities Blank Booklet*. Palo Alto, Cal.: Consulting Psychologists Press, Inc.

Mirenda, J. 1973. *Mirenda Leisure Interest Finder*. Milwaukee Public Schools, Department of Municipal Recreation And Adult Education, Milwaukee, Wisconsin.

Overs, R.P. 1971. *Avocational Activities Inventory (revised)*. Milwaukee Media for Rehabilitation Research Reports No. 5A, Milwaukee Recreation and Adult Education Division, Milwaukee Public Schools.

Overs, R.P. and Page, C.M. 1974. *Avocational Title Card Sort*. Milwaukee Media for Rehabilitation Research Reports No. 5F, Grand Forks, Vocational Adjustment Department, Medical Center Rehabilitation Hospital.

Chapter 11

Exercise

INTRODUCTION

The purpose of this chapter is to provide information on how to adapt appropriate exercises to specific older populations. For the purposes of this chapter, exercise is defined as movement which enhances flexibility, strength, endurance, vents tension, and promotes feelings of well-being. Movement includes both total body involvement and manipulation of isolated body parts. Exercises are described in detail in this chapter in order to provide a basis for leading exercise sessions. In the first section of this chapter, a review of literature on the physical and mental benefits of exercise is presented. In the second section of this chapter, general leadership principles for leading exercise sessions with elders are discussed. The rest of the chapter deals with specific exercises designed for bedridden elders, elders with limited mobility, and high functioning elders. Sample exercise session plans are presented at the end of the chapter.

BENEFITS OF EXERCISE

Exercise in later life has become an area of increasing concern for people of all ages as shown by the numerous articles and studies related to this topic completed in recent years. The physical and mental benefits attained through exercise are discussed in various articles and books.

Physical Benefits

Frankel and Richard (1980) suggested that exercise can retard the aging process. Regular participation in physical activity can improve circulation by enriching the blood with oxygen, strengthen the heart and lungs, prevent bone deterioration, restore muscle tone, improve flexibility, and increase range of motion.

In a related article, Spirduso (1983) stated that physical conditioning may retard the symptoms of an aging motor system. Furthermore, the author noted that exercise has a positive impact on the brain which improves cognitive functioning.

In a similar article describing how exercise can delay changes due to aging, it was determined that exercise can prolong normal walking patterns in later life (Frankel, 1977). Physical activity also keeps the head and back muscles strong to sustain activity. According to Frankel, the positive effects of exercise on the central nervous system may delay changes due to aging. Exercise also stimulates digestion, metabolism, respiration, blood circulation, and glands of external secretion.

In another article describing the benefits of exercise, it was found that exercise in later life helps to maintain flexibility and strength which are the key components in performing activities of daily living (ADL). Self-sufficiency and independence are fostered by the ability to perform ADL skills (Flatten, 1982).

In a related vein, Munns (1979) conducted a study on the effects of an exercise program on the range of joint motion of older subjects. The results indicated an increase in comfort in movement and improvement in the performance of activities of daily living.

Other benefits of exercise were described by Leaf (1975). The rate of arteriosclerosis and coronary disease is reduced with physical activity. Exercise keeps bones and muscles strong, rendering older adults more resilient in the event of falls or accidents.

Lastly, participation in an exercise program will improve coordination of the older adult (Arnold, 1977). Coordination of all body parts can be enhanced through physical activity.

Mental Benefits

Numerous articles discuss the mental benefits achieved through exercise for elders. According to Ingraham (1977), most individuals experience a heightened sense of well-being after exercise. Exercise increases energy levels, improves self-concept, and enhances life satisfaction.

In a related article on the benefits of exercise, Haber (1977) suggested that physical activity creates a state of independence. Furthermore, the author noted that a healthy body achieved through exercise can function more independently and therefore enhance one's psychological well-being.

It was also noted that participation in a group exercise program promotes social growth and development (Arnold, 1977). Through interactions with others in an exercise program, older adults enjoy companionship and feel part of a group.

In a different light, Alexiou (1977) suggested that exercise is an outlet for tension. Without activity, tension accumulates in the individual which can produce muscle contraction causing pain and fatigue. Alexiou also recommended that passive exercise for elders is an effective means of achieving relaxation.

GENERAL LEADERSHIP PRINCIPLES

The leader of an exercise program for older adults should portray constant optimism and cheerfulness (Frankel, 1977). A supportive, encouraging attitude can help to motivate and engage sedentary individuals in activity.

Exercise is too strenuous and should cease if any of the following symptoms are evident: shortness of breath; chest pain; lightheadedness or dizziness; prolonged fatigue; or a heart rate over 120 beats per minute (Harris, 1977). The exercise leader should be cognizant of any of these over-exertion signs and stop exercise immediately if these signs appear.

The exercise leader should involve the total person in an exercise program. Older adults may feel more motivated to participate in a fitness program when physical, psychological, and social needs are being met (Whitehouse, 1977). Obtaining background information on each individual in an exercise program (e.g., habits, goals, etc.), will aid the leader in developing a more personal program. According to Whitehouse (1977), as individuals begin to improve their fitness levels, the leader will be more effective by specifically describing each person's progress rather than merely indicating general improvements.

Another important leadership principle is to recognize participants' problems, physical limitations, and fears. Sensitivity and compassion on the part of the leader can be a motivating factor. The effective exercise leader is enthusiastic and believes in the importance of exercise.

According to Arnold (1977), the leader of an exercise program should relate exercise to the participants' total health to provide a rationale for the importance of exercise. The leader can motivate older adults by clearly defining the benefits of exercise for each individual. However, exaggerated predictions of success should be avoided.

Creating a recreational atmosphere for the exercise session can foster a greater degree of motivation to participate. An effective motivational tool is to incorporate music into the exercise sessions. Ask the participants for a list of their favorite songs, then locate recordings of the songs and play them during the sessions. Just hearing the music may attract individuals to the activity who otherwise may decline from participating.

Another motivational technique is to keep a journal charting progress in an exercise program. In this way, the older adult may be motivated to increase the repetitions of exercise, or at least maintain the existing level. This journal can be a combined effort of both exercise leader and the participants, and can be written at the end of each session.

The exercise leader may occasionally have to physically assist the older adult in performing specific movements. Also, when possible, the leader should demonstrate and participate in the exercise along with the group. Experiencing a sense of joined effort in performing the exercises can be motivating.

The exercise routine should involve all body parts. Relaxation and massage (see the chapter on Adapted Dance) should be interspersed throughout the session. Sessions should progress in a relaxed manner, without undo exertion or fatigue. Furthermore, according to Arnold (1977), the degree of exercise intensity should be individually controlled by discouraging competition and encouraging individualized work-outs.

Knowing about an activity in advance and having the opportunity to make the decision to attend is an important concern. The leader should arrange both oral and written announcements to occur prior to the activity.

Providing leadership roles to individuals in the group can promote a greater sense of involvement. Members should be given the opportunity to demonstrate and lead several exercises. Furthermore, participants should be asked for feedback on the effectiveness of the sessions.

Another motivating ingredient for older adults is the utilization of interesting props in the exercise session. The props can be items found at the center, projects created by participants during crafts activities, or objects brought from home to share with the group, (e.g., colorful scarves, funny hats, costume jewelry, etc.).

The use of physical contact in the exercise session can be a pleasant experience for the participants. Partner exercises utilizing touch can be very rewarding.

Relaxation techniques are an important aspect of an exercise session in that they can penetrate barriers for individuals who insist that exercise is too exerting. Relaxation techniques can act as motivating components of a session to which people look forward.

In summary, motivating older adults to participate in exercise can be a major challenge. The greater the sense of involvement the leader can generate in group members in the exercise session, the greater the attendance, hence, the greater the degree of benefits derived from exercise.

EXERCISES FOR ELDERS

The exercises in this section are based on:

1. Jamieson's (1982) book, *Exercises for the Elderly*
2. Frankel and Richard's (1980) book, *Be Alive as Long as You Live*
3. Norton's (1977) book, *Yoga for People Over Fifty*
4. Anderson and Anderson's (1980) book, *Stretching*

This section has been divided into three sub-sections: exercise for high functioning elders; exercise for elders with limited mobility; and exercise for bedridden elders.

Exercises for Bedridden Elders

The following exercises are designed for elders restricted to bed. Bedridden elders will vary in ability. Higher functioning elders will be able to complete more repetitions, and require shorter rests between exercises. Lower functioning elders may be able to accomplish fewer repetitions, and need more time to converse and rest in between exercises. Exercises are numbered consecutively to facilitate referencing in the sample sessions section.

Exercises for the Neck

1. *Head Raisers*
   a. Slowly raise the head as high as possible, bringing the chin towards the chest.
   b. Gently lower the head back to the pillow.
   c. Repeat this movement two more times.
2. *Head Turns*
   a. Keep the head on the pillow and slowly turn the head as far as possible to the right.
   b. Bring the head back to center position.
   c. Turn the head to the left.
   d. Bring the head back to center position.
   e. Repeat entire exercise two more times.

Exercises for the Face

3. *Mouth Openers*
   a. Open the mouth as wide as possible.
   b. Close the mouth.
   c. Repeat three more times.
4. *Tongue Stretch*
   a. Stick the tongue out of the mouth.
   b. Return the tongue inside the mouth.
   c. Repeat three more times.
5. *Jaw Rotation*
   a. Rotate the lower jaw from side to side.
   b. Repeat six times.
6. *Eye Openers*
   a. Open the eyes wide.
   b. Close the eyes.
   c. Repeat three more times.
7. *Eye Rotation*
   a. Rotate the eyeballs clockwise.
   b. Rotate the eyeballs counterclockwise.

Exercises for the Shoulders

8. *Arm Raisers*
   a. Begin with the arms straight down by the sides.
   b. Lift the arms up toward the ceiling, then up overhead.

    c. Bring the arms back down to the sides.

    d. Repeat three more times.

9. *Overhead Stretch*

    a. Begin with the arms straight down by the sides.

    b. Move the arms out to the sides, then overhead.

    c. Bring the arms back down to the sides, while keeping the arms in a parallel position to the bed.

    d. Repeat three more times.

10. *Elbow Flexors*

    a. Begin with elbows bent, hands pointing upward, palms facing feet.

    b. Move the hands backward and try to touch the back of the hands to the bed.

    c. Bring hands back to starting position.

    d. Move the hands toward the feet and place the palms on the bed while maintaining the arms in the same position.

    e. Move hands back to starting position.

    f. Repeat this exercise three more times.

Exercises for the Arms

11. *Arm Circles*

    a. Begin with hands crossed on abdomen.

    b. Raise hands overhead keeping them crossed.

    c. Circle the arms in opposite directions back to starting position.

    d. Repeat this exercise three more times.

12. *Arm Extensions*

    a. Begin with upper arms on the bed, elbows bent, and hands facing upward.

    b. Straighten the arms and raise the hands toward the ceiling.

    c. Return the arms to starting position.

    d. Repeat this exercise three more times.

13. *Hands Up*

    a. Begin with arms at sides.

    b. Keeping the elbows on the bed, raise the hands upward with the palms facing upward.

    c. Return hands to the bed.

    d. Raise hands upward with the palms facing downward.

    e. Return hands to the bed.

f. Raise hands with the thumbs facing upward.

g. Return hands to the bed.

14. *Hand Circles*

a. Begin with the elbows on the bed, hands held up.

b. Turn the hands in a clockwise direction.

c. Turn the hands counterclockwise.

d. Repeat this exercise four more times.

15. *Wrist Rotations*

a. Begin with arms placed next to the sides, palms down.

b. Bend the wrists and bring the hands upward.

c. Turn hands so that palms are facing upward.

d. Bend wrists so that the hands move toward the head.

e. Return hands to the bed.

f. Repeat this exercise two more times.

16. *Wrist Raisers*

a. Begin with the arms at sides.

b. Without moving the arms, move hands and wrists to the right, then left.

c. Repeat four more times.

Exercises for the Hands and Fingers

17. *Finger Flex*

a. Flex and extend the fingers.

b. Repeat four more times.

18. *Finger Spread*

a. Spread the fingers as wide as possible.

b. Repeat two more times.

19. *Thumb Rotation*

a. Rotate the thumbs clockwise, then counterclockwise.

20. *Finger Stretch*

a. Begin with hands in a fist.

b. Extend one finger at a time beginning with the thumb.

c. After all fingers are extended, return one finger at a time back into a fist position beginning with the pinkie.

Exercises for the Chest

21. *The X*

a. Begin with arms straight out to the sides.

   b. Keep the arms straight, raise them upward in front of the chest to form an "X".

   c. Return the arms to starting position.

   d. Repeat this exercise three more times.

22. *Chest Opener*

   a. Begin with elbows on bed, hands held upward.

   b. Keeping the elbows bent, cross the arms directly over the chest trying to touch the elbows together.

   c. Return elbows out opening up the chest as much as possible.

   d. Repeat this exercise two more times.

Exercises for the Abdomen

23. *Abdomen Contractions*

   a. Contract abdominal muscles for five counts, then release.

   b. Repeat four more times.

24. *Mini Sit-Up*

   a. Raise the head, shoulders, and legs as much as possible off the bed.

   b. Hold for three counts, then slowly lower back to the bed.

   c. Repeat two more times.

Exercises for the Lower Back

25. *Back Press*

   a. Press the lower back to the bed while contracting abdominal muscles, hold for three counts and release.

   b. Repeat two more times.

26. *Knee to Chest*

   a. Begin with legs straight.

   b. Bend one leg and bring the knee towards the chest.

   c. Straighten the leg and return to starting position.

   d. Perform the same movement with the other leg.

   e. Repeat exercise two more times with each leg.

27. *Double Leg to Chest*

   a. Begin with straight legs.

   b. Bend both knees and bring both legs simultaneously to the chest (the hands can be used by placing them on the knees to help the momentum).

    c. Straighten the legs and return to starting position.

    d. Repeat one more time.

Exercises for the Legs

28. *Toe Points*
    a. Begin with legs together.
    b. Point toes downward.
    c. Bring toes upward and point the toes toward the head.
    d. Repeat exercise three more times.

29. *Leg Rotations*
    a. Begin with legs slightly apart.
    b. Rotate legs inward and point the toes toward each other.
    c. Rotate the legs outward and point the toes out to the sides.
    d. Repeat exercise three more times.

30. *Feet Circles*
    a. Begin with legs together.
    b. Slightly lift the feet off the bed, then circle the feet clockwise three times.
    c. Circle the feet counterclockwise three times.

31. *The Walk*
    a. Begin with feet slightly apart.
    b. Alternate lifting one foot slightly off the bed, then the other foot.
    c. Raise each foot four times.

32. *Leg Pushes*
    a. Begin with feet crossed at the ankles.
    b. Simultaneously try to push down with the top leg while trying to raise the bottom leg.
    c. Reverse feet and repeat.
    d. Repeat entire exercise one more time.

Towel Exercises for Bedridden Elders

A towel is an example of one readily available prop which can be utilized in assisting bedridden elders to move their body parts.

A. *The Climb*
    a. The exercise assistant holds a towel vertically above the individual's head.
    b. The elder holds onto the towel and climbs upward using the hands.

B. *Pull-Up*
   a. The exercise assistant holds the towel horizontally above the elder's head.
   b. The elder holds onto the towel and tries to pull the body weight up off the bed.
C. *Push-Down*
   a. The exercise assistant places a towel beneath the lower calves of the elder and lifts the legs six to eight inches off the bed.
   b. The elder tries to push the legs downward towards the bed against the resistance of the towel.

Summary

Exercises for bedridden older adults include simple, non-strenuous movements to stretch and strengthen muscle groups. Achieving movement of most body parts can be accomplished if the exercises are easy and performed in a slow, relaxed manner.

Exercises for Elders with Limited Mobility

In this section, exercises are described which are intended to be performed from a seated position. All the aforementioned exercises for bedridden elders can be adapted to be performed from a seated position for elders with limited mobility.

Exercises for the Neck

33. *Head Circles*
   a. Slowly rotate the head in large circles in a clockwise direction.
   b. Rotate the head counterclockwise.
34. *Chin to Chest*
   a. Bring the chin down to the chest.
   b. Slowly roll the head back as far as possible and look upward.

Exercises for the Shoulders

35. *Shoulder Rotation*
   a. Rotate the shoulders forward, then backward.

36. *Shoulder Rolls*
    a. Bring one shoulder as far forward as possible, while simultaneously moving the other shoulder backward.
    b. Reverse shoulders.
    c. Repeat five more times with each shoulder.

Exercises for the Arms

37. *Arm Rotations*
    a. Begin with arms extended out to the sides.
    b. Rotate arms in circles forward, then backward.
38. *Palms Away*
    a. Begin with hands in lap.
    b. Reach out and upward, palms facing away from the body.
    c. Bring the hands downward, palms facing inward.
    d. Repeat three more times.
39. *The Punch*
    a. Punch out alternating arms, one at a time.
    b. Punch forward, overhead, to the sides, downward.
    c. Punch four times in each direction.
40. *Forearm Stretch*
    a. Place palms of hands on either side of body on the seat of the chair, thumb to the outside and fingers pointed backward.
    b. Slowly lean back in the chair and stretch the forearm. Hold for five counts.
    c. Repeat two more times.
41. *Elbow Pull*
    a. Begin with the right arm overhead, bent at the elbow.
    b. Gently pull elbow behind the head with the other hand. Hold for five counts.
    c. Reverse arms.
    d. Repeat two more times on each side.
42. *Side Stretch*
    a. Begin with arms extended overhead.
    b. Hold the outside of the left hand with the right hand and pull to the left side. Hold for five counts.
    c. Reverse sides.
    d. Repeat two more times on each side.

Exercises for the Chest

43. *Elbow Rolls*
    a. Begin with hands placed on shoulder, elbows extended outward.
    b. Rotate elbows forward, then backward.
44. *The Opener*
    a. Begin with arms crossed in front of chest.
    b. Bring elbows backward as far as possible.
    c. Return arms to original position.
    d. Repeat four more times.

Exercises for the Hands

45. *Hand Spread*
    a. Separate and spread the fingers as much as possible.
    b. Repeat four more times.
46. *The Squeeze*
    a. Squeeze a rubber ball (about 2-1/2 inches diameter) with all the fingers and thumb.
    b. Repeat four more times.
    c. Repeat exercise with the other hand.
47. *Progressive Squeeze*
    a. Squeeze the ball with one finger and thumb.
    b. Start with squeezing the ball between the pinkie and thumb, then ring finger and thumb, and so on.
    c. Repeat with the other hand.

Exercises for the Legs

48. *Under the Chair Point*
    a. Begin with feet together.
    b. Lift the feet and move them beneath the chair as far back as possible, pointing the toes backward. Hold for five counts.
    c. Repeat two more times.
49. *Knee to Chest*
    a. Begin with feet together.
    b. Place hands on one knee and lift the knee towards the chest.

    c. Lower the knee back down and repeat with the other leg.

    d. Repeat four more times with each leg.

50. *Leg Stretch*
    a. Begin with feet slightly apart.
    b. Lift the feet off the floor and extend both legs forward, keeping them straight.
    c. Return the feet to the floor.
    d. Repeat three more times.

51. *Leg Push-Out*
    a. Begin with feet placed next to the inside of the legs of the chair.
    b. Try to push outward against the resistance of the chair. Hold for three counts.
    c. Repeat two more times.

52. *Leg Push-In*
    a. Begin with feet placed next to the outside of the legs of the chair.
    b. Try pushing inward. Hold for three counts.
    c. Repeat two more times.

Exercises for the Abdomen

53. *Tummy Tighteners*
    a. Lift the feet two to three inches off the floor and hold for ten counts.
    b. Repeat two more times.

54. *Tummy Toners*
    a. Lift feet several inches off the floor, turn the knees to the right and extend the arms to the left. Hold for five counts.
    b. Repeat on the other side. Hold for five counts.
    c. Repeat exercise one more time on each side.

Exercises for the Feet

55. *Feet Flexors*
    a. Begin with feet slightly apart.
    b. Lift and arch feet, point toes downward.
    c. Flex feet and point toes upward.
    d. Repeat three more times.

56. *Toe Spread*
    a. Separate and spread the toes as much as possible.
    b. Repeat two more times.

Summary

Exercises for older adults with limited mobility are designed to be performed from a seated position. If practiced regularly, the exercises can increase strength and flexibility, and allow for a greater range of movement.

Exercises for High Functioning Elders

This section will not repeat what has already been described for bedridden and moderately impaired elders. The exercises in the previous section can be performed from a standing position for high functioning elders. In this section, yoga will be discussed as an approach to achieve fitness for high functioning elders. Although most yoga postures would be too difficult for lower functioning elders, yoga can be a very beneficial form of exercise for high functioning elders.

In this section, exercises for elders with little or no impairment are presented. The exercises are not restricted to being performed from a seated position, but can be performed from a variety of positions.

Yoga can be practiced by older adults to improve fitness levels. It can be especially appropriate for the older population in that the system of yoga postures focuses on every aspect of the individual through slow movement and rhythmic breathing. The description of each yoga exercise includes: (1) A description of the benefits of the exercise; (2) A description of the starting position; (3) A step-by-step listing of movements involved in the exercise; and (4) An identification of special considerations for leading the exercise. The following exercises are based on Norton's (1977) book *Yoga for People Over Fifty*.

57. *Overhead Stretch*
Benefits. Stretches the muscles of the arms, feet, legs, and along the sides.
Starting Position. Stand erect, feet flat on the floor, arms at sides.
Movements
    a. Raise the arms high overhead.
    b. Look up.
    c. Stretch through every part of the body.
    d. Rise up on the toes and continue reaching higher.

    e. Relax, lower the heels to the floor and bring the arms back to the sides.

    f. Repeat two more times.

Special Considerations. In the event of balance problems, do not rise up on the toes. It may help to use the support of a chair and reach up with one arm at a time.

58. *Deep Breathing Bends*

Benefits. Stretches lower back, hamstrings, and backs of knees.

Starting Position. Stand erect, arms at sides, and place feet shoulder width apart.

Movements.

    a. Inhale and extend arms high overhead.

    b. Exhale and collapse the body into a slumped position bending from the waist and allow arms to dangle towards the floor.

    c. In this relaxed position, breathe slowly.

    d. Inhale and slowly return to the starting position keeping the chin tucked close to the chest.

    e. Repeat two more times.

Special Considerations. If problems with balance occur, perform this exercise in a circle with everyone holding hands for added support.

59. *Upward Stretch*

Benefits. Stretches muscles in arms, hands, and sides.

Starting Position. Stand erect, arms at sides, and palms facing outward.

Movements

    a. Inhale and slowly raise arms overhead.

    b. Exhale, interlock fingers and turn palms upward.

    c. Take several breaths and reach up as high as possible.

    d. Slowly lower arms back to starting position.

    e. Repeat one more time.

60. *Side Stretch*

Benefits. Stretches arms, hands, wrists, and sides.

Starting Position. Stand erect, arms at sides and palms facing outward.

Movements

    a. Inhale and raise arms.

    b. Interlock fingers and turn palms upward.

    c. Exhale and slowly bend to one side as far as possible keeping the feet flat on the floor.

    d. Inhale and return to center position.
    e. Exhale and slowly move to the other side.
    f. Inhale and return to center position.
    g. Exhale and slowly lower arms.
    h. Repeat one more time.

Special Considerations. For added support, stand sideways, next to a wall and reach for the wall. Perform several repetitions on one side, then switch to the other side. This exercise can also be done in a doorway reaching from side to side.

61. *Pep Up*

Benefits. Promotes circulation to the head, relaxes muscles in back and shoulders, and stretches the legs.

Starting Position. Stand erect, feet twelve inches apart, hands clasped behind the back.

Movements

    a. Inhale, lift clasped hands and arms while squeezing shoulder blades together.
    b. Exhale, bend forward from the waist bringing clasped hands and arms up and away from back as high as possible.
    c. Breathe deeply in this position while relaxing the head and neck.
    d. Inhale and slowly return to starting position.
    e. Repeat one more time.

Special Considerations. Use a buddy system where one person is performing the exercise and the other is spotting to avoid falls or accidents.

62. *Back Stretch*

Benefits. Stretches the back and legs.

Starting Position. Stand three to five feet from a wall, place feet shoulder-width apart. Place palms on the wall a little wider apart than the shoulders.

Movements

    a. Move the buttocks and hips away from the wall and extend the spine.
    b. Flatten the lower back keeping the head down, arms and legs straight, and palms kept firmly against the wall.
    c. Take several deep breaths in this pose.
    d. Slowly return to starting position.

Special Considerations. This exercise can also be performed holding onto a window sill or sturdy chair.

63. *Child's Pose*

Benefits. Relaxes the back and increases circulation to the head and face.

Starting Position. Kneel on floor and sit back on the heels.

Movements
  a. Place the head in front of the knees on the floor.
  b. Move the arms in, back toward the toes, and rest them on the floor. Elbows should be relaxed.
  c. Breathe and relax in this pose for a moment or two.

Special Considerations. If it is uncomfortable placing the head on the floor, try using a pillow under the head.

64. *The Tree*

Benefits. Strengthens the legs, ankles, feet, and improves balance.

Starting Position. Stand sideways next to a wall.

Movements
  a. Place one hand on the wall, raise one leg up and place the sole of the foot against the inside of the thigh of the other leg.
  b. Concentrate on a spot about six feet away.
  c. Slowly release the hand from the wall, then raise both arms overhead and bring the palms together.
  d. Maintain this pose for several breaths.
  e. Repeat the exercise on the other leg.

Special Considerations. While trying to balance on one leg, concentrate on lifting and stretching the body upward. Try not to sink into the hip that is supporting the weight of the body.

65. *Triangle*

Benefits. Stretches and strengthens the legs and opens the hip/pelvic area.

Starting Position. Stand erect, arms relaxed at sides, place feet three to four feet apart.

Movements
  a. Extend arms out sideways at shoulder level, palms down.
  b. Turn the right foot outward to ninety degrees.
  c. Turn the left foot inward so that the heel of the right foot is in line with the arch of the left foot.
  d. Bend to the right side without bending the knees.
  e. Place the right hand on the right knee and extend the left arm upward. The extended arm should be in line with the lower arm.

f. Distribute the weight evenly between both feet.

g. Maintain this pose for several breaths.

h. Return to starting position.

i. Change position of feet and repeat the pose on the other side.

66. *Forward Bend*

Benefits. Promotes circulation to the head, increases flexibility in legs and back.

Starting Position. Stand erect, feet a hip-width apart.

Movements

a. Bend forward bringing buttocks upward.

b. Extend and elongate the spine by flattening the back and reaching with the head as far forward as possible. Concentrate on moving the entire back as one unit from pelvis to neck.

c. Bend forward keeping the back flat and place the hands on the knees. Keep the head down.

d. Maintain this position for a moment and breathe evenly.

e. To return to starting position, tuck the chin to the chest and uncurl up slowly with a rounded back.

Special Considerations. In determining if the back is rounded or flat, try the following: Bend forward from the waist with a round back and straight legs. Reach back with one hand and place the fingers on the lower back and feel the vertebrae sticking out like small bumps on the spine. Straighten the back and feel how the vertebrae move in.

67. *Leg Extensions*

Benefits. Stretches the legs and feet.

Starting Position. Lie on back, knees bent, feet flat on the floor, and arms at sides.

Movements

a. Bring one knee to the chest.

b. Straighten the leg upward.

c. Stretch the foot and point the toes.

d. Flex the foot so that the sole points upward.

e. Return to starting position.

f. Alternate legs and repeat.

g. Repeat entire exercise two more times.

Special Considerations. This exercise is not recommended for people with sciatic pain.

68. *Leg Lifts*
Benefits. Strengthens back and abdominal muscles.
Starting Position. Lie on back, legs straight, arms at sides.
Movements
    a. Raise the right leg while keeping the lower back on the floor.
    b. Slowly lower the leg.
    c. Repeat five times for each leg.

Special Considerations. Try inhaling while raising the leg and exhaling while lowering the leg. To protect the lower back, press the lower back to the floor. At the point where it is not possible to keep contact between the lower back and the floor, bend the knees or quickly lower the leg.

69. *Hand-Foot Extension*
Benefits. Strengthens back and abdominal muscles.
Starting Position. Lie on back, knees bent, and arms relaxed at sides.
Movements
    a. Bend legs and bring both knees to the chest.
    b. Straighten legs upward.
    c. Flex feet and stretch through the heels.
    d. Lift arms and head as high as possible (arms are parallel, palms facing each other, fingers pointed upward).
    e. Take several breaths in this pose.
    f. Slowly lower head and arms.
    g. Bend knees.
    h. Lower legs to the floor.
    i. Repeat one more time.

Special Considerations. If holding the legs up is difficult, try practicing next to a wall so the feet and legs can rest momentarily against the wall, then lift again.

70. *Bridge*
Benefits. Stretches back, thighs, hips, abdomen, and relaxes shoulders.
Starting Position. Lie on back, knees bent, feet flat on the floor, arms at sides.
Movements
    a. Press lower back against the floor (pelvis will naturally rotate forward).
    b. Tighten buttock muscles, inhale, and raise the body as

high as possible (keep feet planted firmly on the floor).
c. Hold this pose two to three breaths.
d. Exhale and slowly lower body to floor.
e. Repeat one more time.

Special Considerations. Keep the neck relaxed and slightly extended during the pose. Keep the feet about a hip-width apart.

71. *Back Twist*
Benefits. Aligns and relaxes the back.
Starting Position. Lie on back, arms extended out at shoulder level, palms down.
Movements
a. Inhale and slowly raise the knees to the chest.
b. Exhale and lower the knees to the floor to the right (keep knees together) and simultaneously move the head to the left.
c. Hold for several breaths and keep both shoulders flat on the floor.
d. Inhale and raise bent legs back to the chest.
e. Exhale and lower legs to the left as head moves simultaneously to the right.
f. Repeat two more times on each side.

Special Considerations. Wrap both arms around the knees to make it easier to bring the knees close to the chest.

72. *Leg Press*
Benefits. Strengthens legs and back, stretches hamstrings.
Starting Position. Sit on the floor with legs extended straight out in front.
Movements
a. Place palms on the floor next to the hips, fingers pointing towards the feet (this helps to lift the back).
b. Keeping the legs together, press the backs of the knees to the floor. Keep the knees facing upward.
c. Flex the feet. Pressing the backs of the knees to the floor will cause the heels to rise off the floor.
d. Hold this pose for several breaths.
e. Repeat two more times.

Special Considerations. If difficulty exists in keeping the back erect, perform the exercise next to a wall and momentarily rest the back against the wall. To maintain a straight back, concentrate on growing taller. Feel the spine to be sure no vertebrae are protruding.

73. *Forward Bend*

Benefits. Stretches and extends entire body.

Starting Position. Sit on the floor with legs extended straight out in front.

Movements

    a. Keeping the back extended, reach with the hands towards the feet.

    b. Reach as far as is comfortable while continuing to elongate the back.

    c. Take several breaths in this position.

    d. Repeat one more time.

Special Considerations. For greater extension, stretch forward over the legs, bending from the hips and exhale. Try to bring the head to the ankles and navel to thighs closing the space between abdomen and thighs. Check the spine for protruding vertebrae and lift the sternum toward the chin for greater extension. The use of a towel may be a helpful aid in this exercise. Wrap a towel around the balls of the feet and with straight arms, pull the towel to draw the shoulder blades back, expand the chest, and straighten the back. Remember to keep the knees facing upward.

74. *Head to Knee*

Benefits. Stretches spine and hamstrings, and relieves tension in the back.

Starting Position. Sit on floor with legs extended straight out in front.

Movements

    a. Bring the right foot to the upper left thigh, keeping the sole of the right foot as close to the body as possible. The left knee should stay flat on the floor.

    b. Inhale and bring arms overhead.

    c. Exhale and reach down the straight leg towards the toes and hold onto the leg at the farthest point that feels comfortable.

    d. Hold this pose for several breaths.

    e. Return to starting position.

    f. Reverse legs and repeat on the other side.

    g. Repeat entire exercise one more time.

Special Considerations. Keep the spine elongated with no vertebrae protruding. The back of the knee on the extended leg should remain flat on the floor, the knee facing upward. A towel can be wrapped around the foot of the extended leg to assist in stretching.

For a greater stretch, exhale while descending down the extended leg.

75. *Frog*

Benefits. Stretches inner thighs, opens up pelvis and hip area.

Starting Position. Sit with back against the wall, legs extended straight out in front.

Movements

    a. Bend the knees and bring the soles of the feet together as close to the body as possible.

    b. Keep the back straight and spine extended.

    c. Gently press the knees to the floor.

    d. Hold this pose for several breaths.

    e. Repeat two more times.

Special Considerations. Avoid this exercise if severe knee problems exist.

76. *Supported Shoulder Stand*

Benefits. Stimulates circulatory and respiratory systems.

Starting Position. Sit on floor with the right hip touching a wall.

Movements

    a. Pivot the body and bring the legs up against the wall.

    b. Scoot up against the wall and rest the buttocks against the wall.

    c. Keep the legs up against the wall at ninety degrees.

    d. Take several breaths in this position.

    e. Keep the back of the neck relaxed and shoulders flat against the floor.

    f. Bring the legs slowly back down to the floor.

Special Considerations. To protect and relax the neck, place a cushion two to three inches in thickness between the floor and the back of the neck.

77. *Shoulder Stand*

Benefits. Same as "Supported Shoulder Stand."

Starting Position. Sit on the floor with the right hip touching a wall.

Movements

    a. Perform same movements as for "Supported Shoulder Stand" to get the legs up against the wall.

    b. Inhale and push the soles of the feet away from the wall.

    c. Bend the knees and raise the hips off the floor.

    d. Support the back with the hands, keeping the elbows close to the body.

e. Try to keep the back straight, move the hands closer to the shoulders, and shift more body weight onto elbows and shoulders.

f. Relax in this pose for several breaths.

g. Come out of the Shoulder Stand by bringing the buttocks slowly down to the floor. To relax a moment, rest with the legs against the wall, then bring the legs slowly down to the floor.

Special Considerations. If discomfort exists at any point during the inverted pose, carefully lower the legs back to the floor. Maintain a straight back during the pose otherwise unnecessary strain is imposed on the neck. When trying to straighten the back, do not bring the chin to the chest as this will constrict the neck, rather bring the chest to the chin. With practice, the chest will naturally come to the chin. This posture is not intended for people with high blood pressure.

78. *Plough*

Benefits. Stretches lower back.

Starting Position. Lie on back, head toward a wall. Lie far enough away from the wall so that fingertips can barely touch the wall when the arms are extended back.

Movements

a. Bend the knees and bring them over the chest so that the soles of the feet touch the wall. Keep the feet parallel and support the back with the hands.

b. Extend the arms back towards the wall and interlace the fingers.

c. Press the arms and hands down on the floor.

d. Extend the spine by bringing the buttocks upward.

e. Breathe evenly and hold the posture as long as is comfortable.

f. For greater stability, bend the knees and place the arms beside the body.

g. To come out of the pose, bend the knees to prevent strain on the lower back.

Special Considerations: To avoid strain on the neck, bring the chest to the chin and not vice versa. Caution should be taken for individuals with high blood pressure.

79. *Meditation Pose*

Benefits. Relieves stiffness in knees and ankles, increases blood supply in lumbar and abdominal areas.

Starting Position. Sit on a folded blanket with legs extended straight out in front.
Movements
    a. Bend the left knee.
    b. Holding the left foot with the hands, place the sole of the foot against the right inner thigh.
    c. Bend the right knee.
    d. Place the right foot over the left ankle and against the left inner thigh.
    e. Breathe evenly, and hold this position as long as possible.

SAMPLE SESSION PLANS

In this section, sample session plans for bedridden, moderately impaired, and high functioning elders are presented.

Bedridden

The exercise leader would most likely lead the exercises for bedridden elders on an individual basis. The proposed time length for the exercise session is twenty to thirty minutes, allowing for periods of relaxation; the session is not designed to be raced through. Only twenty to thirty minutes are allotted for the session in order to avoid over-exerting or fatiguing the bedridden individual. There should be ample time to perform the exercises and converse, creating a friendly and social atmosphere.

The exercise leader should provide gentle physical assistance as necessary to help move body parts. Lower functioning bedridden elders may need assistance raising their head or legs.

The exercises listed are identified by number and name. Refer to the previous section of the chapter for complete descriptions of exercises.

Sequence of Exercises

Exercise Number	Exercise Name	Number of Repetitions
1. #1	Head Raisers	3
2. #2	Head Turns	3
3. #3	Mouth Openers	4

Exercise Number	Exercise Name	Number of Repetitions
4. #5	Jaw Rotation	6
5. #7	Eye Rotation	3
6. #8	Arm Raisers	4
7. ——	Relaxation—deep breathing	4
8. #10	Elbow Flexors	4
9. #11	Arm Circles	4
10. #14	Hand Circles	5
11. ——	Massage—leader massages elder's arms and shoulders	
12. #17	Finger Flex	5
13. #18	Finger Spread	3
14. #21	The "X"	4
15. ——	Relaxation—deep breathing	4
16. #22	Chest Opener	3
17. #23	Abdominal Contractors	4
18. #25	Back Press	3
19. ——	Self-massage: face	
20. #26	Knee to Chest	3
21. #28	Toe Points	4
22. #31	The Walk	4
23. ——	Relaxation—deep breathing	4
24. ——	Relaxation Exercises: shake all body parts.	

In summary, exercises for bedridden older adults include simple, non-strenuous movements to stretch and strengthen muscle groups. Achieving movement of most body parts can be accomplished if the exercises are simple and performed in a slow, relaxed manner.

Moderately Impaired

Moderately impaired elders typically attend adult day care centers and multi-purpose senior centers. The exercise session can accommodate a group of six to twenty senior citizens. The chairs should be arranged in a circle facilitating social interaction, group harmony, and visual contact among group members. Provide enough space between chairs to allow movement safely. The proposed time frame for the exercise session is twenty to thirty minutes depending on the ability and size of the group. The exercises are designed to be performed from a seated position. The exercise session can be a social activity allowing for conversation and feedback from the participants.

Sequence of Exercises

Exercise Number	Exercise Name	Number of Repetitions
1. #33	Head Circles	4
2. #34	Chin to Chest	3
3. #35	Shoulder Rotation	6
4. #36	Shoulder Rolls	5
5. ——	Relaxation—deep breathing	4
6. #37	Arm Rotations	8
7. #39	The Punch	16
8. #40	Forearm Stretch	3
9. #43	Elbow Roll	5
10. ——	Massage—partners: arms and hands	
11. #44	The Opener	5
12. #45	Hand Spread	5
13. #46	The Squeeze	5
14. #49	Knee to Chest	5
15. #50	Leg Stretch	4
16. ——	Relaxation—deep breathing	4
17. #53	Tummy Tighteners	3
18. #54	Tummy Toners	2
19. #55	Feet Flexors	4
20. #56	Toe Spread	3
21. ——	Relaxation Exercises: raise and lower all body parts	

In summary, exercises for older adults with limited mobility are designed to be performed from a seated position to avoid over-exertion. If practiced regularly, the exercises can increase strength and flexibility, and allow for a greater range of movement.

High Functioning

High functioning older adults commonly attend community recreational facilities, continuing education classes, senior centers, and clubs. The types of exercises high functioning elders can participate in are limitless including: aquatics, dance, Tai Chi, aerobics, team sports, etc. In this section, a sequence of yoga postures is presented; the approximate time length is forty-five minutes. Loose comfortable clothing is recommended.

Sequence of Exercises

Exercise Number		Exercise Name	Number of Repetitions
1.	#57	Overhead Stretch	3
2.	#58	Deep Breathing Bends	3
3.	#60	Side Stretch	2
4.	#61	Pep-Up	2
5.	#62	Back Stretch	2
6.	—	Massage—self: head, neck, shoulders	
7.	#64	The Tree	2
8.	#65	Triangle	2
9.	#66	Forward Bend	2
10.	#67	Leg Extensions	3
11.	#69	Hand Foot Extensions	2
12.	—	Massage—self: feet	
13.	#70	Bridge	2
14.	#73	Forward Bend	2
15.	#75	Frog	2
16.	#76	Supported Shoulder Stand	1
17.	—	Relaxation Exercises: squeeze and release all body parts	

In summary, a broad range of exercise possibilities exist for high functioning elders, such as yoga, team, dual, and individual sports, aquatics, self-defense, and dance. In this section, yoga was identified as one approach to improve fitness of high functioning elders.

BIBLIOGRAPHY

Adler, S.S. Seeking stillness in motion: An introduction to Tai Chi for seniors. *Activities, Adaptation, and Aging,* 1983, *3*(4), pp. 1-14.

Administration on Aging. *The fitness challenge in the later years.* Washington, D.C.: U.S. Government Printing Office, 1975.

Alexiou, N.G. Tension control. In R. Harris and L.J. Frankel (Eds.), *Guide to fitness after fifty.* New York: Plenum, 1977.

Anderson, R.A., and Anderson, J.E. *Stretching.* Bolinas, CA: Shelter Publications, 1980.

Arnold, L.C. Organization of exercise programs. In R. Harris and L.J. Frankel (Eds.), *Guide to fitness after fifty.* New York: Plenum, 1977.

Bompa, T.O., Bompa, T., and Zivic, T. *Fitness and body development exercises.* Dubuque, IA: Kendall Hunt, 1981.

Cress, R.H. Rehabilitation exercises for the home bound. In R. Harris and L.J. Frankel (Eds.), *Guide to fitness after fifty.* New York: Plenum, 1977.

de Vries, R.A. Physiology. In R. Harris and L.J. Frankel (Eds.), *Guide to fitness after fifty.* New York: Plenum, 1977.

Flatten, K. Physical fitness and self-sufficiency in persons over 60 years. *Activities, Adaptation, and Aging,* 1982, *3*(2), pp. 69-78.

Fowles, D. The changing older population. *Aging,* May-June 1983, *339,* pp. 6-11.

Frankel, L.J., and Richard, B.B. *Be alive as long as you live.* New York: Lippincott and Crowell, 1980.

Frederick, J.A. Tension control techniques to combat stress. In R. Harris and L.J. Frankel (Eds.), *Guide to fitness after fifty.* New York: Plenum, 1977.

Gurewitsch, E. Switzerland's senior gymnastics program. *Aging,* January-February 1983, pp. 3-7.

Haber, P.S. Developing staff capability for physical fitness. In R. Harris and L.J. Frankel (Eds.), *Guide to fitness after fifty.* New York: Plenum, 1977.

Harris, R., and Frankel, L.J. (Eds.). *Guide to fitness after fifty.* New York: Plenum, 1977.

Ingraham, H.S. Public health and fitness. In R. Harris and L.J. Frankel (Eds.), *Guide to fitness after fifty.* New York: Plenum, 1977.

Jamieson, R.H. *Exercises for the elderly.* Verplank, NY: Emerson, 1982.

Kamenetz, H.C. History of exercise for the elderly. In R. Harris and L.J. Frankel (Eds.), *Guide to fitness after fifty.* New York: Plenum, 1977.

Kulinovich, B. The effects of exercise on the self-concept of physically disabled elderly. *Masters Abstracts,* March 1982, *21,* p. 77. (Abstract)

Leaf, A. *Youth in old age.* New York: McGraw-Hill, 1975.

Lettvin, M. Popularizing physical fitness after fifty via T.V. In R. Harris and L.J. Frankel (Eds.), *Guide to fitness after fifty.* New York: Plenum, 1977.

Mobily, K. Attitudes of institutionalized elderly Iowans toward physical activity. *Therapeutic Recreation Journal,* 1981, *15*(3), pp. 30-40.

Munns, K.M. The effects of a 12-week exercise and dance program on the range of joint motion of elderly subjects. Completed research in *Health, Physical Education, and Recreation,* 1979, *22,* p. 247.

Norton, S. *Yoga for people over fifty.* Old Greenwich, CT: Devin-Adair, 1977.

Padula, H. *Developing day care for older people.* Washington, D.C.: National Council on Aging, 1972.

Rodstein, M. Changing habits and thought patterns of aged to promote better health through activity programs in institutions. In R. Harris and L.J. Frankel (Eds.), *Guide to fitness after fifty.* New York: Plenum, 1977.

Spirduso, W.W. Exercise and the aging brain. *Research Quarterly for Exercise and Sport,* 1983, *54*(2), pp. 208-210.

Subcommittee on Human Services of the Select Committee on Aging. *Future directions for aging policy: A human service model* (2nd ed., 96th Congress, Committee Publication no. 96-226). Washington, D.C.: Subcommittee on Human Services of the Select Committee On Aging, 1980.

Wapner, E.B. *Recreation for the elderly.* Great Neck, NY: Todd and Honeywell, 1981.

Wear, R.E. Conditioning exercise programs for normal older adults. In R. Harris and L.J. Frankel (Eds.), *Guide to fitness after fifty.* New York: Plenum, 1977.

Whitehouse, F.A. Motivation for fitness. In R. Harris and L.J. Frankel (Eds.), *Guide to fitness after fifty.* New York: Plenum, 1977.

Chapter 12

Adapted Dance
for Older Adults

INTRODUCTION

This chapter provides an overview of adapted dance for older adults, including program rationale and guidelines for leading and planning adapted dance sessions. Learning objectives, outlined at the beginning of the chapter, are presented to orient the reader to the purpose and goals of the chapter. Next, a brief review of literature is presented in order to clarify the values and benefits of adapted dance.

In the third section, guidelines for leading an adapted dance session are presented. This section includes a description of the components of an adapted dance program and important considerations in leading a session for impaired elders. In the last section, actual adapted dance programs are presented, including examples of adaptations for folk, square, ballet, tap, and modern dance.

LEARNING OBJECTIVES

1. To understand the importance and benefits of adapted dance for elders.
2. To be able to select appropriate activities for an adapted dance session including opening, warm-up, creative dance patterns, and cooling-off activities.
3. To be able to lead breathing and relaxation exercises and incorporate these exercises appropriately into an adapted dance program.
4. To be able to adapt and lead folk dances suitable for various groups of elders.
5. To be able to adapt and lead square dances suitable for various groups of elders.

6. To be able to conduct a class in simple ballet techniques.
7. To be able to adapt and lead tap dances for various groups of elders.
8. To be able to incorporate modern dance into activity programming and effectively adapt modern dance techniques to fit an older population.

RATIONALE

Adapted dance can be defined as the use of movement as a means of self-expression and communication which promotes a healthy relationship between mind and body. Adapted dance utilizes movement to provide outlets for expression and socialization which can lead to increased feelings of self-worth (Caplow-Lindner et al., 1979).

Adapted dance for elders is attracting increased interest. Older adults are becoming more involved in dance due to the numerous benefits derived from participation in an adapted dance program. One such benefit is improved nonverbal communication skills. According to Wapner (1981), communicating through movement patterns during an adapted dance session can improve one's psychological well-being. Through the use of nonverbal communication, interactions can occur among participants of the dance group which might not have been possible through verbal means. This communication can help to redirect an individual's focus away from self-absorption to an orientation more focused on the external environment.

Other benefits can be derived through adapted dance. Through movement, tension is released which, in turn, reduces stress. Caplow-Lindner, et al. (1979) suggested that emotions, both positive and negative, are expressed through movement. Adapted dance is especially suited for elders in that it provides reality orientation and remotivation. Through participation in an adapted dance program, the older adult is encouraged to utilize both long and short-term memory skills, adjust to reality, and gain new interests or remotivate old interests.

Participation in an adapted dance program provides opportunities to improve socialization skills. The group setting of an adapted dance program encourages a sense of unity, feelings of empathy and support, responses of acceptance, and develops interpersonal relationships (Caplow-Lindner, et al., 1979).

Physical benefits can also be derived through adapted dance. According to Hill (1976), adapted dance can help improve muscular strength and endurance which helps the older individual to engage in activity for longer periods of time. Adapted dance can increase flexibility, allowing a greater range of motion in joints and muscles. In addition, adapted dance improves cardiovascular endurance, permitting a more efficient supply of oxygen to the body. Lastly, adapted dance can increase motor fitness, thereby improving coordination and balance.

GUIDELINES FOR LEADING ADAPTED DANCE PROGRAMS

An adapted dance session should have four components: (1) the opening—participants get acquainted and are oriented to the upcoming activity; (2) the warm-up—the body is prepared for exercise through light movements; (3) the adapted dance patterns—adaptations of folk, square, ballet, tap or modern dance sequences are taught; and (4) the cool-off—light movements are executed to relax and return the body to a nonexercised state.

Opening

The adapted dance leader should welcome the participants, make introductions, and give a brief overview of the upcoming adapted dance activity.

Warm-Up

The purpose of the warm-up is to promote participant involvement in movement from a nonexercised state. Through the use of light movements, the energy level is raised, respiration is increased, and the circulation is stimulated. Eight basic actions which utilize imagery to encourage movement and are appropriate for the warm-up are listed below. (The list is based on Wethered's (1973) book on movement therapy.)

1. Thrusting (hammering and punching)
2. Pressing (pushing and pulling)
3. Wringing (screwing and unscrewing a jar lid)

4. Slashing (cutting wheat or cracking a whip)
5. Flicking (brushing off dust)
6. Dabbing (patting on powder)
7. Gliding (smoothing a tablecloth, ironing clothes)
8. Floating (moving like a feather in a breeze)

The warm-up should utilize body movements with variations of space, time and energy. The following techniques are also appropriate for a warm-up period. (Refer to pages 19-21 of Wethered's (1973) book on movement therapy):

1. Stretching—Stretching all muscle groups causes a limbering up of body parts. Directions, levels, time variations (fast and slow), and energy variations (strong and weak) can all be explored by stretching various muscles.

2. Swinging—Swinging allows individuals to discover the relationship between release and control of different body parts. Swinging aids in exploring one's own natural rhythm.

3. Slapping and Rubbing—Slapping and rubbing different body parts stimulates the circulation and boosts the energy level.

4. Clapping—Clapping hands utilizing different space patterns (up and down, side to side, forward and backward, etc.) increases the movement range. Various forms of energy can also be explored through clapping (heavy and light, etc.).

Breathing exercises and massage are appropriate during the warm-up phase of an adapted dance program but should also be interspersed throughout the adapted dance patterns phase of the session in order to allow participants to rest periodically throughout the session. The breathing, massage, and relaxation exercises described below are based on Caplow-Lindner's et al. (1979) work on expressive movement.

Breathing Exercises

The following are examples of breathing exercises:

1. Abdominal Breathing: Inhale through the nostrils, lowering the diaphragm and pushing out the rib cage. On the exhalation, say "HA" forcing the air from the lungs, raising the diaphragm, and contracting the abdomen. On the exhalation, breathe out as much air as possible.

2. Inhale through the nostrils and push out the abdomen. Exhale slowly through pursed lips.

3. Breathe slowly and deeply through the nose.

Relaxation Exercises

In a supine or sitting position, participants are instructed to progressively relax muscle groups starting from the feet and working toward the head or vice versa. The leader instructs the participants to relax specific body parts, and, in turn, consciously relax that particular body part. Relaxation exercises can be accomplished by squeezing and releasing muscles, shaking body parts, raising and lowering body parts, or curling and uncurling body parts.

Massage

The use of massage during an adapted dance session stimulates circulation and improves skin and muscle tone. Massage can be performed by the group leader, partner, or self. To effectively stimulate circulation, massage should include stroking, kneading, or tapping.

Adapted Dance Patterns

Adapted dance patterns incorporate creative or expressive experiences through movement. This portion of the adapted dance program can include adapted folk, square, ballet, tap or modern dance. Examples of adapted dance patterns are explained in detail later in the chapter.

Cool-Off

Perform movements of decreasing intensity. Slow, controlled movements stretch and relax the muscles and cool down the body (Lopez, 1983).
Some examples of cooling-off exercises are:

1. In a seated position
   a. Reach up with one arm high overhead while the other arm is relaxed and bent at the elbow with the hand touching the shoulder;
   b. Alternate arms by reaching up with the bent arm and bringing the stretched arm back to the shoulder;
   c. Perform this stretching motion for eight counts while concentrating on breathing and stretching;
   d. Then, doing this for eight counts, bring both hands to the

back of the head, elbows out, and gently rotate the head
and spine while allowing the upper torso to relax;
    e. Do this motion for eight counts; and
    f. Repeat complete exercise three more times.
2. In a seated position
    a. Inhale and extend arms high overhead;
    b. Exhale and bring arms back down to sides; and
    c. Repeat three more times.
End the dance session with a relaxation exercise (see page 204).

SPECIAL CONSIDERATIONS IN PLANNING
ADAPTED DANCE SESSIONS

When planning adapted dance sessions for older adults, utilize individual needs to create a more meaningful experience for the participants. The use of repetition and nonstrenuous movement will improve the older adult's ability to succeed in performing the dance
patterns. Providing relaxation and breathing exercises will loosen
muscles and reduce fatigue. Massage is another beneficial diversion, creating feelings of relaxation and reducing stress.

Total body exercise should be an objective for a session of
adapted dance. As many body parts as possible should be involved
in a single dance.

When adapting movement patterns of a dance, an infinite number
of variations exists for each step. The dance leader should not feel
limited to maintaining a similarity between the original and adapted
movements.

Adapted dance programs for elders should facilitate a social and
supportive atmosphere. A special consideration in developing
adapted dances is, when possible, allowing for personal contact.
Personal contact is an integral component of folk and square dance.

A final consideration in programming adapted dance sessions is to
avoid unnecessary accidents. Caution is advised to prevent wheelchairs from colliding, participants from falling, and overexertion.

ADAPTED DANCE PATTERNS

Modified versions of folk, square, ballet, tap, and modern dance
are presented in this section.

Adapted Folk Dance

Folk dance provides specific movement patterns that may be more appropriate for people who feel inhibited with spontaneous movement. The basic nature of folk dance requires a cohesive group setting which creates a group identity and a sharing of experiences. Sharing and being part of a group enhance verbal and nonverbal communication (Feder and Feder, 1981).

Folk Dance Objectives

The following are folk dance objectives as presented by Feder and Feder (1981):

1. The scope of movement patterns is broadened by learning new movement sequences.
2. Body consciousness is heightened as one sees how he/she moves in relation to other group members.
3. An individual's own body alignment can be improved by observing other people's movement styles.
4. Tensions are reduced through movement.
5. Socialization skills can be improved by belonging to a group and sharing interactions with group members.

How to Adapt Folk Dance for an Older Population

Non- or mildly impaired older adults may be capable of performing the actual folk dance steps without modification of movements. For moderately impaired and lower functioning elders, adaptation of folk dance is necessary to enable participation. The following section focuses primarily on adaptations for folk dance for moderately impaired and lower functioning older adults.

Adapted folk dance for impaired elders should be performed from a seated position in order to allow individuals with limited mobility to participate. Movements in the adapted folk dance should concentrate on one body area at a time to achieve easy transitions from one movement to the next. For example, patterns made with the feet should be grouped together into one part of the dance rather than switching from a leg movement to an arm movement and back to the leg. Furthermore, movements of all body parts should be incorporated into the adapted folk dance to accomplish total body involvement.

When teaching an adapted folk dance to impaired older adults, demonstrate the movements first without the music. The participants should have the ópportunity to review the steps slowly, without the music, until they become familiar with the steps and are prepared to keep pace with the music. In addition, the adapted movements should be synchronized with the music.

Dances which are appropriately modified for moderately impaired require further modification for lower functioning elderly, such as elderly nursing home residents. Simple movements, which do not require a large range of motion, are appropriate. Fast movements are replaced by movements which occur on every other beat so that participants are able to keep pace. More repetition is incorporated into the dance, making the dance easier to learn and perform.

A buddy or partner system which matches higher and lower functioning individuals should be established and facilitated through an appropriate seating arrangement. Consequently, the higher functioning participants will be able to assist those individuals experiencing difficulty. If there is a sufficient number of volunteers or assistants available, disperse them among the group members to offer help. Lower functioning individuals may enjoy the activity and merely being part of the group, even though they are not able to keep pace with the movement sequences.

Folk dance is an especially appropriate dance form through which to incorporate physical contact. When seated in a close circle, participants can easily touch their neighbors.

Examples of some adapted folk dances are presented on the following pages. In order to clearly illustrate how to modify folk dances for elders, each dance has been presented in three columns:

1. Dance steps: the actual dance steps for the folk dance are listed in this column.

2. Adapted dance steps: the adapted dance steps for performing the folk dance with moderately impaired elders (e.g., adult day care participants, retirement home residents, or frail elders attending multipurpose senior centers) are listed in this column.

3. Simplified adapted dance steps: a simplified version of the adapted dance steps is described in this column. The simplified version in this column is geared toward the more severely impaired elders typically found in nursing homes. The following is a list of abbreviations used in the folk dance examples presented on the following pages:

(L) = left
(R) = right
CW = clockwise
CCW = counterclockwise

The following adapted folk dances are presented in Tables 1-5.

The record companies from which the music for each folk dance is available are identified at the top of each chart. A list of the record companies and their addresses appears at the end of the chapter.

Table 1 lists the movements for "Ve David," an Israeli folk dance. "Ve David" is a lively Israeli dance performed by couples in a circle formation. The adapted dance steps for moderately impaired elders are designed to be performed from a seated position in a circle arrangement. A movement is performed on every beat. The sim-

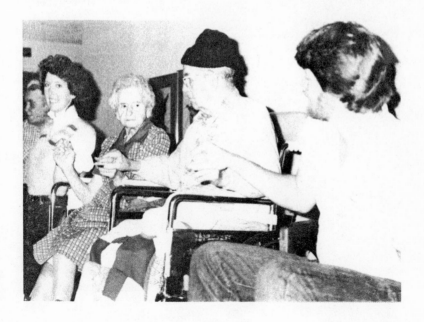

TABLE 1

VE DAVID (Israeli Mixer)

Dance Steps	Adapted Dance Steps	Simplified Adapted Dance Steps
Record: Folk Dancer MH 1153		Music 4/4
Formation:	Formation:	Formation:
Couples Double circle facing counter-clockwise Woman on right side of man Both begin with right foot	Seated in circle, facing center Chairs arranged close enough so that people can hold hands	Seated in a circle, facing center Chairs arranged close enough so that people can hold hands
Steps:	Steps:	Steps:
1. Introduction	1. Introduction	1. Introduction
2. Couples walk counter-clockwise--4 steps	2. Clap hands--count of 4	2. Clap hands--every other count--4 times
3. All join hands facing inward and form a single circle--walk back 4 steps	3. Clap hands high overhead--count of 4	3. Clap hands on knees--every other count--4 times
4. All walk in toward the center of the circle--4 steps	4. Stomp feet--count of 4	4. Thump heels on floor--every other count--4 times
5. All walk back--4 steps	5. Click heels together off the ground--count of 4	5. Snap fingers--every other count--4 times
6. Ladies walk in to the center--4 steps (men clap)	6. Step (R), Step (L), Step (R), Step (L)	6. All join hands and sway from side to side--8 counts

TABLE 1 (continued)

Dance Steps	Adapted Dance Steps	Simplified Adapted Dance Steps
7. Ladies walk back--4 steps	7. Walk forward[1] (remain seated)--count of 4	End of sequence Repeat
8. Men walk in to the center-- 4 steps	8. Walk back[2]--count of 4	
9. Men make a sharp turn and walk 4 steps to the woman on the right of partner	9. Snap fingers--count of 4	
10. With new partners: do a buzz swing[3]--count of 8	10. All hold hands and sway from side to side--count of 8	
End of sequence Repeat	End of sequence Repeat	

[1] Walk forward: Simulate small walking steps forward in a seated position.

[2] Walk back: Simulate small walking steps backward in a seated position.

[3] Buzz Swing: right hips together, right foot carries weight of body, and the left foot pushes. With each push, the left foot momentarily takes the weight. The left foot should not get ahead of the right foot. The right arm holds partner around the waist, left hand held high.

Adapted steps for Ve David include: arm, leg, and upper torso movements; physical contact; and the ability to distinguish musical beats and rhythm.

179

TABLE 2

PATA PATA (African)

Dance Steps	Adapted Dance Steps	Simplified Adapted Dance Steps
Record: Reprise 0732		Music 4/4
Formation: Performed individually Standing facing (N) Feet together	Formation: Seated in a circle facing center (Entire dance per- formed seated)	Formation: Seated in a circle facing center Hands in lap, palms together

(N)

(W) | | (E)

(S)

Steps:	Steps:	Steps:
1. Touch (R) toe to floor to right side (about 12")	1. Touch (R) toe to (R) side	1. Fling (R) hand to right
2. Bring (R) foot back	2. Bring (R) foot back	2. Bring (R) hand back
3. Touch (L) toe to (L) side	3. Touch (L) foot to (L) side	3. Fling (L) hand to left
4. Bring (L) foot back	4. Bring (L) foot back	4. Bring (L) hand back
5. Separate toes (L) (R) \\ / \\/	5. Separate toes (L) (R) \\ / \\/	5. Separate heels of hands (L) (R) /\\
6. Separate heels (L) (R) | |	6. Separate heels (L) (R) | |	6. Separate fingers (L) (R) | |
7. Bring heels together (L) (R) \\ / \\/	7. Bring heels together (L) (R) \\ / \\/	7. Bring fingers together (L) (R) /\\
8. Bring toes together (L) (R) ||	8. Bring toes together (L) (R) ||	8. Bring heels of hands together (L) (R) ||
(Feet are now back together)	(Feet are now back together)	(Hands are now back together)

TABLE 2 (continued)

Dance Steps	Adapted Dance Steps	Simplified Adapted Dance Steps
9. Fling (R) knee up (hip level) and over diagonally left	9. Bring (R) knee up and over diagonally to left	9. Clap hands to knees 4 times
10. Bring (R) foot back to floor	10. Bring (R) foot back to floor	10. Clap hands together 4 times
11. Kick (R) foot across body diagonally left	11. Bring (L) knee up and over diagonally right	End of sequence Repeat
12. Step on (R) foot and pivot 1/4 turn to right (clockwise) to face (E)	12. Bring (L) foot back to floor	
13. Kick (L) foot out	13. Clap hands 4 times	
14. Step backward on (L) foot	End of sequence Repeat	
15. Step backward on (R) foot		
16. Step backward on (L) foot		
End of sequence		
Repeat dance facing (E), then (S), then (W)		

This up-beat dance requires some degree of spatial awareness in order to perform the adapted and simplified dance steps correctly

plified adapted dance steps for lower functioning elders incorporate a smaller range of steps, and movements are performed on every other beat.

Table 2 lists the movements for "Pata Pata," an African folk dance. "Pata Pata" is an African dance performed individually. The adapted dance steps for moderately impaired elders are very similar to the actual dance steps, but are performed from a seated position. The simplified adapted dance steps for lower functioning elders incorporate only arm and hand movements; however, these movements are based on the actual leg movements.

Table 3 lists the movements for "Mayim," an Israeli folk dance. "Mayim" is a high-energy Israeli dance performed in a circle. The

TABLE 3

MAYIM (Israeli)

Dance Steps	Adapted Dance Steps	Simplified Adapted Dance Steps
Record: Folkraft 1108, 1475X45, LP-12		Music 4/4
Formation: Single circle facing center, hands joined	Formation: Seated in a circle facing center	Formation: Seated in a circle facing center, holding hands
Steps:	Steps:	Steps:
1. Grapevine Move clockwise. Cross (R) foot in front of left Step (L) foot to side Cross (R) foot behind left Step (L) foot to side Continue to count of 16	1. Step forward with (R) foot--count of 1	1. Step forward with (R) foot--count of 1
2. Run to center--count of 4	2. Step forward with (L) foot--count of 1	2. Step forward with (L) foot--count of 1
3. Scissor kick	3. Bring (R) foot back--count of 1	3. Bring (R) foot back--count of 1
4. Run backward--count of 3	4. Bring (L) foot back--count of 1	4. Bring (L) foot back--count of 1
5. Run to center--count of 4	5. Repeat this sequence 3 more times	5. Repeat this sequence 3 more times
6. Scissor kick	6. Raise arms up overhead--count of 4	6. Drop neighbors' hands and raise hands to chin level--count of 4

TABLE 3 (continued)

Dance Steps	Adapted Dance Steps	Simplified Adapted Dance Steps
7. Run backward--count of 4	7. Clap overhead--count of 1	7. Clap hands--count of 1
8. Four running steps clockwise	8. Bring arms down--count of 3	8. Bring hands back down to chair--count of 3
9. Face center Hop on (R), touch (L) across front of (R) side Hop on (R), touch (L) to side Hop on (R), touch (L) in front of (R) side Hop on (R), touch (L) to side	9. Bring arms up overhead--count of 4 10. Clap overhead--count of 1 11. Bring arms down--count of 3 12. Stomp both feet--count of 4	9. Raise hands to chin level--count of 4 10. Clap hands--count of 1 11. Bring hands back down to chair--count of 3 12. Shrug shoulders twice--count of 4
10. Hop on (L), touch (R) in front of (L) side Hop on (L), touch (R) to side (arms out to sides shoulder high) Hop on (L), touch (R) in front of (L) side (Hands clap overhead) Hop on (L), touch (R) to side (arms out to sides)	13. Arms out to sides, clap hands with neighbors--count of 8 14. Holding neighbors' hands, make arm circles--count of 8	13. Bring hands out to sides and clap hands with neighbors 4 times--count of 8 14. Holding neighbors' hands, make arm circles--count of 8
End of sequence	End of sequence	End of sequence
Repeat	Repeat	Repeat

This dance incorporates both leg and arm movements. An appealing aspect of the dance is the physical contact which occurs among the dancers.

TABLE 4

MA NAVU (Israeli)

Dance Steps	Adapted Dance Steps	Simplified Adapted Dance Steps
Record: Tikva LP-T 100A		Music 3/4
Formation:	Formation:	Formation:
Circle, facing center Hands joined	Seated in a circle Hands joined	Seated in a circle Hands joined
Part I.	Part I.	Part I.
1. Bring (R) foot forward 6 inches and touch floor-- count "one"	1. Bring (R) foot forward 6 inches and touch the toe to the floor-- count "one"	1. Bring (R) foot forward and touch the toe to the floor-- count "one"
2. Touch (R) foot to (R) side count "two"	2. Touch (R) foot to (R) side-- count "two"	2. Touch (R) foot to (R) side-- count "two"
3. Step (R) foot behind (L) foot--count "three"	3. Step (R)--count "three"	3. Step (R)--count "three"
4. Step (L) foot to (L) side-- count "and"	4. Step (L)--count "and"	4. Step (L)--count "and"
5. Step (R) foot across in front--count "four"	5. Step (R)--count "four"	5. Step (R)--count "four"
6. Rock back on (L) foot-- count "one and"	6. Point (R) toe forward 6 inches and touch floor, lift foot--count "one and"	6. Bring (R) foot forward and touch the toe to the floor, lift foot--count "one and"

184

TABLE 4 (continued)

Dance Steps	Adapted Dance Steps	Simplified Adapted Dance Steps
7. Rock forward on (R) foot-- count "two and"	7. Touch (R) toe again 6 inches forward-- count "two and"	7. Touch (R) toe again-- count "two and"
8. Rock back on (L) foot-- count "three"	8. Bring (R) foot back to (L) foot--count "three"	8. Bring (R) foot back to (L) foot--count "three"
9. (R) foot forward, stepping in place--count "and"	9. Lift both heels off the ground--count "and"	9. Lift both heels off the ground--count "and"
10. Close (L) foot to (R) foot-- count "four"	10. Bring heels back down to floor--count "four"	10. Bring heels back down to floor--count "four"
11. Repeat Part I, beginning with (L) foot	11. Repeat Part I, beginning with (L) foot	11. Repeat Part I, beginning with (L) foot
Part II.	Part II.	Part II.
1. Yemenite step[1] (R) count "one and two"	1. Step (R) foot to (R) side (about 6 inches)-- count "one"	1. Drop neighbors' hands, raise hands up to shoulder level-- count "one, two, three, and"
2. Brush (L) foot across to (R), turning CCW count "and"	2. Step (L) foot in place-- count "and"	2. Snap fingers--count "four"
3. Step (R) foot--count "three"	3. Cross (R) foot over in front of (L) foot-- count "two"	3. Bring hands down--count "one, two, three, four"
		Repeat Part II 3 more times
		End of sequence
		Repeat

185

TABLE 4 (continued)

Dance Steps	Adapted Dance Steps	Simplified Adapted Dance Steps
4. Close (L) foot--count "and"	4. Cross (L) foot over in front of (R)--count "and"	
5. Step (R) foot--count "four"	5. Close (R) foot to (L) foot--count "three"	
6. Face center	6. Step (L) foot in place--count "and"	
Repeat Part II 3 more times	7. Step (R) foot in place--count "four"	
End of Sequence	Repeat Part II 3 more times	
Repeat	End of sequence	
	Repeat	

1 Yemenite Step = Step (R) foot to right side (about 6 inches) with a rocking motion. Step on (L) foot in place. Cross (R) foot in front of (L) foot.

Dancers hold hands throughout most of the dance. Thus, this dance provides a needed outlet for physical contact. The dance moves at a slower pace than the other dances and creates a peaceful atmosphere.

TABLE 5

TROIKA (Russian)

Dance Steps	Adapted Dance Steps	Simplified Adapted Dance Steps
Record: Folk Dancer MH 1059		Music 4/4
Formation:	Formation:	Formation:
Groups of 3, standing side by side holding hands Face counterclockwise in a large circle	Groups of 3, seated in a triangle, one member identified as "center person"	Groups of 3, seated in a triangle, one member identified as "center person"
Steps:	Steps:	Steps:
1. 8 forward running steps	1. Walk forward--8 counts	1. Clap hands every other count--4 times
2. 8 backward running steps	2. Walk backward--8 counts	2. Clap hands to knees every other count--4 times
3. 8 running steps in place; the person on the right goes through the front side of the arch formed by the center person and the person on the left, and back to the original position. The center person follows and makes a left turn under his/her own left arm	3. Center person joins hands with person on the right; then they clap hands together for 8 counts	3. Center person and the person on the right then join hands and push and pull--8 counts

187

TABLE 5 (continued)

Dance Steps	Adapted Dance Steps	Simplified Adapted Dance Steps
4. The person on the left initiates the same sequence as above	4. Center person shifts toward person on the left; they join hands and clap hands together for 8 counts	4. Center person shifts to the person on the left; they join hands and push and pull--8 counts
5. Each trio joins hands, forming a circle of three, and does the grapevine (CW) for 12 counts, then jumps 3 times, shifting directions (left, right, left)	5. Trio joins hands and takes small steps to the left for 12 counts	5. Trio joins hands and takes six steps (step on every other count)
6. Trio does grapevine (CCW) for 12 counts, jumps 3 times, shifting directions (left, right, left)	6. Trio drops hands and claps their own hands 3 times	6. Drop hands and clap 3 times
7. Center person runs forward to join next group	7. Rejoin hands and side step back to the right for 12 counts	7. Trio rejoins hands and takes 6 steps (step on every other count)
8.	8. Trio drops hands and claps 3 times	8. Trio drops hands and claps 3 times
End of sequence	End of sequence	End of sequence
Repeat	Repeat	Repeat

This dance is different from the other dances in that groups of three dancers each join together to perform the dance. Consequently, the dance becomes a more intimate experience, involving the combined efforts of three people.

adapted dance steps for moderately impaired elders require a small stepping motion with the feet, arm movements, and combined movement efforts with individuals seated next to one another. The simplified adapted dance steps for lower functioning elders utilizes leg movements similar to the adapted version; however, the arm movements require a small range of motion.

Table 4 lists the movements for ''Ma Navu,'' an Israeli folk dance. ''Ma Navu'' is a slow dance performed in a circle. The adapted dance steps for moderately impaired elders are performed in a seated position and are very similar to the actual steps. The simplified dance steps for lower functioning elders are identical to Part I of the adapted steps. Part II requires a slow arm motion.

Table 5 lists the movements for ''Troika,'' a Russian folk dance. ''Troika'' is a very fast-paced dance performed in trios. The adapted dance steps for moderately impaired elders require a quick stepping motion. It may be necessary to take very small steps to keep pace with the music. The simplified adapted dance steps for lower functioning elders emphasize a movement on every other beat in order to allow participants to keep pace with the music. In forming trios, try to place the highest-functioning members of the group in trios with the lowest-functioning elders, so that the higher-func-

tioning elders can help the lower-functioning participants to learn the dance.

Summary of Adapted Folk Dances

Adapted folk dance fosters feelings of group harmony and individual acceptance by the group members. The specific movement patterns inherent in folk dance may be more suitable for older adults who feel uncomfortable with spontaneous movement common to modern dance. Lastly, the customary repetitive movements make adapted folk dance easy to learn.

Adapted Square Dance

Square dance is a desirable activity for elders because of its inherent social element. Social interaction is facilitated by the grouping of dancers into units of eight persons each. This unit is known as a square. The development of closer relationships is also fostered by the pairing of dancers into partners. The social nature of square dance can penetrate barriers and draw people out. Being accepted by the group can enhance an individual's psychological and emotional well-being.

Square dancing also contributes to physical fitness. Regular participation in a square dance program can help to develop rhythm, coordination, flexibility, and improve cardiovascular endurance. In addition, performing the skills and dance patterns can aid in memory recall and retention.

How to Adapt Square Dance for an Older Population

Non- or mildly impaired older adults may be capable of performing the actual square dance steps without modification of movements. For moderately impaired and lower functioning elders, adaptation of square dance is necessary to enable participation. The following section focuses primarily on adaptations for square dance for moderately impaired and lower functioning older adults.

A square dance can be adapted so that all the movements can be performed from a seated position. The square should be arranged closely so that each person can easily reach every dancer.

Use only a basic core of square dance movements; the use of too many movements may prove difficult to remember for elders with short-term memory problems. In addition, the movements should be reviewed with the participants numerous times before accompanying the dance with music; consequently, individuals with short-term memory impairment will have had much exposure to the new material.

When developing the lyrics for an adapted square dance, adequate time for performing the movement should be allotted after each call. Including gibberish (e.g., "weave the ring 'til the birdies sing") or phrases that do not dictate a movement allow time to perform the preceding movement.

When working with more impaired elders (e.g., nursing home residents) the sample adapted dances presented in this chapter will need to be simplified further. Delete some of the movement instructions and replace the instructions with gibberish lyrics. Also, try more repetitions of a smaller number of movements within a dance. These adaptations should facilitate the involvement of lower functioning elders.

Lastly, when initially introducing adapted square dance to older adults, having them wear numbered tags indicating the number for each couple may be helpful.

A square consists of four couples. The lady sits on her partner's right. Couples are designated as 1, 2, 3, and 4. Couples 1 and 3 are referred to as head couples. Couples 2 and 4 are the side couples. Couples 1 and 3 are opposites, as are couples 2 and 4. The corner is the person on the man's left and on the lady's right.

For an illustration of the formation of the square, see Figure 1.

Table 6 (pp. 196-199) lists seventeen square dance calls and movements. The table includes the name of the movement, the actual movement description, and its counterpart adapted movement.

The adapted movements are designed to be performed from a seated position. The square consists of four couples seated closely together.

The following are sample adapted square dances utilizing the seventeen basic calls and movements. Lyrics were created to the tunes of old popular songs which can be sung and/or accompanied with musical instruments. There are two versions of each adapted square dance. The first version is designed for moderately impaired elders; the second version is designed for lower functioning elders. The second version uses fewer movements and greater repetition.

FIGURE 1

M = men   L = ladies

```
             3
           L   M



       M                    L
   4                            2
       L                    M



           M   L
             1
```

Sample Square Dances

To the music of "You Got the Whole World in Your Hands"—the following dance is for moderately impaired elders and utilizes the following square dance movements:

—honors
—do-sa-do
—circle left
—alemande left
—circle right
—weave the ring
—right hand star
—pass through
—promenade
—ladies chain
—star promenade
—alemande right

It is necessary to review these movements numerous times before teaching the actual dance. After learning the individual movements, it may be helpful to break the dance down into sub-parts and master one section at a time before attempting the dance from start to finish.

Honor your partner, if you please
And honor your corner, everyone please
Turn towards your partner and do-sa-do
Now, circle left and here we go.

Now when you get through with your circle left
Turn towards your corner for an alemande left
Now that we're here we may dance all night
Let's join hands for a circle right.

Couple #1 please weave the ring
Shake everyone's hand 'til the birdies sing
Now couple #2 go and weave the ring
And now we've all had a little fling.

Come on ladies make a right hand star
Bet you didn't know you could go so far
Couples 2 and 4 let's see you pass through
Then promenade, go two by two.

Couples 1 and 3 let's see the ladies chain
Now all together let's do a star promenade
There's one last thing we'll do tonight
And that's one more alemande right.

The following dance is for lower functioning elders and utilizes the
following square dance movements:

—honors
—do-sa-do
—alemande right
—circle right
—promenade

Honor your partner if you please
Just sit right there and enjoy the breeze
And honor your corner, everyone please
We're gonna' do this dance with ease.

Turn towards your partner and do-sa-do
Look at those dancers just lettin' it flow
Turn towards your corner for another do-sa-do
Get ready, 'cause here we go.

Let's join hands for a circle right
We may just stay and dance all night
Look at our feet movin' oh so light
These dancers are quite a sight.

Couples get ready, we're gonna promenade
It feels so nice in the cool shade
Now corners I bet you can promenade, too
See us dancing proud and true.

Turn towards your partner for an alemande right
I know we can do it without a fight
What a nice day 'cause we all won
This dance has sure been fun.

To the music of "Camptown Races"—the following dance is for moderately impaired elders and utilizes the following square dance movements:

—alemande left
—alemande right
—circle grand
—promenade
—do-sa-do
—ladies chain
—forward and back
—circle left
—weave the ring
—pass through

Alemande left to your left hand,
   doo-da, doo-da

Right to your own and a circle grand
   Oh, doo-da-day

Meet your partner, promenade
   doo-da, doo-da

Do-sa-do, we've got it made
   Oh, doo-da-day

Couples 1 and 3 pass right through
   doo-da, doo-da

Ladies chain couples 4 and 2
   Oh, doo-da-day

Couples 1 and 3 go forward and back
   doo-da, doo-da

Circle left but don't go far
Oh, doo-da-day

Couple #4 will weave the ring
doo-da, doo-da

Let's go back home and we will sing
Oh, doo-da-day

The following dance is for lower functioning elders and utilizes the following square dance movements:

—alemande left
—alemande right
—grand circle
—forward and back
—circle right
—pass through

Alemande left to your left hand
doo-da, doo-da

Right alemande to your own man
Oh, doo-da-day

Let's all form a circle grand
doo-da, doo-da

We're the best in all the land
Oh, doo-da-day

Couples 1 and 3 pass right through
doo-da, doo-da

And couples 2 and 4 will pass through, too
Oh, doo-da-day

Couples 1 and 3 go forward and back
doo-da, doo-da

Now couples 2 and 4 go forward and back
Oh, doo-da-day

Circle right as we sing-a-long
doo-da, doo-da

Now we end this old song
Oh, doo-da-day

TABLE 6

SQUARE DANCE MOVEMENTS

Name of Movement	Movement Description	Adapted Movement
1. Honors	1. Two people acknowledge each other, can be as simple as a tilt of the head or a curtsy and a bow	1. Man bows from the waist. Lady spreads her skirt with her hands, bends slightly and points her left toe toward her partner
2. Do-sa-do	2. Two dancers face one another, walk forward and pass right shoulders, then move to the right as they pass back to back. They then pass left shoulders as they walk backward to their original positions	2. Place both hands behind the lower back and sway from side to side 4 times
3. Circle left or circle right	3. Dancers hold hands and move in a circle either clockwise or counterclockwise	3. All join hands, turn heads to the left if circling left, or right if circling right, and walk in place for 16 counts
4. Forward and back	4. The designated couples walk forward for 4 counts, then back 4 counts to original positions	4. The designated couples take three steps forward, reach forward and clap hands twice with opposite person. Take 3 steps backward
5. Promenade	5. Couples walk side-by-side counterclockwise around the square until they reach their original positions	5. Couples hold hands and sway from side to side

TABLE 6 (continued)

Name of Movement		Movement Description		Adapted Movement
6. Alemande right	6.	Partners face one another and walk around each other in a clockwise circle with right shoulders together	6.	Couples join right hands and slowly lift arms up high, then bring arms back down again
7. Alemande left	7.	Face the corner, join left hands with corner, walk in a counter-clockwise circle, then back to original position	7.	Corners join left hands, raise arms up high, then bring arms back down again
8. Courtesy turn	8.	Partners join left hands. The man places his right arm around the lady's waist and the couple turns counterclockwise half way around. This can be used as an ending for different movements	8.	Lady's left foot touches the man's right foot and keeping their feet together, they form a circle with their feet
9. Weave the ring	9.	Beginning with an alemande left, ladies move clockwise, men move counterclockwise, pass right shoulders with your partner, left shoulders with the next dancer, right with the next and so on until dancers meet their original partners	9.	Designated couple shakes hands with each of the other couples
10. Ladies chain	10.	Two opposite ladies move across the square to the opposite man and are turned with a courtesy turn	10.	Two opposite ladies reach forward and shake hands

TABLE 6 (continued)

Name of Movement	Movement Description	Adapted Movement
11. Right hand star	11. This movement is done by any combination of 4 people (i.e., ladies, men, head couples, side couples). Four people walk to the center of the square, join right hands, advance in a clockwise circle until they meet their partners. A left hand star is done to the left	11. Four designated people reach forward, join hands and take 8 walking steps
12. Star promenade	12. The 4 men form a left hand star and place right arms around their partners' waists. Couples move side by side counterclockwise until they return to original positions	12. Four men reach forward and join left hands, hold their partners with their right hands and all take 8 walking steps
13. All around your left hand lady	13. Similar to "do-sa-do your corner," except the couples continue walking forward keeping right shoulders together	13. Corners join both hands and rotate arms in a big circle
14. Pass through	14. Two opposite couples walk forward, then pass to the right of the person they face. Couples move to their new positions	14. Opposite couples take 4 walking steps forward, lift legs straight out and touch feet with opposite person. Take 4 walking steps backward

TABLE 6 (continued)

Name of Movement	Movement Description	Adapted Movement
15. Alemande that star	15. Men form a right hand star position and hold their partners with a left forearm grip. The men are on the inside of the star facing clockwise. The ladies are on the outside of the star facing counterclockwise. The star rotates in a counterclockwise direction, men moving backward and women moving forward	15. Men form a right hand star while women stomp their feet for 8 counts
16. Split the ring	16. One couple moves forward and "passes through" the couple facing them. The lady turns right, the man turns left and both continue around the outside of the circle, then back to the original position	16. The designated couple claps hands together, then reaches forward, and claps hands with the opposite person, then partners clap hands again
17. Grand circle	17. Dancers form 2 circles; ladies form a circle inside the square and move clockwise; men form a circle outside the square and move counterclockwise. Dancers walk around the circle back to their original positions	17. Men join hands, ladies join hands. Men stomp their left feet and women stomp their right feet for 8 counts

To the music of "Red River Valley"—the following dance is for moderately impaired elders and utilizes the following square dance movements:

- —alemande left
- —circle right
- —weave the ring
- —courtesy turn
- —promenade
- —grand circle

Oh, do an alemande left with your corner
And a circle right all the way round
When you meet up with you partner in the valley
Then promenade her to this pretty sound.

Now the first couple go weave the ring
And let's see that big old grand circle
Don't forget to laugh, smile and sing
And courtesy turn with your Red River Girl.

The following dance is for lower functioning elders and utilizes the following square dance movements:

- —alemande left
- —circle right
- —star promenade
- —do-sa-do

Oh, do an alemande left with your corner
And hold her tight as you swing her round
Let's go a big circle right in the valley
Now let's sit and listen to this pretty sound.

All four couples form a star promenade
That's the best star we've ever made
Find your own partner for a do-sa-do
Now that's the end of our song and show.

In working with impaired elders, learning these seventeen adapted square dance movements may be a sufficient number. Even if the elders know the traditional movements, relearning the adapted movements may prove to be a challenge. Working repetitively with a basic core of movements is desirable when working with elders, especially those with short-term memory deficits.

Summary of Adapted Square Dance

Square dance helps to sharpen socialization skills because of the interaction which naturally occurs due to the physical setting of the square. In addition, the physical activity involved in participating in adapted square dance contributes to improved fitness.

Adapted Ballet

Older adults can restore vitality and release tension by practicing ballet exercises. Simple ballet techniques are an effective form of exercise to improve posture and feel physically and mentally fit. Ballet strengthens the body and allows older adults the opportunity to discover their own inner rhythms. Ballet helps to reshape and control the body (Welles, 1982).

How to Adapt Ballet for an Older Population

Unlike folk and square dance, the adapted movements presented for ballet are very similar to the actual movements. The movements presented are not strenuous but are performed while standing, and can be accomplished by most elders. However, unlike adapted square and folk dance, it would be more difficult to adapt ballet to enable participation by more seriously impaired elders (e.g., nursing home residents). Set up a barre, or horizontal pole, about waist high. During exercise, one hand is placed on the barre for support. Each exercise sequence is performed on both sides, with one hand on the barre.

Adapted Ballet Exercises

The material presented in this section is based on Welles's (1982) book on ballet for women of all ages.

1. First position—heels are together and legs are rotated outward to form a *V* with the feet. The weight of the body is forward over the balls of the feet. The body is erect and extended; the abdomen is pulled in, and the buttocks are squeezed together. One hand is sup-

ported by the barre, and the other arm is lifted to the side and slightly ahead of the body.

2. Second position—feet are twelve inches apart, legs are rotated outward. The body and hand positions are identical to first position.

The following twelve exercises are sample adapted ballet exercises for older adults with moderate to good mobility. These exercises are also based on Welles's (1982) work on ballet for women of all ages.

Demi-plié and relevés in first position. These exercises warm up muscles and tendons and increase flexibility.

1. Bend the knees outward. Keep heels on the floor and the spine erect. The center of the knee should go directly over the foot. Three counts.

2. Straighten the knees and stretch the muscles in the legs. Three counts.

3. Relevé: Raise the heels off the floor. Weight should be evenly distributed over all ten toes. Raise the arm and look up simultaneously. Three counts.

4. Heels are lowered gently back to the floor. Arm returns to side. Three counts. Repeat three more times, then repeat this movement four more times on the other side.

Pliés in second position. This movement stretches the inner thighs:

1. Place feet about twelve inches apart; rotate legs outward.

2. Bend the knees directly over the toes, keeping the heels on the floor. The seat remains exactly in line between the feet; the spine is held straight. Six counts.

3. Straighten knees slowly and pull up thigh muscles. Squeeze buttock muscles together. Six counts. Repeat three more times, then repeat this movement four more times on the other side.

Battements tendus to the front. The following battements are performed in first position. This exercise strengthens abdominal and back muscles. Knees are pointed outward, away from each other in a turned out position. The working leg refers to the leg away from the barre and the supporting leg is next to the barre.

1. Slide the heel on the working leg forward until the foot is entirely stretched and the toes are slightly touching the floor and the heel is naturally forced upward. Two counts.

2. Lift and extend the leg, toes pointed. Two counts.

3. Gently bring the toes back to the floor, keeping the knee straight. Two counts.

4. Slide the foot back to first position without bending the knees.

Lift up on the supporting leg so the working leg fits back easily. Two counts.

Repeat three more times, then repeat this movement four more times on the other side.

Battements tendus to the back. The torso must remain facing straight ahead and not tilted to either side. The body should lean slightly forward as the leg is lifted back to avoid strain on the lower back.

1. Begin in first position. Slide the foot back and point the toes. Two counts.
2. Lift the leg. Two counts.
3. Bring the foot back down to a point. Two counts.
4. Bring the foot back to first position. Two counts.

During this exercise, hold the free arm extended forward. Repeat three more times, then repeat this movement four more times on the other side.

Battements tendus to the side. Keep the supporting knee straight and the spine erect. If the torso sinks, then the kick is too high.

1. Begin in first position. Slide the foot out to the side in the direction the toes are already pointed until the foot is fully stretched with toes pointed. Two counts.
2. Keep thighs in a turned out position and lift the leg. Two counts.
3. Gently lower the leg back down to the floor with the foot still pointed. Two counts.
4. Return the foot back to first position. Two counts.

Repeat three more times, then repeat this movement four more times on the other side.

Battements tendus en croix. This movement strengthens abdomen, back, and thigh muscles.

Tighten the buttock muscles, point the toes and stretch the knees and ankles.

1. Two battements tendus to the front.
2. Two battements tendus to the side.
3. Two battements tendus to the back.
4. Two battements tendus to the side.

Repeat on the other side.

Grand battements. This movement strengthens the back and abdominal muscles and tones the thighs. If the torso buckles during this exercise, the kick to too high.

1. To the front. (In first position.) Legs are straight and turned

out. Swing the working leg up with the knee pointing to the side of the room. Three counts.

Return leg back to first position. Three counts. Repeat three more times.

2. To the side. Keep the torso straight and facing forward. During the kick, the knee should point upward and the toes should be pointed.

—Kick the leg out to the side. Three counts.

—Repeat three more times.

—Repeat entire exercise on the other side four times.

Forward port de bras. Begin in first position. This exercise tones abdominal muscles, stretches the backs of the thighs and the spine.

1. Simultaneously:

—Bend and reach forward, legs straight.

—Bring the chin to the chest.

—Contract abdominal and buttock muscles. Six counts.

2. Gently roll back up. Six counts.

3. Continue into a relevé, bringing the arm overhead. Slightly arch backward, keeping all muscles tight. Six counts.

4. Gently lower the heels back to the floor while slowly bringing the arm back to the side. Six counts. Repeat on the other side.

Balançoire (leg swings). This exercise increases flexibility in the legs. Keep torso erect and stretch the entire working leg. Maintain a turned out position. Begin in a lunge position (supporting knee bent, working leg straight), but as the leg swings foward and up, straighten the supporting leg throughout the exercise. Swing the leg forward and back four times on each side.

Attitude kicks (thigh lifts). This exercise tones the thighs. Keep the spine erect; the supporting leg is straight but the working leg is slightly bent.

1. Begin in first position. Swing the leg up and outward, bending the knee sideways; raise the heel upward and point the toes. Two counts.

2. Bring the leg back to first position. Two counts. Repeat three more times.

3. Swing the leg sideways; the knee is slightly bent, and the toes are pointed downward. Two counts.

4. Return leg to first position. Two counts. Repeat three more times. Repeat the exercise twice on each side.

Side port de bras and stretch. This exercise tones abdominal muscles and firms waistline.

1. Begin with feet in parallel position on the balls of the feet.

Lean sideways away from the barre. With the free arm, reach up and over the head in the direction of the barre until the arm forms an arch. Thighs are touching. Six counts.

2. Bring the arm back to the side while gently lowering the heels back to the floor. Six counts.

3. Bring the free hand to the center of the chest with fingers pointed upward. Extend the arm straight up. Look at the hand moving upward. Lift up on the toes as the hand is raised. Six counts.

4. Allow the arm to drop and let the chin drop to the chest. Allow the knees to bend slightly. Contract abdominal muscles. Six counts.

5. Slowly roll back up to starting position and bring the heels back down to the floor. Six counts.

Repeat two more times; then repeat this movement three more times on the other side.

Battements facing center. This exercise tones the thighs. The legs and spine should remain straight; if the torso buckles, then the kick is too high.

1. Begin in first position with the back to the barre, holding onto the barre with both hands.

— To the front: In a turned out position, kick straight ahead, point the toes. Two counts.

— Bring foot back to first position. Two counts.

2. To the side: Kick out to the side, toes pointed, turned out position. Two counts.

— Return the foot to first position. Two counts.

— While kicking to the side, pull the opposite side of the body in the direction opposite the kick which will create a two-way stretch. Buttock muscles should remain tight. Kick four times to the side. Repeat the entire exercise on the other side.

Summary of Adapted Ballet

Adapted ballet for older adults has both physical and mental benefits. Ballet strengthens and tones the body and simultaneously helps to create a more accurate self-concept. Adapted ballet is different from adapted folk and square dance in that it is performed standing and is very similar to the classical movements.

Adapted Tap Dance

Non- or mildly impaired elders may be able to perform the actual tap movements without modification. For moderately impaired and lower functioning elders, adaptation of tap dance is necessary to enable participation. The following section focuses primarily on adaptations for tap dance for moderately impaired and lower functioning elders.

Tap dance is especially suitable for older adults. Since one can perform the same basic dance patterns in a seated position, the basic steps can be the same no matter if one is standing or seated. The special appeal of tap, the sounds the feet make, remains the same. Tap dance is noisy, expressive and rhythmic. Tap dance utilizes many of the senses, and most dancers can actually hear if the steps are correct.

Taps can be purchased and attached to leather-soled shoes. The purchase of tap shoes is not essential.

How to Adapt Tap Dance for an Older Population

All the basic movements of tap dance can be adapted to a seated position. For older adults with limited mobility, tap dance can be performed sitting in a chair wearing tap shoes. An inexpensive alternative to tap shoes is cardboard tap attachments made in the following way: (1) cut out two cardboard pieces in the shape of a pair of shoes; (2) make one small hole on each side of the insole at the widest part of the foot; (3) make two more holes on each side of the instep; (4) run pieces of yarn or string through the holes and tie the string onto the foot; and (5) attach metal buttons onto the toe and heel areas of the piece of cardboard.

For seniors without use of their legs, adapted tap dance can still be done by making sounds with hands. With the use of tap socks, tap sounds can be simulated with the hands. Wear a sock on each hand and attach metal buttons to the finger and heel areas. A small board or tray placed on the lap of each individual will enable tap sounds to be produced. Use the same terminology as listed. The tap on the fingertips is the counterpart to the toe, and the heel on the hand is the counterpart to the heel on the foot.

The following are basic movement patterns categorized according to the number of sounds each step produces, based on Nash's (1969), Atwater's (1971), and Hungerford's (1939) works.

1. One-sound movements
   —brush (forward): Brush the ball of the foot on the floor as the foot moves forward. This movement can also be done to the side;

—brush (backward): brush the ball of the foot on the floor as the foot moves backward;

—step: transfer the weight to the entire foot;

—toe: transfer the weight to the toe;

—heel: transfer the weight to the heel;

—stamp: same as a step, but use more force to create a louder sound;

—leap: both feet momentarily lose contact with the floor; otherwise, it is the same as a step. Prepare one foot to take off; both feet lose contact with the floor; then the other foot lands on the floor;

—jump: similar to the leap in that there are three parts—take off with one or two feet, a moment in the air, then land on two feet;

—double heel: take off with both feet, knees bent and a moment in the air; land on heels with toes up;

—heel click: hit the inside of the heels together while both feet are off the floor; can occur along with a leap, hop, or jump;

—hop: take off and land on the same foot; no transfer of weight from one foot to the other;

—heel thump: lift the heel, then bring the heel back down to the floor;

—chug: lift the heel; then bring the heel back to the floor as the toe slides forward;

—heel touch: touch the heel of the free foot to the floor;

—toe touch: bend knee of free leg and touch the toe to the floor;

—heel toe brush: no transfer of weight. The sound is made by hitting the shoes together; hit the heel of the free foot against the toe of the other foot as it moves forward and diagonally across supporting foot; and

—toe heel brush: hit the toe of the free foot against the heel of the other foot as it moves diagonally backward across the supporting foot.

2. Two-sound movements

—shuffle: brush forward, then backward; no change of weight;

—flap: toe, then step while walking forward; weight change occurs on second sound;

—heel-toe: transfer the weight on the second sound; touch the heel to make the first sound, then the toe;

—toe-heel: transfer the weight on the second sound; touch the toe to make the first sound, then the heel;

—ball change: shift the weight from one foot to the ball of the other foot; then shift the weight immediately back again to the first foot;

—heel change: shift weight from one foot to the heel of the other foot; then shift immediately back again to the first foot; and

—drawback: while moving backward—toe, then step; transfer of weight.

3. Three-sound movements

—triple: shuffle, then step.

The following adapted tap dances are presented in Tables 7-10.

Table   7. "Love Makes the World Go 'Round' " pp. 210-212.

Table   8. "Sidewalks of New York" pp. 213-215.

Table   9. "Five Foot Two, Eyes of Blue" pp. 216-218.

Table 10. "Won't You Come Home?" pp. 219-221.

These dance sequences are to be read from left to right in each row. The lyrics are found on the first line matched with the tap movement and count or beat on the second and third lines.

Table 7 lists the movements for an adapted tap dance to the music

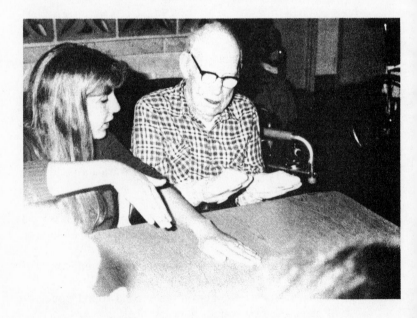

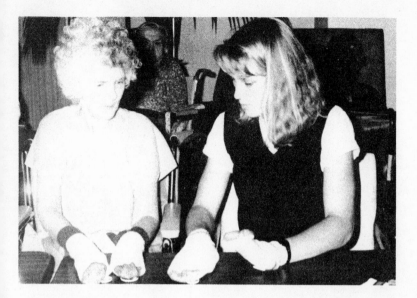

of "Love Makes the World Go 'Round." The dance incorporates
five basic steps for the hands or feet:

— brush forward
— brush backward
— step
— heel touch
— toe touch

A simple sequence of steps is repeated four times.

Table 8 lists the movements for an adapted tap dance to the music
of "Sidewalks of New York." The dance incorporates eight basic
steps for the hands or feet:

— triple
— heel thump
— toe touch
— hop
— jump
— leap
— heel toe brush
— step

TABLE 7

"LOVE MAKES THE WORLD GO ROUND"

Word	LOVE			MAKES		THE	WORLD		GO
Action	(R) brush forward	(R) step	(L) step	(L) Brush forward	(L) step	(R) step	(R) brush backward	(R) step	(L) step
Count	1	2	3	1	2	3	1	2	3

Word	ROUND			LOVE		MAKES	WORLD		GO
Action	(L) brush backward	(L) step	(R) step	(R) heel touch	(L) heel touch	(R) heel touch	(L) toe touch	(R) toe touch	(L) toe touch
Count	1	2	3	1	2	3	1	2	3

Word	ROUND			-----		THE	SOME - BODY		SOON
Action	(R) heel touch	(L) heel touch	(R) heel touch	(L) toe touch	(R) toe touch	(L) toe touch	(R) brush forward	(R) step	(L) step
Count	1	2	3	1	2	3	1	2	3

Word	WILL			LOVE		YOU	-----		
Action	(L) brush forward	(L) step	(R) step	(R) brush backward	(R) step	(L) step	(L) brush backward	(L) step	(R) step
Count	1	2	3	1	2	3	1	2	3

TABLE 7 (continued)

Word	Step	Beat	Word	Step	Beat	Word	Step	Beat
IF	(R) heel touch	1	NO	(L) heel touch	2	ONE	(R) heel touch	3
LOVES	(L) toe touch	1		(R) toe touch	2	YOU	(L) toe touch	3
NOW	(R) heel touch	1		(L) heel touch	2		(R) heel touch	3
SI	(R) brush backward	1	-	(R) step	2	LENT	(L) step	3
HIGH	(R) brush forward	1		(R) step	2		(L) step	3
IN	(L) brush forward	1		(L) step	2	SOME	(R) step	3
SKY	(L) brush backward	1		(L) step	2		(R) step	3
LOVE	(R) heel touch	1	SINGS	(L) heel touch	2	A	(R) heel touch	3
SIL	(L) toe touch	1	-	(R) toe touch	2	VER	(L) toe touch	3
SONG	(R) heel touch	1		(L) heel touch	2		(R) heel touch	3
----	(L) toe touch	1		(R) toe touch	2		(L) toe touch	3

TABLE 7 (continued)

MAK -	ING THE	EARTH
(R) brush forward	(R) step	(L) step
1	2	3

-----		WHIRL
(L) brush forward	(L) step	(R) step
1	2	3

SOFT	-	LY
(R) brush backward	(R) step	(L) step
1	2	3

(L) brush backward	(L) step	(R) step
1	2	3

LOVE	MAKES	THE
(R) heel touch	(L) heel touch	(R) heel touch
1	2	3

WORLD		GO
(L) toe touch	(R) toe touch	(L) toe touch
1	2	3

ROUND		
(R) heel touch	(L) heel touch	(R) heel touch
1	2	3

(L) toe touch	(R) toe touch	(L) toe touch
1	2	3

This tap dance can be performed as slowly as is appropriate, to allow the dancers to keep pace.

TABLE 8

"SIDEWALKS OF NEW YORK"

EAST (R) Triple 1 2 3	SIDE (L) Triple 1 2 3	WEST (R) Triple 1 2 3
SIDE (L) Triple 1 2 3	ALL A - (R) heel thump / (R) heel thump / (R) heel thump 1 2 3	ROUND THE (L) heel thump / (L) heel thump / (L) heel thump 1 2 3
TOWN (R) toe touch / (L) toe touch / (R) toe touch 1 2 3	THE (L) toe touch / (R) toe touch / (L) toe touch 1 2 3	TOTS SANG (R) hop / (R) hop / (R) hop 1 2 3
RING A (L) hop / (L) hop / (L) hop 1 2 3	ROS - IE Jump / Jump / Jump 1 2 3	LON - DON Leap / Leap / Leap 1 2 3

TABLE 8 (continued)

TRIPPED THE LIGHT FAN - TAS - TIC

TRIPPED	THE		LIGHT		FAN -	TAS -		TIC
(R) hop	(R) hop	(R) hop	(L) hop	(L) hop	(L) hop	Jump	Jump	Jump
1	2	3	1	2	3	1	2	3

ON THE SIDE - WALKS OF NEW

ON	THE		SIDE -		WALKS	OF		NEW
Leap	Leap	Leap	Heel toe brush to (R). . .		(L) step	Heel toe brush to (L). . .		(R) step
1	2	3	1	2	3	1	2	3

YORK

YORK								
(L) step	(R) step	(L) step	-----			(R) step	(L) step	(R) step
1	2	3				1	2	3

This adapted tap dance uses more steps and less repetition than the first dance, consequently the dance may be more challenging.

TABLE 8 (continued)

Measure 1	Measure 2	Measure 3
BRIDGE IS . . . Heel toe brush to (R) . . . (L) step 1 2 3	FALL - ING Heel toe brush to (L) . . . (R) step 1 2 3	DOWN (L) step (R) step (L) step 1 2 3
----- (R) step (L) step (R) step 1 2 3	BOYS . . . . AND (R) triple 1 2 3	GIRLS . . . . TO- (L) triple 1 2 3
GETH - ER . . . . (R) triple 1 2 3	----- (L) triple 1 2 3	ME . . . . AND (R) heel thump (R) heel thump (R) heel thump 1 2 3
MA - ME . . . . O' (L) heel thump (L) heel thump (L) heel thump 1 2 3	ROURKE (R) toe touch (L) toe touch (R) toe touch 1 2 3	----- (L) toe touch (R) toe touch (L) toe touch 1 2 3

TABLE 9

"FIVE FOOT TWO, EYES OF BLUE"

FIVE	FOOT	TWO		EYES	OF	BLUE ,	BUT	OH	WHAT	THOSE	FIVE
(R) flap. . .		(L) flap. . .		(R) drawback. .		(L) drawback. .		(R) flap. . .		(L) flap. . .	
1	2	3	4	1	2	3	4	1	2	3	4

FOOT	COULD	DO	HAS	AN -	Y	BOD -	Y	SEEN		MY	
(R) drawback. .		(L) drawback. .		Heelclick. . .		Heelclick. . .		(R) heel thump	(L) heel thump	(R) heel thump	(L) heel thump
1	2	3	4	1	2	3	4	1	2	3	4

GIRL?				-----				TURNED	UP	NOSE	
(R) toe touch	(L) toe touch	(R) toe touch	(L) toe touch	Jump	Jump	Jump	Jump	(R) flap. . .		(L) flap. . .	
1	2	3	4	1	2	3	4	1	2	3	4

TURNED	DOWN	HOSE	NEV -	ER	HAD	NO	OTH -	ER	BEAUS	HAS
(R) drawback. .		(L) drawback. .	(R) flap. . .		(L) flap. . .		(R) drawback. .		(L) drawback. .	
1	2	3	1	2	3	4	1	2	3	4

TABLE 9 (continued)

Box 1

Lyric	1	2	3	4
AN - Y . . . BOD - Y	Heelclick. . .		Heelclick. . .	
SEEN MY	(R) heel thump	(L) heel thump	(R) heel thump	(L) heel thump
GIRL?	(R) toe touch	(L) toe touch	(R) toe touch	(L) toe touch

Box 2

Lyric	1	2	3	4
NOW IF YOU	Jump	Jump	Jump	Jump
RUN IN TO A	(R) flap. . .		(L) flap. . .	
FIVE FOOT TWO	(R) drawback. .		(L) drawback. .	

Box 3

Lyric	1	2	3	4
COV - ERED WITH FUR	(R) flap. . .		(L) flap. . .	
- - - -	(R) drawback. . .		(L) drawback. . .	
DIA - MOND RINGS AND	Heelclick. . .		Heelclick. . .	

Box 4

Lyric	1	2	3	4
ALL THOSE THINGS	(R) heel thump	(L) heel thump	(R) heel thump	(L) heel thump
BET - CHA LIFE IT	(R) toe touch	(L) toe touch	(R) toe touch	(L) toe touch
IS - N'T HER BUT	Jump	Jump	Jump	Jump

TABLE 9 (continued)

COULD	SHE	LOVE		COULD	SHE	WOO?		COULD	SHE	COULD	SHE
(R) flap . .		(L) flap . . .		(R) drawback . .		(L) drawback . .		(R) drawback . .		(L) drawback . .	
1	2	3	4	1	2	3	4	1	2	3	4

COULD	SHE	COO?	HAS	AN –	Y	BOD –	Y	SEEN		MY	
(R) drawback . .		(L) drawback . .		Heelclick . . .		Heelclick . . .		(R) heel (L) heel	(R) heel (L) heel		
								thump thump	thump thump		
1	2	3	4	1	2	3	4	1	2	3	4

GIRL?				– – – –	Jump	Jump	Jump	Jump
(R) toe touch	(L) toe touch	(R) toe touch	(L) toe touch					
1	2	3	4		1	2	3	4

This lively dance includes basic movements which can be performed with either the hands or feet.

TABLE 10

"WON'T YOU COME HOME?"

Panel 1

1	2	3	4
WON'T	YOU		COME
(R) brush forward	(R) step	(L) step	(R) step

1	2	3	4
HOME		BILL BAI –	LEY
(L) brush to side	(L) step	(R) step	(L) step

Panel 2

1	2	3	4
WON'T	YOU		COME
(L) brush forward	(L) step	(R) step	(L) step

1	2	3	4
HOME?		SHE	MOANS
(L) brush backward	(L) step	(R) brush backward	(R) step

1	2	3	4
WHOLE		DAY	THE
(L) brush backward	(L) step	(R) step	(R) step

Panel 3

1	2	3	4
LONG			
(R) toe-heel . .	(L) toe-heel . .		

| ----- | | | |

1	2	3	4
I'LL	DO	THE	
(R) stamp	(L) stamp	(R) stamp	(L) stamp

Panel 4

1	2	3	4
COOK –	IN'	DAR –	LING
(R) stamp	(L) stamp	(R) stamp	(L) stamp

1	2	3	4
I'LL PAY		THE	THE
(R) heel-toe . .	(L) heel-toe . .		

1	2	3	4
RENT			
(R) heel-toe . .	(L) heel-toe . .		

TABLE 10 (continued)

	1	2	3	4	1	2	3	4	1	2	3	4
Lyric	I	KNOW		I'VE	DONE		YOU		WRONG			
Step	(R) stamp	(L) stamp	(R) stamp	(L) stamp	(R) stamp	(L) stamp	(R) stamp	(L) stamp	Jump	Jump	Jump	Jump
Lyric	——				'MEM –	BER	THAT		RAIN –	Y	EVE	THAT
Step	Jump	Jump	Jump	Jump	(R) brush to side	(R) step	(L) step	(R) step	(L) brush to side	(L) step	(R) step	(L) step
Lyric	I DROVE			YOU	OUT		WITH		NOTH' –	IN	BUT	A
Step	(R) brush forward	(L) step	(R) step	(R) step	(L) brush forward	(L) step	(R) step	(L) step	(R) brush backward	(R) step	(L) step	(R) step
Lyric	FINE	TOOTH			COMB?							I
Step	(L) brush backward	(L) step	(R) step	(L) step	(R) toe-heel . .	(L) toe-heel . .	.	(L) step	(R) toe-heel . .	(L) toe-heel . .		(L) toe-heel . .

TABLE 10 (continued)

KNOW	I'M		TO	BLAME		WELL		AIN'T	THAT		A
(R) heel-toe ..		(L) heel-toe ..		(R) stamp	(L) stamp	(R) stamp	(L) stamp	(R) heel-toe ..		(L) heel-toe ..	
1	2	3	4	1	2	3	4	1	2	3	4

SHAME?			BILL	BAI -	LEY	WON'T	YOU	PLEASE		COME	
(R) heel-toe ..		(L) heel-toe ..		(R) stamp	(L) stamp	(R) stamp	(L) stamp	(R) stamp	(L) stamp	(R) stamp	(L) stamp
1	2	3	4	1	2	3	4	1	2	3	4

HOME?				----			
Jump	Jump	Jump	Jump	Jump	Jump	Jump	Jump
1	2	3	4	1	2	3	4

This dance incorporates only two movement sequences. The movements within each sequence are repetitious and easy to learn.

221

A basic sequence of steps is repeated two times.

Table 9 lists the movements for an adapted tap dance to the music of "Five Foot Two, Eyes of Blue." The dance incorporates six basic movements for either the hands or feet:

- — flap
- — drawback
- — heelclick
- — heel thump
- — toe touch
- — jump

A basic sequence of movements is repeated four times.

Table 10 lists the movements for an adapted tap dance to the music of "Won't You Come Home?" The dance incorporates six basic movements for either the hands or feet:

- — brush
- — step
- — toe-heel
- — stamp
- — heel-toe
- — jump

A basic sequence of movements is repeated two times.

Summary of Adapted Tap Dance

Adapted tap dance is an appropriate activity for the elderly because the basic steps remain unchanged regardless of whether one is standing or sitting. For elders with limited mobility, adapted tap dance can be performed with the feet, in a seated position. For elders without the use of their legs, tap sounds can be simulated by the hands with the use of tap socks.

Adapted Modern Dance

Modern dance can help the older adult gain increased awareness of the sensation of motion within his/her own body. It aids in the ability to express oneself creatively and can expand the movement potential. Modern dance allows the individual the freedom to create his/her own unique movements; through this physical involvement, a sense of well-being is fostered.

How to Adapt Modern Dance for an Older Population

Non- or mildly impaired elders may be able to perform modern dance without modification. For moderately impaired and lower functioning elders, adaptation of modern dance is necessary to enable participation. The following section focuses primarily on adaptation of modern dance for moderately impaired and lower functioning older adults.

Adapted modern dance allows for spontaneity of movement. There are no right or wrong steps. Ideas or themes are suggested and each individual has the liberty to create movement patterns within his/her own unique framework. A supportive and accepting atmosphere must exist to eliminate inhibitions and to encourage this type of sharing.

Adapted Modern Dance Patterns

The following modern dance patterns are based on Caplow-Lindner's et al. (1979) and Wethered's (1973) works. These patterns illustrate the potential for using a theme to stimulate movement in modern dance.

1. Movement sequences are created where different body parts come together, meet and then part again, e.g., finger to toe, nose to knee, etc. This basic theme can be expanded to include meeting and clashing, meeting and passing, and meeting and joining to create another movement. This movement exercise can be done alone or with partners.
2. Explore movement principles such as free flow and controlled flow, light and strong energy, direct and indirect movement, body oriented movement and environment oriented movement, and simultaneous and successive movement.
3. Create movement patterns using different verbs, e.g., turning, exploding, digging, zigzagging, climbing, etc. This theme is called "Word-Movement Association."
4. Create a sequence of movements to develop a whole scene, e.g., a basketball game, an orchestra, a fishing trip, etc.

5. Explore locomotor movements, e.g., walk, slide, gallop, hop, etc. These movements can be done seated.
6. Experiment with movements as they relate to sounds, e.g., clicking, whistling, tapping, etc.
7. Use adjectives to elicit movement, e.g., scary, gooey, hot, etc.
8. Recite poems and/or stories to the group to stimulate movement.
9. Use sensory recall that evokes energy, space, and rhythm to elicit movement, e.g., raking leaves, walking in mud or snow, etc.
10. Use oppositional movement factors as an impetus to create movement, e.g., toward and away, high and low, large and small, slow and fast, open and closed, etc.
11. Use hand dancing as a form of self-expression to elicit movement. Two people face each other and place their palms together. One is designated as the leader and guides the movement of the other. The action can be performed in place, sitting or standing, and with changing levels and directions. Due to the physical contact which occurs between the pairs, this activity may be especially rewarding.
12. Try using a mirror image. One person initiates movement, while others mirror the movement. This activity can be performed in a partner situation or small groups. The passive and active roles should be reversed.

Exploring themes in modern dance may help to elicit imagery which can spark impetus for movement. Ideas for themes are limitless. Creating themes based on individuals' backgrounds in the group may stimulate movement and simultaneously induce interaction through a sharing of interests and experiences.

Dynamics of movement is often studied in modern dance classes. The degree of force and energy a dancer expends in his/her movements allows for variety and contrast in the quality of those movements (Duffy, 1982). Table 11 lists the common categories of energy, approaches to each category, and adapted versions of each approach for impaired older adults.

Summary of Adapted Modern Dance

Adapted modern dance fosters creativity and spontaneity for elders. The freedom to invent and express original movements helps

TABLE 11

MODERN DANCE: DYNAMICS OF MOVEMENT

Name of Movement	Sample Movement	Sample Adapted Movement
1. Sustained movement: Occurs with a smooth, continuous release of energy. There is a strong sense of control from beginning to finish.	1. Move an imaginary heavy box across the floor. Midway, switch from moving the box with the arms to moving the box with the legs.	1. Sitting in a circle, pass a very heavy imaginary box around the circle. One at a time, each person lifts the box from his/her lap and places it on a neighbor's lap. Continue this motion around the circle.
2. Percussive movement: Uses a lot of energy, starts and stops suddenly. The movements are strong, sharp and explosive.	2. Simulate a baseball game using percussive movements.	2. In a seated position, experiment with motion by percussively moving each finger, one at a time. After each finger is involved, try it with the whole hand.
3. Swinging movement: A small movement begins the momentum, then gravity takes control which causes a swinging motion, a suspension in the motion, then uncontrolled flow again until finally the movement stops.	3. Swing different body parts: legs, arms, head, torso, and in different combinations, creating as much space as possible.	3. While seated in a circle, have each person find a different body part that can swing; allow the whole group to try the same motion. Have another person demonstrate swinging a different body part, then the group will imitate. Continue until everyone has had a chance to lead the motion.

TABLE 11 (continued)

4. Vibratory movement: A succession of many quick and pulsating movements.	4. While walking across the floor, try quivering or shaking a series of body parts, beginning with the head and working progressively down toward the feet.	4. Pass a prop around the circle, e.g., scarf, paper cup, book, etc. As the prop touches a person's hands, that person's hands and arms begin to vibrate as he/she is passing it to the next person. After the object is passed, the vibrations cease.
5. Collapse: The body gives into gravity by releasing energy.	5. The total body or isolated body parts can be involved. Collapse to the ground from an erect position, then from a squatting position. Allow one body part to collapse while another body part is vibrating.	5. In a seated position, experiment with collapsing different body parts. Raise one arm and allow it to collapse, raise the other arm and experience its collapse, then raise both arms. Try the same thing with the legs, head, torso.
6. Ballistic movement: An explosive, vigorous movement, used to gain speed or power, ending with a follow-through. This forceful movement is usually directed at an object.	6. Pass around various props, e.g., a ball, a hat, a broom, etc., so that each individual can create a ballistic movement utilizing the prop, then collapsing to the floor.	6. Begin by powerfully pointing with both arms and feet at a person in the group and yelling out his/her name, then collapse in the chair. This person must initiate the next explosion by pointing with arms and legs and yelling out someone else's name, then collapsing. Continue until everyone has had a turn.

226

to expand movement potential. Themes, movement principles, sounds, props, and poems are a few of the aids which can be utilized in adapting modern dance.

CONCLUSION

Participation in dance in later life can have both physical and mental benefits. It can enhance coordination, muscular strength, flexibility, and cardiovascular efficiency. Mental health can be improved through the opportunity for creativity and self-expression. Folk, square, tap, ballet, and modern dance can provide rewarding experiences for older adults if adapted appropriately. Using the guidelines presented, a limitless number of adapted dances can be created.

BIBLIOGRAPHY

Atwater, C. *Tap dancing: Techniques, routines, terminology.* Rutland, VT: Tuttle, 1971.

Caplow-Lindner, E., Harpaz, L., and Samberg, S. *Therapeutic dance movement: Expressive activities for older adults.* New York: Human Sciences Press, 1979.

Duffy, N.W. *Modern dance: An adult beginner's guide.* Englewood Cliffs, NJ: Prentice-Hall, 1982.

Evans, J. *Let's dance: A movement approach to folk dance.* Canada: an-Ed Media, 1981.

Feder, E., and Feder, B. *The expressive arts therapies.* Englewood Cliffs, NJ: Prentice-Hall, 1981.

Hays, J.F. *Modern dance: A biomechanical approach to teaching.* St. Louis: Mosby, 1981.

Hecox, B. Movement activities for older adults. *Journal of Physical Education, Recreation, and Dance,* 1983, *54*, pp. 47-48.

Hill, K. *Dance for physically disabled persons: A manual for teaching ballroom, square, and folk dances to users of wheelchairs and crutches.* Reston, VA: American Alliance for Health, Physical Education, and Recreation, June 1976.

Hungerford, M.J. *Creative tap dancing.* Englewood Cliffs, NJ: Prentice-Hall, 1939.

Jensen, C.R., and Jensen, M.B. *Square dancing.* Provo, UT: Brigham Young University Press, 1973.

Kraus, R. *Square dances of today and how to teach and call them.* New York: A.S. Barnes, 1950.

Lopez, T. Guidelines for using dance with older adults. *Journal of Physical Education, Recreation, and Dance,* 1983, *54*, pp. 44-45.

Munns, K.M. The effects of a 12-week exercise and dance program on the range of joint motion of elderly subjects. *Completed Research in Health, Physical Education, and Recreation,* 1979, *22*, p. 247.

Nash, B. *Tap dance.* Dubuque, IA: Brown, n.d.

Preston-Dunlop, V. *A handbook for modern educational dance.* London: McDonald and Evans, 1980.

Wapner, E.B. *Recreation for the elderly.* Great Neck, NY: Todd and Honeywell, 1981.

Welles, L. *Ballet body book.* Indianapolis/New York: Bobbs-Merrill, 1982.

Wethered, A.G. *Movement and drama in therapy.* Boston: Plays, n.d.

SONG BOOK RESOURCES FOR TAP DANCE MUSIC

Estella, J.M. *Easy to play! Well known melodies for the piano.* New York: Kamnaen Music Co., 1953.
Sixty-four popular standards. The Montgomery Ward Electronic Organ. Registrations by Russ Taylor. New York: Robbins Music, 1968.

RECORD COMPANIES LISTED
IN THE ADAPTED FOLK DANCE SECTION

Tikva. 1650 Broadway, Room 301, New York, New York 10019.
Folkraft. 1159 Broad St., Newark, New Jersey 07114.
Reprise. c/o Warner Brothers, 3300 Warner Blvd., Burbank, California 91510.
Folkdancer. P. O. Box 201, Flushing, New York.

Chapter 13

Recreational Techniques
and Activities

INTRODUCTION

A wide range of recreational activities can work successfully with elders. The purpose of this chapter is to foster a greater awareness and understanding of some of the diverse recreational activities and techniques possible with elders. Information on a variety of recreational activities and techniques is presented in this chapter, including: massage; clowning; drama; music; arts and crafts; horticulture therapy; pet therapy; and the uses of humor and laughter with elders. There is enough information available on some of the techniques (e.g., arts and crafts, horticulture therapy, music, and drama) to write an entire textbook on that one topic. Thus, the discussion of some of these techniques is not intended to be a thorough overview. Rather, the intention is to increase the reader's awareness and understanding of the use of these techniques with elders, and alert the reader to resources for obtaining further information and specific program ideas.

MASSAGE

Massage is an exceptionally beneficial and enjoyable leisure activity for elders. The information presented in this section is intended to prepare one to be able to perform massage with elders, although a massage training course is strongly recommended for someone seriously interested in massage. Also, Downing and Rush's (1972) book on massage is highly recommended as a reference for techniques. Much of the information presented in this section is based on Downing and Rush's (1972) book, *The Massage Book*. For the purposes of this book, massage is defined as a handling and manipulation of flesh, such as stroking, kneading, and pressing, for therapeutic purposes (Nissen, 1929).

In the first sub-section, the benefits of massage are described in order to foster a clear understanding of the value and importance of massage to elders. In the second sub-section, general considerations in massaging elders are discussed. In the last sub-section, specific massage techniques and strokes are clearly explained.

Benefits of Massage

The benefits of massage for elders are quite impressive. Massage is a unique form of non-verbal communication. It is an effective way of expressing caring and warmth. Through massage, deeper levels of communication can be established between two individuals.

Massage is one of the most relaxing leisure activities one can enjoy. Relaxation has very important health benefits, especially for elders, and massage is certainly one of the most relaxing forms of recreation in existence. Unlike most drugs used as sedatives and relaxants, massage has a relaxing effect without any harmful side effects (Downing and Rush, 1972).

Massage, especially facial massage, can have cosmetic benefits. Massaged areas have a less wrinkled, smoother, and more youthful appearance. This cosmetic benefit of massage often leads to enhanced self-esteem and a greater sense of well-being.

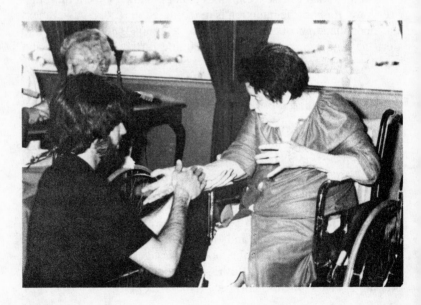

The emotional benefits of massage are very significant. In addition to enhanced self-esteem and general sense of well-being, the experiencing of such a pleasurable, enjoyable leisure activity contributes to higher morale and happiness.

The physiological benefits of massage are equally impressive. Massage has the following general effects (Nissen, 1929): Increased circulation and respiration; improved digestion; sleep is facilitated; and pain is relieved.

In particular, massage can help relieve the pain of arthritis, an ailment which affects approximately 50 million Americans. According to Jayson and Dixon (1974), massage can relieve arthritic pain because firmly rubbing in a liniment massages the underlying tissue and relieves the muscle spasm that produces the aches and pains.

General Considerations

Downing and Rush (1972) identify numerous considerations and helpful hints for making massages more effective and more enjoyable:

1. The least expensive, yet most effective liniment to use is a mixture of vegetable oil with some fragrance (e.g., a few drops of musk). Be sure that the oil is at least room temperature or warmer. For easy use, pour the oil into a plastic container with a narrow opening.
2. If the recipient of the massage feels awkward, or a group massage activity is being conducted, the massage recipients can remain seated in wheelchairs or chairs, fully clothed. However, the optimal conditions for a massage are to have the recipient undressed, lying on a massage table or gurney (usually available in a nursing home). Massage on a bed could be effective primarily for the face, arms, hands, legs, and feet, but not for the back, abdomen, and other body parts because of the lack of underlying support. Massage on the floor is also possible (use a foam pad for comfort and sheets to prevent staining the floor or carpet), but it tends to strain the massager's back.
3. The room temperature should be warm (over 72 degrees). It is difficult to warm someone once they are chilled.
4. The massager's hands should be warm, and fingernails should be short.

5. Do *not* use bright lighting.
6. Experiment with using soft, relaxing music in the background, but if the massager and/or the recipient seem to focus more on the music than on the massage, try massaging without music. Regardless of whether or not music is used, the environment should be quiet, relatively private, and free from distractions.
7. Talk as little as possible during the massage. However, one might find (especially when working with nursing home residents) that the recipients become extremely friendly, uninhibited, and expressive. Perhaps a reasonable compromise is to request silence and concentration on the sense of touch during some of the strokes, and allow free flowing conversation at other times.
8. Ask the recipient for feedback during the massage, in order to know whether to apply more pressure, less pressure, or whether to massage a particular area for a shorter or longer duration of time.
9. Hairy body areas require more oil.
10. Apply oil only on the body part immediately to be massaged.
11. Try to never lose contact with the recipient's body during the massage. When pouring oil, keep one arm or hand on the body, and pour the oil with the other hand into the hand on the recipient's body.
12. Relax hands, and apply pressure by using body weight, *not* muscles.
13. Involve the whole body in the massage, not just the hands.
14. If the massager is standing, try to keep the back straight, feet apart, and knees bent.
15. The speed and pressure used during the massage can vary once in a while to avoid monotony, but in general, maintain a flowing, even speed and degree of pressure.
16. Mold hands to fit the contours of the body parts over which they are passing.
17. Be especially gentle with very dry, chapped, injured, or sensitive body parts.
18. Prolonged, gentle pressure can loosen and relax tight and constricted body parts (e.g., curled fingers and toes can be straightened).
19. Do *not* force a joint to move.
20. Hands should be clean—wash with warm or hot water before beginning the massage.

21. Allow approximately 45 minutes for the massage. The last few minutes of the massage should be devoted to silent thought and self-awareness of how one's body parts feel.
22. As identified in the following section, there are a variety of strokes which can be utilized. Try to use as many of these different strokes as possible.

Massage Techniques/Strokes

There are numerous different massage strokes:

1. Massage the muscles with the ball of the thumb.
2. Move the fingertips in circles.
3. Knead the body with the fingers and hand.
4. Rake the body with the fingers.
5. Stroke the muscles with the heels of the hands.
6. Stroke the muscles with the undersides of closed fists.
7. Drum the muscles with the fingertips.
8. Move the undersides of the forearms in large sweeps and circles.
9. Press tightly over the muscles with the flat part of the elbow.
10. Lightly slap the body with cupped hands.

The following is a suggested sequence for a 45 minute massage session. The session begins with facial massage, because: (1) people identify themselves more by their face than any other part of their body; and (2) touching the face is less taboo than touching other body parts (Downing and Rush, 1972). The session outlined below can be adapted for a group of nursing home residents in wheelchairs by allowing them to remain dressed, merely taking off shoes and socks for foot massage, rolling up pants legs for lower leg massage, and rolling up shirt sleeves for arm massage. The back and shoulders can be massaged gently without oil if the massage recipient remains clothed.

Suggested Sequence

1. Massage the forehead with the thumbs.
   a. Begin with the thumbs flat on the center/top of the forehead.
   b. Exert firm pressure, bringing the thumbs across the forehead in a horizontal line.
   c. Bring the thumbs down to the temples, and massage the temples *very lightly*.

    d. Repeat this procedure until the entire forehead has been massaged.

2. Massage the cheeks with the fingertips.
    a. Begin massaging the lower area of the face.
    b. Gradually work upward to the eyes.
    c. Fingers should rotate in tiny circles as they move slowly up the face.

3. Similarly, massage the neck and chin with the fingertips, working upward to the chin.

4. Massage just the neck with the hands.
    a. Begin with the hands on the neck.
    b. Move the hands in circles around the entire neck area.

5. Massage the scalp with a clawing motion.
    a. Begin with the fingertips at the hairline.
    b. With the fingertips, claw the scalp towards the nape.
    c. Repeat this motion several times until the entire scalp has been massaged.

6. Massage the chest and stomach with both hands (use discretion).
    a. Stand behind the person's head.
    b. Place both hands palms down, thumbs touching, on the top of the chest.
    c. Glide hands down towards the stomach.
    d. Move hands out towards the sides.
    e. Glide hands along the sides back up towards the head.
    f. Move hands back to center position.
    g. Repeat this motion several times.

7. Massage the forearms.
    a. Place the person's elbow on the armrest and bring forearm to a vertical position.
    b. Place both hands on the wrist.
    c. Move hands down the forearm towards the elbow. Apply a great deal of thumb pressure.
    d. Repeat this motion several times.

8. Similarly, massage the upper arms.
    a. Lift upper arm and bring the person's hand to the opposite shoulder.
    b. Place both hands on the elbow.
    c. Move hands down the upper arm towards the shoulder. Apply a great deal of pressure.
    d. Repeat this motion several times.

9. Massage the hands.
   a. Place the thumbs on the palms of the recipient's hands.
   b. Rotate the thumbs in circles.
10. Similarly, massage the backs of the hands.
11. Massage the fingers.
    a. Gently pull each finger.
    b. Slide the fingertips along each of the recipient's fingers.
12. Make a hand sandwich.
    a. Place the recipient's hand in between both of the massager's hands.
    b. Gently squeeze the hand.
    c. Repeat with the other hand.
13. Massage the front of the leg.
    a. Place both hands on the recipient's skin, palms down, fingers facing in opposite directions.
    b. Glide hands up the leg, including the sides of the leg.
    c. Repeat with the other leg.
14. Massage the knee.
    a. Criss-cross thumbs over the knee.
    b. Move thumbs in opposite directions, making a circle around the knee cap.
    c. Repeat with the other knee.

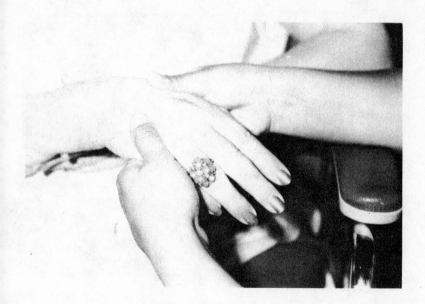

15. Massage the foot.
   a. Place thumbs on heels.
   b. Rotate thumbs firmly in a circular motion.
   c. Slowly work up the foot.
   d. Repeat with the other foot.
16. Make a foot sandwich (similar to the hand sandwich [#15]).
17. Massage the back of the leg (similar to the front of leg massage [#16]).
18. Massage the calf by rotating the thumbs in tiny circles.
19.-21. These strokes are not feasible unless the recipient is unclothed and lying on a massage table, gurney, or on the floor (use discretion).
19. Massage the thighs.
   a. Place the palms of both hands on the inside of the recipient's thigh.
   b. Glide hands across the thigh with a pulling motion going toward the outside of the thigh.
   c. Repeat with the other thigh.
20. Knead the buttocks with both hands.
21. Place one hand on the buttocks, palms down, and rotate the buttocks in a circular motion.

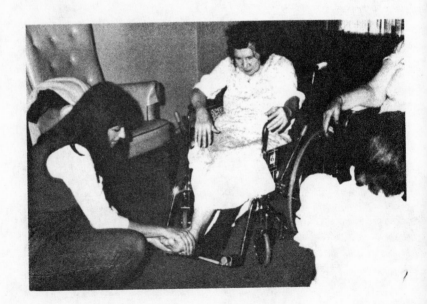

Summary

The massage sequence described in this chapter can be adapted for elders in a variety of settings. In a nursing home, massages can be given to bed-ridden elders on an individual basis, omitting some of the strokes if the elder remains clothed. Higher functioning nursing home residents can be massaged in a group setting (seated in wheelchairs and clothed), hopefully with a 1:1 or 1:2 ratio of staff and volunteers to elders. Groups which are comprised of a mixture of high functioning and low functioning elders can utilize the higher functioning elders as aides to staff in massaging low-functioning elders. The high functioning elders can also be trained to massage each other, or perform self-massage. For high functioning groups of elders, the massage session can involve elders pairing up, lying on the floor, and taking turns massaging each other. Thus, elders of almost any functioning level can enjoy the benefits of massage.

CLOWNING

Benefits of Clowning

Another beneficial and enjoyable recreational activity for elders not usually associated with elders is clowning. Clowning is not only amusing; it is also an excellent activity for improving the mental and physical functioning of impaired elders. In the physical domain, clowning can help improve coordination, balance, and reduce stress. The psychological benefits are numerous: (1) improved communication skills, especially non-verbal communication skills such as body language and eye contact; (2) mental stimulation, especially for mentally impaired elders; (3) because clowning is so unusual, it can prod the memory of someone with poor short-term memory; (4) clowning can be a creative outlet for elders, if they dress up and put on make-up to be a clown themselves; (5) clowning can provide an outlet for the expression of emotions; and (6) many times, withdrawn elders are seemingly miracuously drawn out. Clowning also promotes group interaction and socialization. Certainly, clowning is a desirable activity for elders because of its potential benefits. Guidelines for leading a clowning activity with elders are presented in the next sub-section.

Guidelines

There are three different types of clowns:

1. The mime—This clown is white-faced, and not much make-up is used. The clown acts out stories and expresses emotions non-verbally.
2. The traditional clown—This clown has a big smile and rosy cheeks, and usually a baggy, funny costume.
3. The character-type clown—This clown dresses up to play a specific comedic role. For example, rodeos often have clowns dressed up as cowboys.

The procedures described below pertain more to traditional clowns than to mimes or character clowns.

Materials Needed

1. Ping pong balls
2. Brightly colored nail polish
3. Funny hats
4. Old, baggy clothes
5. Mirrors
6. Balloons
7. Strings
8. Pictures of different clowns
9. Skin lotion
10. Water-based clown white
11. Grease paints

Becoming a Clown

The clown-to-be should put on the make-up and costume in front of the participants so that they can see the transformation take place, and possibly become motivated to become clowns later during the activity. First, the clown should put on the funny clothes. Next, skin lotion should be applied, as this application of lotion makes it easier to take off the make-up later. The clown white should then be applied, followed by the colorful grease paints. Make funny noses by cutting ping pong balls in half and painting them with nail polish. For finishing touches, attach funny-shaped balloons, and wear unusual hats and wigs.

Once the clown has completed dressing and applying make-up, elders should be encouraged to get dressed up as clowns. One motivational technique is to show elders pictures of different clowns and ask them which one they'd like to be made up to look like. Assure people that the make-up is very easy to remove. Sit people in front of mirrors so that they can enjoy seeing themselves being transformed into clowns.

Once people have been transformed into clowns, a drama session can be conducted. Pantomimes and short humorous skits are very effective because clowning tends to allow people to more freely express emotions, play roles they normally don't play in day-to-day life, laugh freely, and generally be less inhibited. Clowning can also be a very well-received intergenerational activity. Young children are fascinated to watch elders transform themselves into clowns, and then are very amused by humorous performances by a group of clowns.

Summary

Clowning is a very beneficial and enjoyable activity for elders. It allows elders to use their imagination and creativity, and enables one to express their individuality. Above all, clowning can generate quite a few laughs!

DRAMA

In this section, drama activities for elders are discussed. The topics covered in this section include: the benefits of drama for elders; components of a drama program; and special considerations in leading a drama session. This section is based on Thurman and Piggins' (1982) and Burger's (1980) works.

Benefits

The following are emotional and psychological benefits of drama for elders:

1. Reduces feelings of loneliness, isolation, and depression;
2. Promotes social interaction;
3. Validates personal experiences by remembering past events;
4. Establishes a bridge between the past and the present; and
5. Can enhance one's self-esteem.

Thus, the benefits of drama activities for elders are numerous. In the next sub-section, components of a drama program are discussed.

Components of a Drama Program

There are six components or phases of a drama program for elders: the introduction; sensory exercises; movement and pantomime; imagination stretchers; improvisations; and session plans with a unifying theme. In addition, five to ten minutes at the end of each session should be allotted for a discussion of participants' impressions of the session. All drama sessions should include both the introduction and time for the concluding discussion, with any combination of the other phases enacted in between. The sensory exercises, movement and pantomime, imagination stretchers and improvisations are most appropriate for the first few meetings of a drama group. Session plans with a unifying theme should be attempted after the group has met a few times and seems ready to try something more difficult. The session plans with a unifying theme are more involving and should be rehearsed several times until the group is able to master the session plan.

1. Introduction to the Session

The introductory phase of the session is used to gain the group's interest. Open-ended questions are asked relevant to the upcoming theme of the session. To encourage participation, all responses are accepted; no answers are considered wrong.

Icebreakers can also be used as an element of the introductory phase to help the group members get acquainted and feel comfortable interacting with one another. Icebreakers are effective in: heightening concentration; increasing the attention span; creating a supportive environment; and increasing energy levels.

An example of an appropriate icebreaker for the introductory phase of a drama session is the activity "How Do You Feel About . . ." Participants should sit in a small circle, facing each other. The leader begins by reciting a phrase such as "I feel . . . ," "I like . . . ," "My pet peeve is . . . ," etc. and then looks to the participant nearest to her to complete the phrase by briefly and openly expressing whatever comes to mind. Every person in the group is called upon to give their answer. Similar responses among different individuals help to validate one's feelings. Humorous responses elicit laughter, which in turn makes the group more relaxed and less inhibited.

2. Sensory Exercises

Many older adults experience a decline in their ability to distinguish sensory stimuli, resulting in a loss of self-esteem. By practicing sensory exercises, the ability to recognize senses can be heightened, renewing self-reliance in daily functioning.

An example of an appropriate sensory exercise is "Sleuth."

> *"Sleuth" (Thurman and Piggins, 1982)*
> *Objectives:* increase concentration and ability to focus on visual stimuli.
> *Directions:*
> a. Pair all participants with a partner.
> b. Direct the partners to observe each other for 60 seconds, carefully noticing one another's appearance e.g., clothes, jewelry, hair, etc.).
> c. At the end of one minute, ask the partners to turn their backs on each other and change three things about themselves.
> d. Ask the partners to turn and face each other and share the changes they detect.

"Sleuth" can be especially challenging and humorous if partners make very subtle changes in appearances (e.g., remove a ring, unfasten one button).

3. Movement and Pantomime.

These activities increase the energy level, enhance body awareness and coordination, and stir the imagination. Pantomime involves the use of imagery and characterization.

An example of a movement and pantomime activity is "Adverbs."

> *"Adverbs" (Thurman and Piggins, 1982)*
> *Objectives:* "to communicate ideas through actions and observe and discriminate among different qualities of movement."

Directions:
  a. Divide the group in half.
  b. Group A decides on an adverb and keeps it a secret from group B. Some examples of adverbs are lazily, nervously, intensely, cautiously, and frantically.
  c. Group B decides on actions they want group A to perform.
  d. Group B tells group A what action they would like group A to perform.
  e. Group A performs the action in the manner of the chosen adverb.
  f. Group B tries to guess what adverb group A has chosen.
  g. After a few attempts, the groups can reverse roles.

4. Imagination Stretchers

The imagination of elders will diminish if it is not exercised. Imagination stretcher activities involve sharing memories, associations, and ideas in a supportive environment, and most importantly, force people to use their imagination.

An example of an imagination stretcher is "Transformation of Real Objects."

"Transformation of Real Objects" (Thurman and Piggins, 1982)
Objectives: to exercise the imagination and share ideas.
Directions:
  a. The leader presents an object (e.g., rope, yardstick, cup, etc.) and demonstrates its normal use.
  b. Through movement, the leader transforms the object to have a different use. For example, one can hold and swing a ruler so as to transform it into a baseball bat.
  c. The leader passes the object around to each person in the group to pantomime a different use for the object.
  d. The rest of the group members try to guess the pantomime.
  e. The activity continues until all group members have had an opportunity to transform at least one object.

5. Improvisations

Individuals become emotionally involved in the activity while they actually become part of the scene. The group members are asked to experiment with dramatic principles, sensory skills, and create an impromptu scene incorporating interaction and movement. The higher the emotional involvement, the higher the level of belief.

An example of an improvisation is "Living Pictures."

> *"Living Pictures" (Thurman and Piggins, 1982)*
> *Objectives:* Explore feelings through body language and experience a common group effort.
> *Directions:*
>   a. Divide the group into groups of four or five people each.
>   b. Present a picture title (e.g. the Wedding, the First Baby, the Picnic, etc.) to each group.
>   c. Direct the group to physically arrange themselves according to the theme of the picture. Each group decides on the setting, relationships, body positioning, etc. of their picture.
>   d. Each group presents their picture while the other groups try to guess the title of the picture.

6. Session Plans with a Unifying Theme

This component is more involving than the other components. The session plan with a unifying theme should be a dramatic activity which needs to be rehearsed several times in order to master. Hopefully, once the session plan has been mastered, a performance can be arranged (e.g., at a nursing home, or a performance for children). The following are some ideas for session plans:

   a. A melodrama involving audience participation (the audience cheers, boos, and makes other noises in response to cue cards, while the characters act out a comedy/drama, perhaps a spoof of a western hero/villain story).
   b. An enactment of a popular television show or movie. The memories of group members can be stimulated to write a script for the simulation of a familiar old movie or television show.

c. A reader's theater activity is an excellent choice for elders with poor short-term memory. In the reader's theater, characters are not required to memorize their lines but rather expressively read and act out their parts. There are numerous books available in most libraries which have appropriate plays for a reader's theater activity.

d. A biblical role play is another appropriate type of session plan. The biblical role play can either be in the format of a reader's theater (characters read expressively and play the parts of characters in a familiar story in the bible) or can be an improvisational activity if the group members are very familiar with the story.

Videotaping the drama session can add a great deal of excitement to the session. Videotaping can be a strong motivational force during rehearsals. Playback of the videotape at the end of the session can be an image-booster, as well as a great laughter-inducing stimulus.

7. Concluding the Drama Session

Allow five to ten minutes at the end of the session for individuals to share their impressions of the drama session.

Special Considerations in Leading a Drama Session

It is imperative for the leader of a drama session for elders to create a warm, supportive atmosphere to reduce inhibitions and foster feelings of acceptance. The use of physical contact can be helpful in creating this type of environment. In addition, sensory input should be offered to individuals with impaired eyesight and/or hearing.

The leader of a drama class should always overplan the session. The drama class will appear much more invigorating when there is not quite enough time to finish all the material, rather than running out of material when there is still time remaining in the session.

A variety of stimuli should be incorporated into each session. Various props, music, sounds, mentally challenging activities, and opportunities for movement exploration enhance the successfulness of drama sessions. At times, the drama leader may feel the need to share personal experiences to spark an interchange for others to relate their own personal experiences.

As in any other recreational activity for elders, match the pace of the activity to the pace of the group members and be prepared to adapt activities according to the functioning level of the participants. A major challenge for the leader is maintaining the interest of higher functioning group members while simultaneously slowing the pace of the activity to ensure the full participation of lower functioning group members.

MUSIC

Music is one of the most universally enjoyable and beneficial forms of recreation. People of all ages and functioning levels can be

positively affected by music. The possibilities for utilizing music with elders are endless. In this section, the use of music with elders is examined briefly (further reading and musical training is strongly recommended). Topics discussed in this section include: benefits of music; and ideas for music activity sessions.

Benefits

Wapner (1981) identifies several benefits of music:

1. Music can have a relaxing, stress-reducing effect.
2. Music can have a stimulating, energizing effect.
3. Musical activities can provide much needed sensory stimulation which can contribute to higher functioning of senses such as hearing, speech, and touch (if rhythm instruments are used).

In addition, Douglass (1978) states that music can:

1. Motivate even depressed elders to participate in activities.
2. Stimulate social interaction and improve socialization and communication skills.
3. Provide a creative outlet for individuals.
4. Allow individuals to physically and emotionally express themselves.
5. Help elders feel better about themselves and enhance one's self-concept.

Thus, musical activities are very beneficial for elders. One only needs to think of how enjoyable and integral an aspect of one's life music is in order to appreciate the benefits of musical activities for elders.

Program Ideas

A selected few of the many musical activity possibilities for elders are described in this section. For additional musical activity ideas, consult Douglas' (1978), Schulberg's (1981), and Wapner's (1981) books. Also, refer to the chapter in this book on intergenerational recreational activity for ideas for intergenerational musical activities. Some of the more popular musical activity possibilities are:

1. Listening Activities

    a. Live performances by either a visiting performer, or a field trip to a performance can be extremely entertaining. Even very confused elders are drawn out and hum along to old familiar tunes.

    b. Listening to and critiquing or discussing recorded music.

    c. A music appreciation activity, involving listening to different types of music or music of different countries.

    d. Listening to and analyzing the meaning of song lyrics. Songs dealing with a specific topic (e.g., serious topics such as love, aging, or social issues) can be listened to in order to generate discussion on the particular topic of the songs. Such an activity can prove to be quite enlightening and mentally stimulating.

2. Singing Activities

    a. For higher functioning elders, a choral group can be formed which has regularly scheduled rehearsals and performances.

    b. An intergenerational singing group can be formed, as depicted in the award-winning film, "Close Harmony."

    c. Large print song sheets can be distributed for a sing-a-long with impaired elders. Those who can not read and do not know the lyrics should be encouraged to hum along.

3. Playing Musical Instruments

    a. High functioning elders might be interested in forming a performing ensemble.

    b. High functioning elders might also be interested in taking music lessons in order to learn how to play the guitar, piano, recorder, and other instruments.

    c. Moderately impaired or lower functioning elders not able to play a band instrument or learn how to play an instrument can still enjoy being part of a rhythm band, accompanying a pianist, guitarist, or recorded music with simple rhythm instruments (e.g., sandpaper blocks, triangles, bells, maracas, and tambourines.

4. *Composing Activities*

    a. An excellent creative outlet is the composing of original music and lyrics. This activity has the potential to be very rewarding and greatly enhance one's self-esteem.

    b. A creative and humorous activity is the composing of satiric lyrics to replace the existing lyrics of a popular song.

5. *Movement to Music*

A variety of music (various tempos and rhythmic patterns) should be utilized in order to elicit different types of movements.

6. *Musical Games*

    a. Musical bingo is a great favorite (the author recently led a two-hour game in a nursing home—the participants didn't even want to quit after two full hours of playing the game). There are several versions of this game; the directions for one of the more popular versions are:

    1) Players receive regular bingo cards and chips.

    2) The leader calls out the numbers.

    3) As each number is called, players that have the number on their card notify the leader.

    4) An excerpt from a popular song is hummed or played on an instrument. The players must correctly guess the title of the song in order to place a chip down on their card.

    Naturally, the rules of this game can be made more flexible when working with a lower functioning population.

    b. A variety of musical quiz games are possible, such as musical tic tac toe, musical baseball, musical anagrams, and others (refer to Douglass' [1978] and Schulberg's [1981] books).

Summary

This section presented a very small sample of the musical activity possibilities which exist. It is important to remember to utilize music which is suited to the interests of the group one is working with.

People in different age groups tend to prefer music from different time periods. Because teenagers and young adults tend to be the most avid followers of popular music, elders tend to be most familiar with music and performers most popular during the time period when they were in their teens and twenties. Thus, a person age 60 in the year 1990 might be most familiar with the music of the 1940s and early 1950s. Meanwhile, a person age 90 in the year 1990 would probably be most familiar with the music of the early 1900s and 1920s. Thus, the varying musical interests of different age groups of elders must be considered in selecting music for musical activities. Just think: persons ages 60-65 in the year 2010 will probably be filling senior centers with the sounds of rock and roll music!

ARTS AND CRAFTS

In this section, an overview of arts and crafts activities for older adults is presented. There are many books written on this topic. The aim of this section is *not* to provide an in-depth discussion of arts and crafts for elders which has already been completed in other books. Rather, this section is intended to give the reader a basic understanding of arts and crafts activity possibilities and practical guidelines for leading arts and crafts activities. Wilkinson and Hester's (1979), Williams' (1962), Merrill's (1967), Fish's (1971), and Wapner's (1981) books are recommended as resources for further information on arts and crafts for elders.

This section has been divided into the following sub-sections: goals and objectives of arts and crafts for elders; benefits of arts and crafts; guidelines in programming arts and crafts activities; special considerations; and a listing of arts and crafts activities.

Goals and Objectives

Arts and crafts activities should augment other programs occurring at the facility or institution. A unifying theme involving other events may provide motivation and a purpose to participate (e.g., making decorations for an upcoming party, or creating special place mats for a family luncheon). The gathering of needed materials is an integral part of an arts and crafts session and participants can be involved in the planning and budgeting of materials (Wapner, 1981).

An effective arts and crafts program for elders is concerned with the creative and productive process of the group members (Wilkinson and Heater, 1979). In addition, the group members should be allowed to demonstrate their individuality in the arts and crafts they produce (Wapner, 1981). This allows the opportunity for self-expression which can enhance emotional growth.

Another objective of an arts and crafts program is to utilize the older adult's inherent capacities and interests (Wilkinson and Heater, 1979). Consequently, varying levels of abilities and interests are accounted for in planning the arts and crafts sessions.

An important objective of an arts and crafts program is to improve skill levels. Skill levels are enhanced as a consequence of working on different projects. This is achieved by the necessity to focus one's attention on the project, and utilize cognitive, perceptual, and motor capacities in a constructive fashion.

Participation in an arts and crafts program gives the older adults a lasting object of personal value (Wapner, 1981). Thus, the individual may experience the sense of achievement and productiveness.

Benefits of Arts and Crafts

Participation in an arts and crafts program enhances physical, cognitive, social, and emotional growth.
1. Physical Benefits:
    a. Strengthens and tones muscles;
    b. Increases range of motion;
    c. Heightens tactile stimulation;
    d. Improves manual dexterity; and
    e. Improves eye/hand coordination.
2. Cognitive Benefits:
    a. Enhances perception;
    b. Increases concentration;
    c. Provides reality orientation;
    d. Increases the attention span;
    e. Increases concentration;
    f. Evokes color identification; and
    g. Enhances the ability to adhere to directions.
3. Social Benefits:
    a. Promotes social interaction;
    b. Creates an opportunity for service to others; and
    c. Promotes group cohesion.
4. Emotional Benefits:
    a. Channels energy;
    b. Enhances self-esteem;
    c. Provides an outlet for creativity;
    d. Recognizes individual achievement;
    e. Allows for ego satisfaction; and
    f. Provides an avocational interest.

Guidelines in Programming Arts and Crafts

The following are practical guidelines in programming arts and crafts for elders:

1. Sufficient time should be allotted for set-up and clean-up of art activities;

2. Specific tasks should evolve from simple procedures to more complex (Wilkinson and Heater, 1979);
3. Discuss the activity ideas with the elders prior to their occurrence;
4. Specific tasks should be broken down into basic steps to allow for greater participation (Wapner, 1981); and
5. Plan projects which are economical, since funding for activities is usually limited (Wapner, 1981).

Special Considerations in Programming Arts and Crafts

The following are special considerations when programming arts and crafts activities for an older population:

1. Special attention is required for very confused older adults in a group arts and crafts setting. These individuals must be observed to avoid the possibility of them injuring themselves or digesting the art materials.
2. Crafts projects should not be so simple that they are boring, and on the other hand, they should not be too difficult so as to be frustrating (Wapner, 1981).
3. A higher degree of involvement can be obtained by allowing elders' input into choosing the crafts projects (Merrill, 1967).
4. Crafts that are very fine or intricate in detail may be difficult for elders with impaired vision (Williams, 1962).
5. The availability of a specific crafts room can generate the involvement of individuals working on their own time.
6. The use of bright colors may be helpful.
7. A discussion of the meaning of the project may increase motivation to participate.
8. Demonstrations, combined with clear instructions are most effective. Try to relate one step at a time (Fish, 1971).

Arts and Crafts Activity Ideas

Place Mats	Mobiles	Leathercraft
Collage	Stuffed Animals	Painting
Stained Glass	Mosaics	Papercraft
Plaques	Sewing	Metalwork
Table Decorations	Signs and Posters	Quilting

Bookmarks	Sketching	Calligraphy
Greeting Cards	Wood Working	Ceramics
Decorated Flower	Caning	Weaving
Pots	Knitting	Cloth Flowers
Wreaths	Hooked Yarn	Door Mats
Holiday	Rugs	
Decorations		
Costume Jewelry		

The activity ideas listed represent only a small range of the arts and crafts activities possible in working with elders. There are numerous books available (see the bibliography at the end of the chapter) which can be consulted for arts and crafts activity ideas.

HORTICULTURE THERAPY

In this section, an overview of horticulture therapy for elders is presented, based on Olszowy's (1978) book, *Horticulture for the Disabled and Disadvantaged*. This section is intended to enhance the reader's awareness and understanding of the use of horticulture therapy with elders. Further reading on this topic is strongly recommended for those interested in incorporating horticulture therapy into a therapeutic recreation program for elders. This section has been divided into several sub-sections: benefits of horticulture therapy; background of horticulture therapy; and a listing of horticulture activity ideas.

Benefits of Horticulture Therapy

Horticulture activities can be used for therapeutic purposes. Such services as physical therapy, occupational therapy, recreational therapy, and vocational therapy can incorporate horticulture as a rehabilitative mechanism. Manual dexterity, the ability to understand instructions and follow directions, and the ability to concentrate are important skills utilized in horticulture therapy (Olszowy, 1978).

Horticulture as therapy is unlike many other therapies in that the focus is on living beings. Research indicates (Olszowy, 1978) that there is a symbiotic relationship between humans and plant life.

Plants seem to thrive best under human care, and likewise, a psychological need in people is fulfilled through horticulture because a bond is created with the environment.

Caring for plants fulfills different needs in different people. For some, caring for plants poses a challenge, for others it becomes a responsibility and a desire for accomplishment. Caring for plants also provides an exposure to coping with loss (Olszowy, 1978).

Another therapeutic value of horticulture therapy is that it teaches patience. Waiting for the seed to germinate, the cutting to root, or the plant to flower requires patience (Olszowy, 1978).

Horticulture therapy can occur in a group setting conducive to social interaction, thereby helping to fill a void in the lives of socially isolated elders. Caring for plants also helps elders feel a greater sense of control over the environment. This is an important benefit, because a loss of control over the environment is a concern for many elders (Olszowy, 1978).

According to Hefley (Olszowy, 1978), the following are intellectual, emotional, and physical benefits of horticulture therapy:

Intellectual Benefits

1. New skills are learned.
2. Vocabulary and communication skills are enhanced.
3. Curiosity is heightened.
4. Observation skills are increased.
5. Sensory perception is improved.
6. Training for vocational and prevocational opportunities are provided.

Emotional Benefits

1. Confidence and self-esteem are enhanced.
2. Outlets for aggressive behavior are provided.
3. Opportunities for self-expression are offered.
4. Activities arousing interest in the future are provided.

Physical Benefits

1. Basic motor skills are enhanced.
2. Outdoor activities which improve physical and mental health are participated in regularly.

Background of Horticulture Therapy

For hundreds of years, garden activities have been used as a form of preventive medicine. Before the science of psychiatry was developed, physicians advocated working in the garden for patients with emotional problems. According to Olszowy (1978), in 1798, Benjamin Rush prescribed digging in the soil as a curative agent for the mentally ill. Agricultural activities were viewed as helpful to mental patients in Spain dating back as early as 1806. In the early 1900s, garden activities were established in many hospitals and institutions for therapeutic purposes. After World War I and II, many veteran's hospitals developed garden therapy programs for their patients (Olszowy, 1978).

Today, many diverse institutions across the country have incorporated horticulture therapy into their activity programs, including: schools, hospitals, arboreta, community centers, and correctional institutions. The growth in horticulture therapy is expected to continue producing many, new innovative programs which can be adapted for elders (Olszowy, 1978).

Activity Ideas

The following is a brief overview of activity ideas for a horticulture program for elders (Olszowy, 1978):

1. Drying plants and flowers
2. Flower arranging
3. Terrariums
4. Window box gardening
5. Growing herbs
6. Hanging baskets
7. Forcing bulbs
8. Vegetable gardening
9. Flower gardening

In addition to Olszowy's (1978) book, the following books and organizations should be consulted for additional information on activity ideas, and on horticulture therapy in general.

American Horticulturist, American Horticulture Society, Mount Vernon, VA 22121.

Brooks, H., and Oppenheim, C., *Horticulture as a Therapeutic Aid.* Monograph 49, Institute of Rehabilitation Medicine, New York University Medical Center, 1973.

Flower and Garden Magazine, Mid-American Publishing Corp., 4251 Pennsylvania Street, Kansas City, MO 64111.

McDonald, E. *Plants as Therapy.* Praeger Pubs., Inc., New York, 1976.

Men's Garden Clubs of America News, 5560 Merle Hay Road, Des Moines, IA 50023.

National Council for Therapy and Rehabilitation through Horticulture, Mount Vernon, VA 22121.

Watson, D.P., and Burlingame, A.W., *Therapy Through Horticulture,* Macmillan Co., New York, 1960.

Summary

Horticulture therapy is a rapidly expanding field, and this growth is expected to continue (Olszowy, 1978). Horticulture is a valuable therapy for older adults due to the many benefits derived from participation in such a program.

PET THERAPY

Another therapy which focuses on living beings is pet therapy. According to Cusack and Smith (1984), the benefits of companion animal association are especially significant for elders. An overview of the benefits of, considerations in, and program ideas for the use of pets with elders is presented in this section.

Benefits

Physiological Benefits

Cusack and Smith (1984) cite several research studies which indicate that pets can physiologically benefit people in several ways:

1. Pet ownership stimulates and facilitates recovery from illness.
2. Interaction with pets lowers blood pressure.
3. People who care for a pet tend to also take better care of themselves with regard to nutrition, hygienic and health conditions, adequate shelter, and creating a caring living environment.

Psychological Benefits

Pets can also psychologically benefit elders in several ways:

1. Pets provide a much-needed outlet for affectionate, cuddling behavior (Corson and Corson, 1981).
2. Pets can allay anxiety (Cass, 1981).
3. Pets provide the opportunity to be involved in a loving relationship with minimal risks for the elder. In a relationship with an animal, the person can choose the rules for the relationship and choose the degree of closeness, without fear of rejection (Cass, 1981).
4. Pets provide companionship and can reduce feelings of loneliness and isolation (Cusack and Smith, 1984).
5. Pets can help elders feel safer and more secure, especially in novel situations (Cusack and Smith, 1984).
6. Caring for a pet's needs provides elders with daily responsibilities and activities which can enhance reality orientation (Cusack and Smith, 1984).
7. Animals provide elders with amusing and entertaining experiences. Pets can induce laughter, prompt a sense of humor, and in general, improve morale (Cusack and Smith, 1984).

Social Benefits

According to Cusack and Smith (1984), pets can positively affect elders' social behavior:

1. Activities with pets can occur in a group setting conducive to forming new friendships.
2. Pets are an excellent topic for conversation, and can help people ease into social interaction.

Activity Benefits

Cusack and Smith (1984) also discuss how pets can facilitate a variety of activities:

1. Animals often motivate elders to engage in higher levels of physical activity and exercise. For example, the responsibility of needing to walk a dog can cause a sedentary person to walk much more than they would if they did not have a dog.
2. Animals are sometimes able to prompt noncommunicative elders to speak.
3. Pets can stimulate creativity (e.g., in terms of grooming or decorating a pet for display).
4. Pets can stimulate elders to engage in educational activities (e.g., research aspects of pet care).

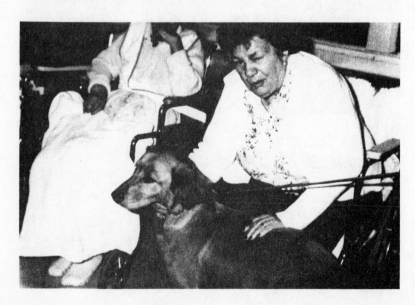

Thus, elders can benefit in numerous ways from interaction with animals. In the following section, recreational program ideas involving animals are discussed.

Program Ideas

Numerous types of animals can be utilized in a pet program for elders, such as dogs, cats, caged birds, rabbits, small caged mammals, aquarium fish, and vivarium reptiles and amphibians. Dogs are perhaps the most popular pets, because of the numerous activities possible with dogs, such as:

1. A dog show, in which elders groom, decorate, and display their dogs. The local humane society will often be able to provide puppies for such an activity. Local pet stores might be able to loan grooming brushes for the activity. The dog show activity gives elders an opportunity to have a great deal of much-needed tactile contact with a living being. The activity can also stimulate creativity in decorating the dog and enhance self-esteem in displaying the dog.
2. A dog obedience show can be a very stimulating and entertaining activity. Local dog fanciers clubs or pet shops are often willing to provide assistance for such an activity.
3. A "dog day" special event can be held, in which staff, program participants, and their families bring their dogs to the center or nursing home for a dog show and social activity.

According to Corson and Corson (1981), the best types of dogs to use in a pet program for elders are: Wirehair Fox Terriers, small Poodles, Border Collies, Labrador Retrievers, Dobermans, Cocker Spaniels, Dachshunds, and some Mongrels. Dogs can be utilized with elders in several ways: as occasional visitors; as individual pets; and as group mascots.

Considerations

Cusack and Smith (1984) identify several considerations in establishing a pet program for elders:

1. The estimated yearly upkeep costs for different types of pets are: $500-$700 for large dogs; $150-$200 for cats; and $150-$400 for large birds.

2. Allergic reactions of some elders to certain types of hair and fur should be considered.
3. The death of a pet can be very devastating. Try to select young and healthy animals for mascots and individual pets, animals which are likely to outlive the people caring for them.
4. Legal restrictions regarding pets (especially relevant to institutional settings) must be considered.
5. A staff member must be responsible for overseeing that program participants properly care for the pet.

Summary

A variety of recreational activities and programs for elders involving animals are possible. As discussed earlier, pet activities and programs have great potential physical, psychological and social benefits for elders.

LAUGHTER AND HUMOR

Humor and laughter-inducement have been cited as important benefits of many of the recreational activities, programs, and techniques previously discussed. The purpose of this section is to further clarify the importance and benefits of laughter and humor for elders.

Laughter and humor are expressive and social outlets. Laughter is also an outlet for releasing excess or surplus energy. Thus, laughter can have a relaxing, stress-reducing effect on people.

According to Moody (1978), laughter and humor can be very valuable in facilitating interaction between doctors and their patients. Similarly, humor and laughter can open up avenues of communication between senior center, day care, hospice, or nursing home staff and their elderly clients.

Laughter can also produce some very impressive physiological benefits:

1. Relief of tension headaches through laughter's relaxing effect on the tightened muscles in the back of the head and neck which cause the pain associated with tension headaches (Moody, 1978);
2. Laughter's pain-relieving, stress-reducing and relaxing effects on the body in general (Schelle, 1979); and

3. Increased oxygen saturation levels caused by sustained laughter. The increased oxygen saturation levels lend support to the old adage: "laughter is the best medicine" (Schelle, 1979).

A striking example of the physiological benefits of laughter is the story of Norman Cousins (Moody, 1978). Norman Cousins was suffering from a devastating terminal illness, and decided to take control of the treatment of his illness. A major component of Cousins' treatment program was several hours per day of laughter-inducing activities, such as watching humorous films. Cousins found that one hour of laughter allowed him to enjoy two hours of painless sleep. This much-needed deep rest, along with the positive emotions brought about by laughter seemed to make a great contribution to Cousins' miraculous recovery.

In summary, laughter and humor can greatly enhance the physical, mental, and emotional health of elders. Conscious efforts to include humor and laughter in recreational activities and programs can make recreation for elders much more enjoyable and beneficial.

BIBLIOGRAPHY

Burger, I.B. *Creative drama for senior adults.* Wilton, CT: Morehouse-Barlow, 1980.

Bustad, L.K. *Animals, aging and the aged.* Minneapolis: University of Minnesota Press, 1980.

Cass, J. Pet facilitated therapy in human health care. In B. Fogle (Ed.), *Interrelations between people and pets.* Springfield, IL: Charles C. Thomas, 1981.

Corson, S.A., and Corson, E.O. Companion animals as bonding catalysts in geriatric institutions. In B. Fogle (Ed.), *Interrelations between people and pets.* Springfield, IL: Charles C. Thomas, 1981.

Cusack, O., and Smith, E. *Pets and the elderly: The therapeutic bond.* New York: Haworth Press, 1984. (Also published as volume 4 (2/3) of *Activities, Adaptation, and Aging.*)

Douglass, D. *Happiness is—Music! Music! Music! Music activities for the aged.* Salem, OR: LaRoux Enterprises, 1978.

Downing, G., and Rush, A.K. *The massage book.* Berkeley, CA: The Bookworks, 1972.

Fish, H.U. *Activities programs for senior citizens.* West Nyack, NY: Parker Publishing Company, Inc., 1971.

Hosler, R. *Massage book.* Mountain View, CA: Runners World Book, 1982.

Jayson, M., and Dixon, A. *Understanding arthritis and rheumatism.* New York: Pantheon Books, 1974.

Merrill, T. *Activities for the aged and infirm: A handbook for the untrained worker.* Springfield, IL: Charles C. Thomas, 1967.

Moody, R.A. *Laugh after laugh: The healing power of humor.* Jacksonville, FL: Headwaters Press, 1978.

Nissen, H. *Practical massage and corrective exercises.* Philadelphia: F.A. Davis, 1929.

Olszowy, D.R. *Horticulture for the disabled and disadvantaged.* Springfield, IL: Charles C. Thomas, 1978.

Schelle, S.C. Humor and tension: The effects of comedy. In T.J. Scheff, *Catharsis in healing, ritual, and drama.* Berkeley, CA: University of California Press, 1979.

Schulberg, C. *The music therapy sourcebook: A collection of activities categorized and analyzed.* New York: Human Sciences Press, 1981.

Thurman, A.H., and Piggins, C.A. *Drama activities with older adults: A handbook for leaders.* New York: Haworth Press, 1982. (Also published as volume 2 (2/3) of *Activities, Adaptation, and Aging.*)

Towsen, J.H. *Clowns,* New York: Hawthorn Books, 1976.

U.S. Department of Health, Education, and Welfare. *Activities coordinator's guide.* Washington, D.C.: U.S. Government Printing Office, 1978.

Wapner, E.B. *Recreation for the elderly: A leadership, theory, and source book.* Great Neck, NY: Todd and Honeywell, Inc., 1981.

Wilkinson, V.C., and Heater, S.L. *Therapeutic media and techniques of application: A guide for activities therapists.* New York: Van Nostrand Reinhold Co., 1979.

Williams, A. *Recreation in the senior years.* New York: Association Press, 1962.

Chapter 14

Recreational Programs
and Special Events

INTRODUCTION

The purpose of this chapter is to describe several recreational program ideas appropriate for elders in almost any community, or any setting. The programs discussed in this chapter are: camping for senior citizens; Elderhostel; Adult's Health and Development Program; Senior Olympics and other sports programs; and Elderfest.

CAMPING

Senior adult camping has been very successful throughout the country. Based on a successful program coordinated by the University of Oregon, Armstrong (1979) developed a manual for people interested in senior adult camping. The information in this section is based on this manual. Topics discussed include philosophy, practical considerations, and program ideas.

Philosophy

As documented by research studies cited in the first chapter of the book, elders can and do enjoy outdoor recreation experiences. Even impaired elders can enjoy a camping experience, as long as necessary adaptations are provided. Some appropriate goals and objectives for a senior adult camp are:

1. To provide opportunities for social interaction.
2. To expose elders to new leisure activities in order to develop new activity interests and skills.
3. To learn about and gain a greater appreciation for nature.
4. To provide enjoyable activities which are physically and mentally stimulating.
5. To provide the opportunity to experience an aesthetically pleasing environment (an important objective, especially for

urban elders). Winfrey's (1977) article on camps for elders in
New York State illustrates the value of camping as a relief
from the tensions of the city. Approximately 8,000 New
Yorkers aged 60 to 104 visited 9 camps in four states in 1977
(Winfrey, 1977). The camps were supported by churches,
community centers, and private individuals under the auspices
of Vacations for Aging and Senior Citizens Association.

Practical Considerations

Armstrong (1979) identifies several considerations in planning a
successful camping experience for elders:

1. Involve the participants in the planning process.
2. Expose participants to new activities. Elders are as willing to
   learn as any other people.
3. Schedule religious activities, such as morning worship and
   quiet times before meals.
4. As much as possible, provide historical background information on the places to be visited.
5. Take photographs during the outing; many people enjoy seeing
   pictures of themselves in camp after the experience is over.
6. Make provisions for those who have special dietary needs.
7. Schedule an orientation meeting for all staff and participants to
   be held approximately two weeks before the trip. The meeting
   gives participants a chance to meet staff and ask questions.
   Suggested topics for the orientation meeting are: general camp
   policies; necessary items to bring to camp; health and safety
   considerations; emergency procedures; and schedule of activities. Participants can be asked to complete a health questionnaire and a leisure interest inventory.
8. Determine methods of evaluating camp programs before the
   camp begins.

Program Ideas

Leisure interest inventories should be reviewed to obtain program
ideas. Armstrong (1979) identifies numerous sample program ideas:

1. Arts and crafts, such as sketching, oil painting, puppetry, and
   woodworking.

2. Sports and games, such as volleyball, horseshoes, table games, canoeing, frisbee, yoga, and swimming.
3. Music and drama activities, such as singing, folk dancing, and short sketches.
4. Special events, such as a Cabaret night, travelogues, and an international dinner.
5. Nature activities, such as birdwalks, all-day hikes, night hikes, and environmental education discussions and hikes.
6. Sightseeing trips to points of interest.

Summary

Camping for elders is a relatively new concept, but has already proven to be successful. Camping can provide elders with new experiences, stimulate new activity interests, enhance individuals' knowledge of the environment and natural resources, and provide excellent opportunities for socialization and the development of new friendships. Thus, senior adult camping is a desirable program to expand to reach more elders.

ELDERHOSTEL

Elderhostel, though vastly different from camping, does share a few similarities. Participants are exposed to new experiences and are provided with numerous opportunities for enjoyable mentally and physically stimulating recreation activities. Also, Elderhostelers are provided with excellent opportunities for socialization. In addition, program participants must adapt to less-than-luxury living accommodations during their stay.

The Elderhostel program began at the University of New Hampshire in 1975 based on the idea of providing elders with a mentally and physically stimulating experience. Elderhostelers live on a college campus for a one-week period during which they attend educational classes and participate in a variety of recreational activities on campus. Thus, Elderhostel is a unique one-week college experience program designed especially for persons age 60 and older.

Elderhostel has been an extremely popular program. In 1978, 200 colleges and universities offered programs in 38 states; by 1984, over 700 colleges and universities offered programs in the U.S. and overseas. According to Gurewitsch (1980), 13,000 elders enrolled in Elderhostel programs in 1979; approximately 20,000 were enrolled in 1980; and the number of enrollees grew to approximately 78,000 in 1983.

Most programs are limited to 35 to 40 participants. Programs cost slightly under $200. The fee includes: registration costs; six nights accommodation; all meals; five days of classes; and a variety of extra-curricular activities. Elderhostel is a non-profit international organization which receives no public funds. The Elderhostel office is responsible for coordinating all of the available programs, registering participants, disseminating information, and publishing catalogs. In order to obtain further information on Elderhostel and obtain a copy of their latest catalog of programs, write to: Elderhostel, 100 Boylston Street, Boston, MA 02116.

ADULTS' HEALTH AND DEVELOPMENTAL PROGRAM

College and universities are excellent resources for programs for elders. In particular, a uniquely enjoyable and beneficial program is the Adults' Health and Developmental Program, directed by Dr. Dan Leviton at the University of Maryland. Leviton founded the program based on a desire to contribute to the health, life satisfaction, and morale of elders through a program providing elders with opportunities to participate in enjoyable activities and form friendships with same-age peers and college students. Research on evaluating the effects of this program on its participants indicates that the program has been very successful in meeting its aims (Leviton and Santa Maria, 1979).

The program is a nine-week, once-a-week clinic, in which each participant (ranging in age from 55 to 87) is matched with their own student staff member (usually in their late teens or early twenties) for ninety minutes of physical activities, such as creative dance, brisk walks, swimming, tricycling, trampolining, and bowling, followed by an hour of discussion on topics such as loneliness, communication, and sexuality in later life.

A very positive aspect of the program has been the formation of intergenerational friendships among participants and the student staffers. Not only has the program had a positive impact on participants' health and morale, but it has also had a positive effect on the student staffers' attitudes toward aging. The program costs approximately $10 per semester and has served as many as 120 elders in a semester. It is certainly a worthwhile program for other colleges and universities to adopt. For further information, write: Dr. Dan Leviton, Adults' Health and Developmental Program, PERH Building, University of Maryland, College Park, MD 20742.

SPORTS PROGRAMS

A number of new sports programs for elders have been developed in recent years. For example, in 1977, a ski school in Keystone, Colorado started the first learn-to-ski program for persons age 50 and older ("Never too late for ski school," 1977). The learn-to-ski program consists of a package including: accommodations; lift tickets; lessons; a race; and a party. Every morning throughout the week, warmup exercises, followed by two-hour group lessons are scheduled. Afternoons are devoted to cross-country ski tours, mountain ecology sessions, videotaping sessions to improve skiing techniques, and opportunities for relaxation in the swimming pool or whirlpool.

Another interesting sports program is the senior recreational doubles program offered by the United States Tennis Association (USTA). The USTA senior doubles program gives players the opportunity to play with different partners and opponents in progressive doubles. For further information, contact: Senior Tennis Programs, USTA Education and Research Center, 729 Alexander Road, Princeton, NJ 08540.

Numerous other sports programs are offered by the National Senior Sports Association (NSSA). The NSSA is a non-profit national organization dedicated to helping people age 50 and older to enjoy participating in recreational and competitive tournaments in golf, tennis, bowling, skiing, and other sports. The NSSA events include social as well as sports activities, in order to promote the fellowship of participants in the sporting events. The NSSA also offers a Vacation Home Exchange program, which allows members to enjoy a lodging-free vacation by exchanging homes with another member in a desired location.

One of NSSA's very successful programs has been the seniors tennis program. For example, approximately 2,500 men compete in the Super Senior Tennis program for people ages 55-80. According to Hal Demoody, director of the NSSA tennis programs, the tennis programs not only enhance the health and fitness of elders, but also facilitate the development of friendships ("Kretschmer Sponsors Seniors Tennis Classic," 1982). For further information on NSSA programs, contact: National Senior Sports Association, Inc., 317 Cameron Street, Alexandria, VA 22314.

SENIOR OLYMPICS

Another sports program of interest is the Senior Olympics, founded in 1969 by Warren Blaney. The Senior Olympic movement is sponsored by a non-profit corporation called Senior Sports International, Incorporated. The movement has been very successful in encouraging growth in the Senior Olympics. The Senior Olympics began in 1969 with 175 people participating in three events (marathon, swimming, and track and field) over a four-day period. In 1980, its twelfth year of existence, over 4,000 people participated in more than 50 athletic events and other recreational activities throughout the year (Provost, 1981). In order to encourage the growth of this movement, information on the philosophy of the Senior Olympics, and guidelines for developing local Senior Olympics programs are presented, based on Provost's (1981) book.

Philosophy

The goals of the Senior Olympics are:

1. "To encourage all adults to exercise regularly for better health, greater happiness, and higher productivity." (Provost, 1981)
2. "To give recognition to all adult athletes in every sport, at every age level." (Provost, 1981)
3. To contribute to enhanced international relations through opportunities provided to form international friendships through the Tour of Champions and the attendance of athletes from foreign countries at the Senior Olympics in the U.S.
4. "To bring adults and youth together in a positive environment." (Provost, 1981)

The Senior Olympics are based on the belief that athletics are very physically, mentally, and emotionally beneficial for people, and that participation in athletics throughout one's life can help to retard the aging process. The Senior Olympics aims to involve adults in athletics as early in one's life as possible so that participation in sports can continue throughout one's lifespan and produce maximal benefits for the individual.

The Senior Olympics are also based on the belief that competition can be very enjoyable and healthy. The positive value of competition as a means of reinforcing one's sense of self-worth and dignity is emphasized. Also, competition can be physically beneficial because it can motivate people to do a great deal of training and physical conditioning.

The Senior Olympics emphasizes that winning isn't the only measure of success; all participants are recognized for their involvement. The Senior Olympics are an excellent opportunity for people ages 20 to 120 to compete against same-age peers in a variety of sports. The physical, psychological, and social benefits of participating in the Olympics are enormous.

Guidelines

Some guidelines for developing a local Senior Olympics program are (Povost, 1981):

1. Establish an executive committee which will be responsible for establishing policies and procedures, preparing a budget, and publicizing the event. The committee's membership should be a representative cross-section of the community, including recreation and physical education students and faculty, members of service clubs and the chamber of commerce, media personnel, and representatives of senior citizens' clubs and organizations.
2. Expenditures should be minimal. Use of athletic facilities should be obtained at no cost. Volunteer staff should be able to plan and lead all activities. Donations of awards and prizes for the events should be solicited from local businesses. Any other expenses should be covered by entry fees. Entry fees should be set as low as possible in order to ensure maximal participation, yet be set high enough to ensure that all expenses are covered.
3. Select sports for the program which are most popular in the community. International rules for all sports should be used wherever possible. Distances should be measured in meters.
4. Keep complete and accurate records of results in all events, and develop a record book which will give each year's participants goals to strive to attain.

5. Age classifications for events should begin with the age 20-24 category, and continue in five year increments, *without* an upper limit. If there are a large number of entries of varying ability levels in one age category, then divide the age category on the basis of ability (e.g., A, B, C, and D levels). The winners of one ability level should compete in the next ability level in the next Olympics.
6. Modification in rules and equipment (e.g., reducing heights, weights, game time, etc.) should be made as necessary for participants age 50 and older.
7. All participants should be required to submit a medical release form from their physician. A doctor and/or nurse should be available at most events.
8. Liability and accident insurance coverage should be obtained.

For further information on the Senior Olympics Movement and guidelines for conducting a local Senior Olympics, contact: Mr. Warren Blaney, Senior Olympics, Senior Sports International, Inc., 5726 Wilshire Blvd., Suite 360, Los Angeles, CA 90026.

ELDERFEST

Elderfest is a festive community event designed to destroy myths and stereotypes of aging by involving people of all ages in a celebration of the multi-faceted talents of local elders. Numerous businesses, senior citizens organizations, the Chico Area Recreation District, and numerous departments at California State University, Chico (CSUC) have assisted the students and faculty of the Department of Recreation and Parks Management at CSUC to coordinate four successful Elderfests, from 1981-1984. The number of exhibitors and attendees of the event has grown, from approximately 300 participants in 1981, to well over 1,000 in 1984. In order to assist communities interested in organizing an Elderfest, philosophy and guidelines, and considerations for coordinating an Elderfest are presented, based on Leitner's (1983) article in *Parks and Recreation*.

Philosophy

Many elders and younger people believe that later life is a sad and lonely time of life, a time when there is a great deal of leisure time available, but limited opportunities available for utilizing that time in an enjoyable and meaningful way. Belief in such myths and stereotypes can prove to be a significant barrier to involving elders in recreational activities. Elderfest seeks to destroy these myths and stereotypes, and enlighten both younger and older people to how productive and enjoyable leisure in later life can be. Elderfest attempts to attain this goal through a festive display of the arts and crafts, hobby, dance, and musical talents of local elders.

Guidelines

Elderfest is a community project which naturally lends itself to university/community cooperation. Committees, composed of students, faculty, elders, and merchants, should be formed to coordinate the different aspects of the event.

General Steering Committee

This committee is responsible for the overall coordination of the event, setting guidelines and policies, and ensuring that all of the other committees are sufficiently staffed. This committee is also responsible for fund raising, overseeing the budget, and determining the location, date(s), and time(s), for the event.

Displays/Exhibits Committee

This committee is responsible for identifying and contacting elders to exhibit art work, and demonstrate hobby and craft skills. Exhibits can include painting, dolls, woodworking, and clocks; demonstrations can include chair caning, lace making, and gourd carving, just to name a few. Talented elders are identified through local senior citizens organizations, arts and crafts shops, and notices in local newspapers. The 1984 Chico Elderfest boasted approximately 50 high-quality exhibits. The displays/exhibits committee is also responsible for obtaining necessary display equipment (e.g., easels and display boards can be borrowed from the university at no charge) and determining a floor plan for the exhibits and demonstrations. In addition, this committee should make security arrangements for the exhibits. An excellent way to involve college students, service clubs, boy scouts, and girl scouts in Elderfest is to enlist their help as volunteer security guards.

Yet another responsibility of this committee is to organize an exhibit of local historical artifacts. The historical display can include: a slide show of local area history; a genealogical display; and a display of artifacts from the 1800s and early 1900s, such as postcards, pictures, and articles of clothing. Local historical clubs and organizations can be contacted to organize this display. The historical display is an excellent way to enlighten younger Elderfest attendees of the changes our elders have experienced and helped to create in their lifetime.

Entertainment Committee

This committee has the very important task of making arrangements to have local talented elders perform at Elderfest. The entertainment schedule can include diverse acts such as a dixieland band, square dancing, belly dancing, a symphonette, and a "kitchen klatterer" band. In connection with the entertainment schedule, this committee must devise a time schedule of performances and ensure a smooth transition between acts. This committee also is responsible for obtaining needed equipment, such as a public address system (a

The Senior Men's Singers, one of the many groups who entertained the attendees of the 1984 Chico Elderfest.

local music store is likely to be willing to loan such equipment at no cost).

Yet another concern of this committee is organizing a variety of contests to be included in the entertainment schedule. The contests are intended to be an opportunity for people of all ages to participate in a common activity and share some laughs. Some popular contests are: animal and bird calling; old and/or unusual hat contest; and a 60 and over "body beautiful" contest. In addition, awards are given to recognize the oldest person attending Elderfest; the couple married the most years; and the family with the most generations present at Elderfest. The entertainment committee is responsible for soliciting prizes for all of the contests from local merchants. In addition, the committee obtains judges for the contests. Judges are selected on the basis of three criteria: expertise in the contest to be judged (e.g., have an agriculture professor judge animal and bird calling); potential publicity benefits (e.g., have the editor of the food page in the local newspaper judge the dessert baking contest); and popularity/ familiarity with the public (e.g., a Congressman).

Refreshments Committee

In order to encourage people to stay at Elderfest all day to enjoy the exciting schedule of contests and entertainment, low-cost snacks and lunches are served throughout the day. This committee needs a large staff of volunteers (elders and college students work well together) and the cooperation of a local supermarket to sell food at a discount. Prices should be set as low as possible, just high enough to enable meeting costs. Elderfest is a non-profit community event, and the food service aspect of the event should be designed to be non-profit as well.

Outreach/Transportation Committee

This committee is responsible for ensuring the full participation and attendance of elders in nursing homes and retirement homes. Initial contacts with the activity directors in these homes are made, followed with visits to the homes to inform the residents about Elderfest and motivate them to attend, and possibly have an exhibit, perform, or enter some of the contests. On the day of Elderfest, this committee provides transportation to and from Elderfest for the residents of these homes (use of the van and gasoline donated by local merchants and organizations).

It is very important for people in the community to understand that even elders in institutional settings can be creative and productive in their leisure time. Thus, it is very desirable to try to obtain as much participation from elders in institutional settings as possible.

Publicity Committee

The task of this committee is to attract people of all ages to attend Elderfest. Effective publicity techniques include: flyers posted at senior centers, retirement homes, nursing homes, senior citizen apartment complexes, churches, storefront windows, and bulletin boards at the university; presentations about Elderfest at meetings of senior citizen organizations such as the local AARP chapter; outreach visits to nursing homes, retirement homes, churches, and elementary schools; presentations and announcements in college classes; announcements in senior citizens newsletters; announcements in local newspapers, and on television and radio (solicit free air time); and, of course, word of mouth. In addition, the local newspaper might be able to arouse interest in Elderfest by publishing some related human interest stories a few weeks prior to the event. For example, in Chico, the local newspaper published a series of interviews with some of the more extraordinary Elderfest exhibitors and performers (e.g., a 65 year-old bellydancer and a 90 year-old chair caner) several weeks before the event in order to arouse the public's interest in Elderfest. Despite massive publicity efforts, attracting younger generations to Elderfest is still a major challenge, as discussed in the next section.

Special Considerations

Attracting Younger Generations

Because Elderfest is designed to break myths and stereotypes of aging, it is especially important to have as many young people as possible attend Elderfest in order for them to have an experience which is likely to improve their attitudes toward aging. Some ideas for encouraging children and college students to attend Elderfest are:

1. A poster/essay contest for elementary school children can be organized. Children in grades 1-3 can be encouraged to draw

posters, and children in grades 4-6 can be encouraged to write essays on the general topic of aging. Contest entrants are then asked to attend Elderfest to see their posters displayed, or to read their essays.

2. Enlisting college students and children as volunteers is another method of assuring their attendance. Appropriate volunteer roles are: exhibits security; ushers for the entertainment room; refreshments preparation and serving; and individual assistance for impaired attendees.

3. An intergenerational dance held during the evening (after all exhibits have been cleared) has been a successful part of the Chico Elderfest. With the cooperation of the social dance classes at the university, an intergenerational dance contest (partners must be a minimum of 30 years apart) can be an effective means of drawing college students to Elderfest.

4. The appearance of a celebrity at Elderfest can help to draw younger generations, and the public in general, to the event.

5. Instead of Elderfest being a one-day (Saturday or Sunday) event, it can be expanded to two days (e.g., Friday and Saturday). The Friday portion of the event could be devoted to class tours by elementary schools, junior high and high schools, and

A youngster admiring one of the many outstanding exhibits at the 1984 Chico Elderfest.

even college classes. Tours can be arranged with the local school district, and the individual public and private schools to make sure that a steady flow of visitors continues throughout the day. Arranging class tours is perhaps the surest way to ensure that younger people attend Elderfest.

Location and Date

Chico has been fortunate that the Chico Area Recreation District has donated the use of their community center building for Elderfest. The community center building is ideal because it is conveniently located, has a large assembly room for entertainment and numerous smaller rooms for exhibits, and is a very familiar place for most elders in town. Because of the uncertainty of weather conditions (a windy or rainy day is almost always a possibility), an indoor location is much preferred to an outdoor location.

Because of weather considerations and the reliance of Elderfest on volunteers from the college, April is a good month for this event. College students have enough time to prepare for the event during the spring semester, and weather conditions are usually not severe enough to deter a substantial number of potential attendees.

Policies

There are several issues which the general steering committee must discuss and reach agreement on:

1. What is the minimum age requirement for exhibitors and performers?
2. Can exhibitors sell merchandise?
3. Can a local business be allowed to have a display table in return for a generous contribution?
4. What are the geographical limitations on participation? (e.g. Must one be a resident of the city in order to have an exhibit or perform?)

Determination of policies in matters such as those listed above can help prevent difficult or sensitive situations from arising later on.

Budget and Fundraising

Elderfest is a self-sufficient event. Prizes for contests are donated by local merchants. Refreshment sales should cover food costs. Donations for facilities and equipment needed should be solicited. Free media publicity should also be solicited. Fundraising activities such as a car wash or even an airplane wash can raise additional money needed to cover stationery, mailing, xeroxing and other miscellaneous costs. In addition, funds can sometimes be obtained from local organizations (e.g., a sorority in Chico donated $300 for the 1983 Elderfest). Recognition for these contributions should be included in a printed program distributed at Elderfest.

An expensive item in the budget is the cost of printing a collection of poems and essays by local talented elders. Such a booklet is greatly appreciated by both the contributors and the general public, but the cost can be prohibitive ($500). The poetry and essay collection should be an optional item in the budget, contingent on obtaining adequate funds for its printing.

Summary

Elderfest is a festive event which can be replicated in almost any community with a sizable older population. The event reminds people of all ages that later life can be a rich, rewarding, active, and creative time of life. In summary, Elderfest is guaranteed to be the experience of a lifetime!

BIBLIOGRAPHY

Armstrong, C.H. *Senior adult camping.* Martinsville, IN: American Camping Association, 1979.
Gurewitsch, E. Elderhostel: A good idea is growing and growing. *Aging,* 1980, *303-304,* pp. 12-16.
Kretschmer sponsors seniors tennis classic. *Parks and Recreation,* December 1982, pp. 12; 13; 53.
Leitner, M.J. Elderfest . . . Sharing our lives (videotape). Chico, CA: Instructional Media Center, CSU, Chico, 1983.
Leitner, M.J. Elderfest: The experience of a lifetime! *Parks and Recreation Magazine,* 1983, *18*(8), pp. 56-58.
Leviton, D., and Santa Maria, L. The adults' health and developmental program: Descriptive and evaluative data. *Gerontologist,* 1979, *19*(6), pp. 534-543.

Never too late for ski school. *New York Daily News*, November 13, 1977, p. 10 (travel section).

Provost, C.A. *The Senior Olympics, preventive medicine with findings pertaining to health and longevity.* Warren W. Blaney, Publisher, 1981.

Winfrey, C. For the aged, camp life's slower, but much like that for young. *New York Times*, July 16, 1977, pp. 23; 26.

Section IV:
Issues in Providing Leisure Services to Elders

Chapter 15

The Role of Recreation
in Hospice Care

INTRODUCTION

Hospice care refers to programs which provide health and supportive services to help dying patients and their families live their lives as fully as possible during the final stages of a terminal illness (U.S. DHEW, 1979). The growth of hospice programs in the United States is quite impressive. Only a handful of programs were in existence prior to 1972, but by 1980, a National Hospice Organization directory identified 138 member organizations providing services (Buckingham, 1983). According to the National Hospice Organization (1985), estimates run as high as 1500 hospices in varying stages of development in the United States in 1985.

Hospice care is an area of concern to the fields of recreation and gerontology in that most hospice patients are between 60 and 70 years old, (U.S. DHEW, 1979) and as stated by the National Hospice Organization (NHO, 1979), "one of the greatest problems of the dying is the boredom that comes out of not doing anything." Although recreational activity would seem to be an effective means of alleviating the boredom many hospice patients face, recreation is an area which has been neglected in much of the literature on hospice care programs.

The purpose of this chapter is to discuss the role of recreation (in particular, therapeutic recreation) in hospice care. Topics discussed in this chapter include: background on hospice care; goals, objectives, and components of hospice care; research and case studies on hospice care and recreation with the terminally ill; and practical examples of recreational activities appropriate for terminally ill elders.

OVERVIEW OF HOSPICE CARE

Hospice care is a philosophy and program of care for dying and terminally ill patients. Dr. Cicely Saunder's work with the St. Christopher's Hospice in London, England has been the inspiration for many of the newly formed hospice groups in the United States (Stoddard, 1978).

Although the modern hospice movement has its origins in England, one can find traces of the hospice philosophy in the ancient Greek and Roman "healing places." Similar to modern hospices, these Greek and Roman places of healing emphasized "total treatment" of the individual—maximization of comfort, physical and mental stimulation, as well as medical treatment. However, dying and terminally ill persons could not take advantage of these healing places, because such persons were felt to have little value to the state. On the other hand, modern hospices are specifically designed to help terminally ill and dying persons live as fully as possible until death, and to die peacefully. Unlike the Greek and Roman philosophy of "value to the state," Dr. Saunders states that "an individual matters up until the last moment of his life," (Stoddard, 1978).

Because Dr. Saunders and the St. Christopher's Hospice have been so influential in the evolution of the hospice movement, a description of the St. Christopher's program can help one better understand hospice care.

St. Christopher's Hospice is a free-standing facility, surrounded by beautiful landscaping. There is a reflecting pool and flower beds, a lawn, chapel, study center, and out-patient clinic. Large paintings are found on most walls inside the buildings. Staff, visitors, and patients of all ages are found; the sound of laughter fills the air (Stoddard, 1978).

St. Christopher's is perhaps a "model" hospice program; there is great variation among hospice programs. Some are free-standing facilities, such as St. Christopher's, while others are part of a hospital or nursing home. Hospice programs can offer services to dying and terminally ill people in the patient's place of residence (private home or institution) or in the hospice facility (on an in-patient or out-patient basis) (Osterweis and Champagne, 1979).

The goals and objectives of hospice programs vary, but some generally applicable goals and objectives are: to help terminally ill and dying persons maintain a personally acceptable quality of life until death; to help patients maintain and/or improve their mental and/or physical functioning so as to promote their independence; to keep pain to a minimum and comfort at a maximum for patients; to help patients find meaning in their life and death; and to facilitate patients' families to respond *appropriately* to their family member's death (Alsofrom, 1977; Cunningham, 1979; National Hospice Organization, 1979; Osterweis and Champagne, 1979; U.S. DHEW, 1979).

Hospice programs include an array of services designed to meet the aforementioned goals and objectives. Some of the components of hospice care are: pain control through the use of drugs and comfort maximization; home health care or in-patient care including physician services, skilled nursing, and psychiatric consultation; physical, speech, and occupational therapy; day care for the patient; homemaker services; meal preparation at home; transportation to and from treatment centers; education about death, emotional counseling; spiritual support; and bereavement services after the patient has died. Above all, an essential aspect of hospice care is loving kindness (Osterweis and Champagne, 1979; Stoddard, 1978; U.S. DHEW, 1979).

Some of the staff needed in a hospice program are: a hospice administrator; a medical director; a director of patient/family services; a pastoral counselor; volunteers, and a volunteer coordinator; and a medical records consultant. In addition, an interdisciplinary hospice team should include: a physician; registered nurse; social worker; nutritionist; occupational therapist; and other rehabilitation therapists (National Hospice Organization, 1979; U.S. DHEW, 1979).

RESEARCH AND CASE STUDIES

Value of Hospice Care

Hospice care seems to be beneficial in several ways. Economic savings is one clear-cut benefit of hospice care; Wald (1979) states that the New Haven Hospice was serving patients for an average time of 76 days for slightly over $1,000, while a hospital in New Haven was charging patients $285 per day.

Although economic benefits are fairly easy to document, it is more difficult to find clear-cut evidence that hospices actually help dying patients enjoy life more or maintain better physical and mental health in their last days. Hospice care is an area which does not readily lend itself to well-controlled, experimental study, thus the difficulty in inferring cause-effect relationships based on the literature.

However, case studies of hospice programs support the notion that hospice care is beneficial for its patients and their families (Ingles, 1974; Wentzel, 1976; Stoddard, 1978; Ward, 1978; and Wald, 1979). Ingles' article provides insight into the value of hospice care through an in-depth description of the St. Christopher's Hospice program. According to Ingles, St. Christopher's provides the love, kindness, and attention that dying patients so desperately need. The well-being of patients is enhanced through the provision of activities and services such as: discussion groups; arts and crafts; group sing-a-longs; flowers and plants in patients' rooms; television and radio; preparation of patients' favorite foods; and above all, companionship.

Wentzel's (1976) description of the St. Christopher's Hospice also indicates that hospice care has a positive effect on terminally ill persons. According to Wentzel, many patients at St. Christopher's feel better than they have in years. Wentzel's article indicates that patients at St. Christopher's are relatively free of pain, and surrounded by love. Both Wentzel's and Ingles' articles create the impression that St. Christopher's hospice patients are living their last days to their fullest.

Stoddard (1978) presents an overview of the Marin Hospice in California, and the New Haven Hospice in Connecticut. Both of these hospice programs emphasize a humane approach toward treatment of terminally ill persons. Much like St. Christopher's, the Marin and New Haven hospices attempt to enrich the lives of its patients through the devoted efforts of paid staff and volunteers.

In a related vein, Ward (1978) describes the development and implementation of a hospice home care program connected with Overlook Hospital in Summit, New Jersey. The intent of this program is to help terminally ill persons live in their own home for as long as it is feasibly possible. Ward concludes that through an expansion of home care services, the hospital was able to better meet the needs of terminally ill patients and their families.

Wald's (1979) article conveys the value of hospice care through quotes from hospice patients and staff of the New Haven Hospice, Hospice Orlando, and Hospice of Central Pennsylvania. According to a spokesman for the New Haven Hospice, "there's never a point at which nothing can be done to make the patient more comfortable.'' This statement accurately sums up the rationale for hospice care.

Although the aforementioned studies provide evidence that hospice care can be beneficial for dying persons and their families, there is a need for more scientific evaluation research on hospice care (Buckingham, 1978). Clearly, not only is further research needed on evaluation of hospice programs, but evaluation research is also needed on specific components of hospice care. One such component of hospice care in need of further study is recreation.

Value of Recreational Activity to the Dying

Several case studies and programs discussed in the literature lend support to their notion that recreation and related activity therapies can work well with dying patients. Rogers (1978) cites the need to support the creativity of dying patients. Rogers describes the value of creative activities such as poetry writing, music, arts and crafts, dance, and drama to patients of the Hillhaven Hospice in Tucson, Arizona. According to Rogers, artistic stimuli helped create a more relaxed atmosphere for the Hillhaven Hospice patients.

According to Gilbert (1977), music therapy is a potentially beneficial resource for terminally ill patients and their families. Gilbert states that music is an activity which helps draw people closer together and that music therapy can open lines of communication between patients and their families.

Similarly, Cannon (1974) states that recreation can help an individual find meaning in one's death. Furthermore, Lovelace (1974) points out that in play, one's ego can feel superior to time, space, social, and physical limitations (all of these limitations are particularly relevant to terminally ill persons).

Both Newman (1974) and Cannon (1974) describe how recreational activity can help improve the quality of life of a dying person in the final stages of life. Newman states that recreational activity can help dying persons keep their mind off their disease; recreation gives a person something to do and something to talk about. Cannon cites an example of how recreation activity can be adapted for a terminally ill person in poor physical condition. The author describes how a sportsminded boy too sick for participation in active sports became the "sports editor" of his hospital ward—the boy collected sports information from newspapers, television, and radio sports reports and wrote a sports newsletter for the other patients on his floor.

RECREATIONAL ACTIVITIES
FOR ELDERLY HOSPICE PATIENTS

The case studies and programs discussed in the previous section lend support to the notion that recreation can benefit hospice patients. Theory also dictates that recreation can benefit elderly hospice patients. According to hospice philosophy, the health, overall functioning, morale, life satisfaction, and self-esteem of clients are all very important concerns. Research indicates that recreation can effect positive change in these areas of elders' lives. Thus, why not provide recreational activities and programs for dying and terminally ill elders?

An often-cited argument against providing recreational activities and programs for elderly hospice patients is that dying and terminally ill elders have very limited abilities or desires to recreate. As illustrated in the following examples, this argument is false. Almost any person in a conscious state can enjoy and benefit from recreational activities.

Example #1

The Client

Mr. C. is 68 years old, a cancer patient diagnosed to have only a few months left to live. He is in a weakened state and is unable to walk. He is able to sit up in a chair, but usually for no longer than two hours at a time. Mr. C. still has use of his arms, although his muscles are deteriorating due to lack of use. His favorite leisure activity throughout his life has been tennis. Unfortunately, he is physically unable to play tennis due to his weakened state.

Appropriate Activities

Based on Mr. C.'s love for the game of tennis, and considering his level of functioning, there are numerous appropriate recreational activities he could enjoy, such as:
1. Adapted forms of wheelchair tennis, for example:
   a. Playing on a regulation-size tennis court, modifying the rules and boundaries to enable a desirable level of success. If the tennis racket is too difficult to manipulate, a small wooden paddle can be tried.

    b. Playing an adapted version of tennis on a smaller court with a lower net.

    c. Mr. C. could practice hitting tennis balls against a backboard, or hit balls driven at him by a ball machine, tossed gently to him by someone, or even practice hitting a stationary tennis ball attached to a string.

2. Mr. C. might enjoy playing a tennis video game, while sitting in his wheelchair, or sitting up in bed (if a portable unit is available).

3. Giving bedside tennis lessons could enhance Mr. C.'s self-esteem and provide much needed mental stimulation. Mr. C. could demonstrate proper grips and explain strokes to tennis students.

4. A simple, yet physically beneficial activity would be to periodically squeeze tennis balls, in order to increase arm and hand strength.

5. Tennis-related spectator activity might also be stimulating. Mr. C. could watch tennis matches on television and keep abreast of tennis news by reading newspapers and magazines. Mr. C. might also enjoy going to nearby tennis courts to watch some local players in action.

6. Mr. C. might also enjoy playing racket sports similar in nature to tennis, such as table tennis and badminton. Such sports could probably be performed at a higher skill level than tennis by a person in a weakened state. Also, playing new sports and learning new activity skills can be an exciting challenge.

Thus, there are a variety of recreational activities Mr. C. could enjoy, based on his love for tennis, and adapted to his level of functioning.

Example #2

The Client

Mrs. A. is 75 years old, suffering from lung cancer, and diagnosed to have only a few months to live. She has been widowed for the past fifteen years and has one daughter who lives 2,000 miles away.

Mrs. A. lives in a personal care home and receives assistance with most of her personal care needs. She spends most of her time lying in bed or sitting up in a chair, because she suffers from shortness of breath with the smallest amount of exertion. Mrs. A. has had very few recreational interests throughout her life. She was a dedicated housewife and mother who "never had time to do much else." She never sought a career and had few friends. However, one aspect of housework Mrs. A. always enjoyed was cooking. She said it was always important to her to serve her family good, nutritious meals.

Appropriate Activities

Based on Mrs. A.'s interest in cooking, and considering her level of functioning, there are numerous recreational activities she could enjoy, such as:

1. Writing a cookbook would be a time-consuming, involving activity which could enhance Mrs. A.'s self-esteem, and maintain Mrs. A.'s interest for a sustained period of time. Mrs. A. could dictate the recipes from her bedside; the recipes could then be typed, and placed in a folio. The cookbook project would be exciting and challenging, yet it would be an activity Mrs. A. could definitely engage in, despite her poor physical condition.
2. An excellent activity for strengthening the fingers and hands would be to help knead bread as part of a bread baking activity.
3. Mrs. A. could act as a consultant for meal planning for the impaired elders residing in the personal care home.
4. Home Economics students from a local school could visit with Mrs. A. for tips on bread baking or other aspects of cooking.
5. Mrs. A. could be involved with a local nursing home in helping to plan the refreshments to be served to the residents for parties.
6. Mrs. A. could subscribe to various nutrition magazines and be informed of any cooking or nutrition-related television programs that might be of interest to her.
7. Mrs. A. could assist in the preparation of simple snacks or meals at the personal care home.

Obviously, there are numerous recreational activities Mrs. A. could enjoy, based on her interest in cooking, and adapted to her level of functioning.

SUMMARY

Through recreational activity, one can add a new dimension of meaning to the final stages of life. Recreation can serve as a major motivational force to continue living. For some people, life isn't worth living if it means an existence of pain, devoid of enjoyment. Recreational activity cannot only provide enjoyable experiences and laughter which can help motivate one to keep living, but it can also give an individual feelings of competence and self-esteem.

The value of recreation for hospice patients has thus far been relatively neglected in the hospice movement. However, both theory and practice indicate that recreational activity can greatly benefit hospice patients. Further research in this area can help provide an even stronger case for expanding recreation as a component of hospice care.

BIBLIOGRAPHY

Alsofrom, J. The hospice way of dying. *American Medical News*, February 21, 1977, pp. 7-9.

Bertman, S.L. The arts: A source of comfort and insight for children who are learning about death. *Omega*, 1979, *10*(2), pp. 147-162.

Buckingham, R.W. *The complete hospice guide*. NY: Harper and Row Publishers, 1983.

Buckingham, R.W., and Foley, S.H. A guide to evaluation research in terminal care programs. *Death Education*, 1978, *2*(1/2), pp. 127-141.

Cannon, K.L. Death and attitudes toward death—Implications for therapeutic recreation service. *Therapeutic Recreation Journal*, 1974, *8*(1), pp. 38-41.

Craven, J., and Wald, F.S. Hospice care for dying patients. *American Journal of Nursing*, 1975, *75*(10), pp. 1816-1822.

Cunningham, R.M. When enough is enough. *Hospitals*, July 1, 1979, pp. 63-64.

DeFouw, R. Hospices for the dying. *The Humanist*, July/August 1974, pp. 28-29.

Downie, P.A. Havens of peace: Hostels for terminal patients. *Nursing Times*, 1973, *69*, pp. 1068-1070.

Gilbert, J.P. Music therapy perspectives on death and dying. *Journal of Music Therapy* 1977, *14*(4), pp. 165-171.

Hackley, J.A. Full service hospice offers home, day, and in-patient care. *Hospitals*, 1977, *51*, pp. 84-87.

Ingles, T. St. Christopher's Hospice. *Nursing Outlook*, 1974, *22*(12), pp. 759-763.

Jordan, L. Hospice in America. *The Coevolution Quarterly*, Summer 1977, pp. 112-115.

Kastenbaum, R. Healthy dying: A paradoxical quest continues. *Journal of Social Issues*, 1979, *35*(1), pp. 185-206.

Kerstein, M.D. Care for the terminally ill: A hospice. *American Journal of Psychiatry*, 1972, *129*, pp. 237-238.

Kron, J. Designing a better place to die. *New York Magazine*, March 1, 1976, pp. 43-49.

Kubler-Ross, E. *Death, the final stage of growth*. Englewood Cliffs, NJ: Prentice-Hall, 1975.

Lamerton, R. The need for hospices. *Nursing Times,* 1975, *71,* pp. 155-157.

Lovelace, B.M. The role of the recreation therapist with the terminally ill child. *Therapeutic Recreation Journal,* 1974, *8*(1), pp. 25-28.

National Hospice Organization (NHO). *Frequently asked questions about hospice: A working paper.* Vienna, VA: NHO, 1979.

National Hospice Organization. Personal Communication, April 3, 1985.

Newman, B. The role of paramedical staff with the dying adult patient. *Therapeutic Recreation Journal,* 1974, *8*(1), pp. 29-33.

Osterweis, M., and Champagne, D.S. The U.S. hospice movement: Issues in development. *American Journal of Public Health,* 1979, *69*(5), pp. 492-496.

Rhein, R.W., Jr. The health cost crisis. *Medical World News,* February 21, 1977, pp. 57-72.

Rogers, B.L. Using the creative process with the terminally ill. *Death Education,* 1978, *2*(1/2), pp. 123-126.

Ryder, C.F., and Ross, D.M. Terminal care: Issues and alternatives. *Public Health Reports,* 1977, *92*(1), pp. 20-29.

Saunders, C. The last stages of life. *American Journal of Nursing,* March 1975, pp. 70-75.

Stoddard, S. *The hospice movement.* New York: Vintage Books, 1976.

The hospice: An alternative. *Journal of the American Medical Association, 236*(18), p. 2047.

United States Department of Health, Education and Welfare (U.S. DHEW). *Hospice.* Washington, D.C.: U.S. DHEW, 1979.

Wald, M. Hospices give help for dying patients. *New York Times,* April 22, 1979.

Ward, B.J. Hospice home care program. *Nursing Outlook,* 1978, *26,* pp. 646-649.

Wentzel, K.B. Dying are the living: St. Christopher's Hospice, London. *American Journal of Nursing,* 1976, *76,* pp. 956-957.

Chapter 16

Recreation and the Rural Elderly

INTRODUCTION

This chapter addresses the issue of recreational services for rural elders. Special areas of concern include recreation needs, attitudes, and interests of rural elders, factors affecting the provision of recreational services to rural elders, and suggestions for improving service provision.

The information presented in this chapter is based on an extensive review of literature and contacts with national organizations such as the National Recreation and Park Association, National Rural Center, National Council on Aging, and Rural America. For the purposes of this chapter, the term rural refers to all people who live outside of Standard Metropolitan Statistical Areas (SMSAs)—whether they live on farms, open countryside, or in villages, towns, or cities of up to 50,000 population—and all residents of those towns within SMSAs which are defined as rural because of small populations (50,000 or less). (Vinson, 1980).

This chapter is organized into six sections:

1. *Needs of rural elders*: This section presents an overview of pertinent value and socio-economic characteristics of rural elders.
2. *Leisure activities of rural elders*: This section presents studies on the leisure interests and recreation participation patterns of rural elders. Topics covered include: studies on the attitudes of rural elders toward leisure and recreation; studies on activity interests of rural elders; studies comparing recreation interests and participation patterns of rural and urban aged; and research

Leitner, M.J., Shepherd, P.L., and Ansello, E.F. College Park, MD: University of Maryland Center on Aging. Prepared under contract for the Heritage Conservation Recreation Service, U.S. Dept. of the Interior.   *291* on recreation needs and interests of rural persons of different age groups.

3. *Existing recreation programs for rural elders*: This section is a compilation of representative program descriptions.

4. *Factors affecting the provision of recreation services to rural elders*: Factors discussed include: transportation; attitudes of rural persons; publicity needs; living conditions and socio-economic status; ethnic and cultural diversity; sex differences; educational level; health status of service recipients; climate and geographic location; and staff considerations.

5. *Approaches to meeting the recreational needs of rural elders*: Approaches discussed include: improved transportation and access services; citizen input and natural focal points; publicity and outreach techniques; institutional improvements; removal of architectural barriers to recreation participation; and funding possibilities.

6. *Summary, conclusions and recommendations*: This section presents an overview of the state-of-the-art in the provision of recreation services to rural elders, as well as conclusions and recommendations related to improving the quality of recreation services for rural elders.

NEEDS OF THE RURAL ELDERLY

Of particular interest to the planner of recreation services for the rural elderly are the values, needs, and attitudes of this population. These seem to differ not only from those of the urban elderly, but also, to some degree, from those of younger rural persons (Blake and Lawton, 1980). Ansello (1980) suggests that the rural elderly may constitute a sub-culture within the rural environment. More than their urban counterparts rural elderly tend to value independence, work or "doing," and the informal support network of friends and family. This may require differential planning for the rural elderly, as well as an awareness that even in the same environment elderly recreation "consumers" and younger "service providers" may see recreation needs and importance differently (Berry and Stinson, 1977).

Adding to the difficulty in planning recreation services for the rural elderly is the tremendous size and diversity of this population. While those over age 60 account for about 3 people out of every 20 of America's total population, they comprise some 5 of every 20 rural inhabitants. Depending on one's definition of "rural," rural elderly total upwards of two-fifths of the nation's elderly. Further, in 28 of the 50 states, 40% or more of the state's older population lives in rural areas (Harbert and Wilkinson, 1979). Rural elderly are also very diverse. Their recreation needs and practices are expressed differently by region; in Appalachia, the Deep South, the north central plains and elsewhere. This makes drawing conclusions from the limited research extremely tenuous.

Compounding the problems that size and diversity create for the planner of recreation services is the economics of aging in a rural area. Almost half of all elderly citizens who live at or below the poverty level are rural residents; the median income of a rural family with an elderly head-of-household is approximately 80% that of their urban counterparts; the incidence of poverty among the rural elderly (21%) is nearly twice that among the urban elderly (12%); and, although some 44% of all poor elderly live in rural areas, these areas receive only 18% of the federal grant money targeted for the elderly (Harbert and Wilkinson, 1979).

Another consideration is that the recreational needs of rural elderly men and women must also be differentiated. Kivett and Scott (1979) and Hooyman and Scott (1980) note that the numbers of elderly rural women are growing disproportionately, and that widows and women with no children or only one child comprise significant percentages of all rural eldery. These data have implications for program planning, especially with regard to the social element of recreation services. Jacobs (1974) points out that the primarily female orientation of senior center activities and an emphasis on the "leisure ethic" may conflict with the "work ethic" of many rural older men. Additionally, recreational needs of rural elderly minorities remain to be clarified, as very little research has been conducted in this area. Lambing (1972) and Watson (1980) examine differences in recreational activities between blacks and whites, while the Goldenrod Hills Community Action Council (n.d.) contrasts recreational pursuits of native Americans and whites. It is not clear, however, if observed differences are due to race or to socio-economic status, health, education or other characteristics.

Other considerations in designing recreation programs for the rural elderly include misconceptions held by service providers and planners who may not have been raised in rural settings, difficulties in locating interested participants because of geography and lack of outreach mechanisms, financial and administrative insufficiencies within programs, and the attitudes of the rural elderly themselves toward government programming in general and recreational programming in particular.

Although there is some disagreement among authors, Ward (1979) notes that the rural elderly see activities as being more meaningful if they yield feelings of achievement, creativity, or helping others, and that perceived meaningfulness is an important factor in determining whether or not a program will be used. Coward (1979) notes the need for diverse programming, as the rural elderly present a greater diversity than their urban counterparts, and as the elderly population in a rural area likely encompasses a thirty to forty year span. A primary concern in determining the kinds of services to be delivered should be that adequate opportunity for input by the rural elders of the region and by respected local citizens be provided, as only through such input will programs be consistent with the values, needs and attitudes of the local older citizenry; and only through such efforts will the local elderly come to identify with the program. Reiss (1979) observed that rural older people want "to be asked", rather than to "be told". Local value, needs and identity must be maintained if a program is to succeed.

LEISURE ACTIVITIES OF THE RURAL AGED

Considerations in Interpreting the Literature

As has been noted earlier, the rural elderly demonstrate a great diversity in backgrounds and interests. It is important to recognize, therefore, that research findings drawn from one particular subgroup may have limited generalizability. Inter-regional differences are likely to be persistent, as well as intra-regional differences. Further, different cohorts, or age groups, within the sixty-plus age bracket are likely to demonstrate different recreational interests (Hoar, 1961).

Much of the literature on leisure activity interests involves interviews or self-report questionnaires as primary data collection techniques. One of the short-comings of this methodology is the tendency of subjects to give responses that they think are socially acceptable, rather than to divulge their true feelings. Suspicion on the part of the rural elderly towards outsiders, government, and "being helped" may further undermine response data (DeJong and Bishop, 1980). Rural older people seem reluctant to divulge "private" information.

Indeed, Auerbach (1976), reports that eighty-five percent of his respondents reported no needs at all. Another limitation is the difficulty in obtaining information from the frail and impaired rural elderly. Recognizing the shortcomings of such research techniques, future studies should employ a variety of methods of data collection including the use of archival data and behavioral observation. These points notwithstanding, the present literature on the leisure activities of the rural aged provides some valuable insights.

Studies of Attitudes Toward Leisure and Recreation

Several studies deal with the attitudes of the rural elderly toward leisure and recreation. DiGrino and McMahon (1979) examine the relationships among early recollections of older persons, their leisure attitudes, and recreation participation patterns by conducting interviews with 90 elderly residents of a small west-central Illinois community. This study reports that early childhood recollection is not significantly related to leisure attitudes nor to hours of recreation participation. The data of the study do indicate a significant positive relationship between leisure attitude scores and weekly hours of participation in recreational activities. Although the small sample size might limit the generalizability of the study, this research nevertheless indicates the importance of leisure attitudes in determining recreation activity patterns.

In a related vein, Gunter (1979) assesses the recreational needs of 250 rural older persons. The majority of the study subjects indicate satisfaction with their lives, do not consider health or economic problems to interfere with recreational pursuits, and prefer intergenerational versus age-segregated activity.

Keating and Marshall (1980) examine the recreation orientation of 25 farm and 24 non-farm couples retiring in rural Alberta. The subjects report that the most desirable aspects of retirement are increased time for involvement in hobbies and for travelling. Another finding is that 70% of the sample view making friends as relatively unimportant, most subjects seeing no need to develop new hobbies or join clubs once retired.

These results suggest that recreation planners should *not* assume that the rural aged have a greater need than other populations to develop activity interests and social relationships.

With regard to activity interests, several studies focus on recreational interests of the rural aged. Barnett's (1975) study on the leisure activity preferences of older persons indicates that they prefer activities participated in as youths. The implication here is that rural recreation workers should build first upon recreation interests the rural aged pursued earlier in their lives, before trying to introduce "new" or unfamiliar activities. The Goldenrod Hills Community Action Council (no date) reinforces the point, saying that "it is impossible to graft recreational past-times of an intellectual or cultural nature onto the tag ends of working class lives." Although this statement should not be generalized to all older persons, the useful suggestion it makes is: do *not* force upon older people activities in which they have never been interested. The Goldenrod Hills project, involving nutrition and social interaction programs for elderly Nebraskans, shows mixed results. The authors report that some of the more successful activities in the program include looking at photograph collections, talking about grandchildren, bingo, and visiting the sick among their peers, while unsuccessful activities in this program include watching movies, discussions on current events and books, and listening to records of talking books. The study shows some variation in activities among the target populations, bingo being the favorite activity of Caucasian elderly; a mixed group of Winnebago Indians and Caucasians showed little interest in activities; and Omaha Indians preferred Indian games and visiting. Regional, ethnic and linguistic considerations, however, may confound these findings.

Several surveys investigate the recreational interests of the rural aged. Hoar (1961) reports the leisure activities of 200 elderly in Oxford, Mississippi. In this study, characteristic activities of males in their sixties include gardening, television viewing, and fishing or hunting. Men in their seventies participate in television viewing, resting, gardening, and reading, while men in their eighties mainly engage in loafing, reading, and gardening. Women in their sixties and seventies enjoy reading, visiting, and watching television, while women in their eighties participate more in sewing, reading, resting, and gardening. Similarly, Grant's (1980) survey on the recreational interests of older people suggests that favorite activities are entertainment, picnics, concerts, bingo and festivals.

In contrast, Ward (1979), having interviewed 323 elderly Wisconsin residents in a study on the meaning of voluntary association to the aged, concludes that certain types of activity are more meaningful when they yield feelings of achievement, creativity, or helping others. Purely social activities, such as games, are seen as less meaningful by the subjects.

Youmans and Larson's (1977) study of 399 elderly residents of Powell County, Kentucky indicates that 30% of the subjects feel a need for recreational activities such as "playing games, doing crafts, or visiting." Forty-five percent of the female subjects and 29% of the males emphasize this need.

A larger study on this topic was conducted by Pihlblad, Hessler, and Freshley (no date). Some 1,700 elderly in rural areas of Missouri were interviewed in 1966; follow-up interviews were conducted in 1973-74 with 568 of these subjects (representing 69% of the survivors from the 1966 interviewees). The subjects report low participation in formal social activity aside from membership and attendance at religious services. The female subjects have higher rates of participation in clubs, societies, and other social and recreational organizations than males, with membership in purely friendship and social groups being limited almost exclusively to women. Kivett and Scott (1979) examine the leisure activities of 418 elderly residents of rural Caswell County, North Carolina. Eighty-five percent of the subjects rate television viewing as their favorite pastime. This corroborates Hoar's (1961) study in which television viewing was also identified as a favorite pastime. Hughston, Axelson and Keller (1979) report the leisure time preferences of 150 elderly residents of a small Virginia community as being church activities (70%), cooking (45%), and gardening (43%).

Studies on Specific Activity Interests

Several studies have also been conducted on highly specific activity interests of the rural aged. Kamaiko (1965) and Winfrey (1977) discuss the success of camping for senior citizens. Burch (1966) discusses the exclusion of senior citizens from wilderness camping because of the lack of adaptation of wilderness areas for the handicapped and the elderly. In a different area of recreational activity, Hoffman (1979) elaborates the benefits of art programs for the rural elderly. According to Hoffman, art can ease isolation, promote socialization, and aid self-concept. And, finally, examining the reading needs and interests of the rural elderly, Murray (1979) suggests that non-institutionalized rural aged read primarily to learn, whereas institutionalized rural elderly read mainly to pass the time.

Rural-Urban Differences in Activity Interests

Some studies compare the attitudes and activities of urban and rural elderly persons. DeJong and Bishop (1980) note that rural persons are more resistant to receiving help than are their urban couterparts. Youmans (1962) finds only small differences in the leisure activities of urban and rural older persons, the major differences being higher participation in *formal* community activities for urban elderly and higher participation in *informal* activity (e.g., visiting friends) for rural elderly. Auerbach (1976) states that television viewing is the favorite activity of both rural and urban elderly subjects in his study. Urban subjects tend to read more newspapers, books, and periodicals, while rural subjects attend church and social clubs more often. Related to DeJong's and Bishop's (1980) assertion that the rural elderly do not as readily accept help as the urban elderly, Auerbach notes that 85% of the rural subjects in his study maintain that they need nothing.

Cohort Differences in Attitudes and Activities

Attitudes and activities may also be compared among different age groups in rural areas. Hoar (1961) analyzes differences in activity interests among persons over age 60 according to age. Blake and Lawton (1980) measure differences among rural persons over age 60 and those under age 60. In this study, persons over age 60 view senior centers as essentially recreational in nature, whereas persons under age 60 consider senior centers to be an opportunity for personal growth. Caution should be exercised in interpreting the results of studies on age differences in leisure activities. Cross-sectional studies merely describe extant differences in activities among different age groups; one should not infer from such studies that increasing age causes these changes in recreation participation patterns. Clearly, further longitudinal or time-lag study on this topic would yield insight into the changes in leisure activity among rural persons across the lifespan.

The preceding literature focuses on leisure interests rather than on evaluation of on-going programs. Research on program evaluations can provide valuable insight into how to improve recreation services for the rural aged. The following section of the chapter presents descriptions of various programs serving the recreational needs of the rural aged, as well as information on evaluation of some of these programs.

EXISTING PROGRAMS OF RECREATION FOR THE RURAL AGED

Exercise and Physical Fitness

Exercise and physical activity programs have been conducted with a great deal of success with the rural aged. An article in *Chronic Disease Management* (1973) extolls the virtues of an exercise program for older persons in rural West Virginia. According to Dr. Raymond Harris, keynote speaker of the First Appalachian Conference on Physical Activity and Aging, "exercise keeps people too fit to die." Fitness crusader Lawrence J. Frankel believes that physical activity "can ameliorate the plight of the aging population, enrich the lives of the sick, the disadvantaged, the hopeless—the millions living in darkness and despair, friendless and alone." Frekany and Leslie (1974) report on their experimental exercise program for senior citizens in a seven county area of east central Iowa. The researchers conclude that an exercise program can make a significant contribution to the well-being of the aged, and recommend that exercise programs be incorporated into activity programs for the aged. Gullie (1978) provides information on aquatic exercise for the aged. The author describes a recreational aquatic exercise program conducted in the small community of Cohoes, New York and lists twenty-three exercises used in this program.

In the Upper Cumberland Development District of Tennessee senior citizens who participated in activities sponsored by the district named physical fitness programming as their number one need. As a result, participants travel from throughout the fourteen counties of the district to a central physical fitness program that is offered regularly. The program includes bicycling and walking, as well as exercise. Demand for the program exceeds available resources. In Vermont physical fitness activities are provided to formerly institutionalized elderly through Project Independence. This program sponsors swimming, physical fitness and arts activities for handicapped elderly, and all participants assume responsibility for the program's operation. Some answer telephones, some wait tables, and others keep track of administrative matters. In this way, each participant is active and responsible for the success of Project Independence. Likewise, a daily exercise program is a major component of an adult day care center located in Lima, Ohio. The center also functions as the link between the thirty or so disabled elders in the program and existing in-home service providers.

In a related vein, Gissal (1979) reports the effects of a twelve week progressive walking and exercise program on morale of older persons. Using a two group pre-test and post-test design with 29 subjects in the experimental group and 40 subjects in the control group, Gissal measured the impact of the program on residents of two small towns of southeastern Wisconsin. Although tests indicate no statistically significant difference in morale scores between groups over time, participants' comments demonstrate that social, psychological, and physical benefits are derived from the exercise program. Gisall recommends that future research efforts focus on variables other than morale, such as stress and tension which can be measured by Galvanic Skin Response tests and biofeedback machines.

MacCullum (1978) describes the value of a fitness maintenance program in promoting senior citizens' involvement in outdoor recreation activities. The fitness program program described by Mac-Cullum helps its participants to gain and maintain a functional level required to enjoy outdoor recreation activities. The rural elderly in particular can benefit from such a program in that rural persons tend toward participation in outdoor recreation activities such as fishing and hunting.

Camps

Camping activities for the elderly are promoted in numerous areas throughout the nation. Accommodations generally include lodging in cabins or an inn. Near Burlington, Vermont 150 elders enjoy a week at the Tyler Place Inn. Activities include recreational and educational programs. Campers attend for a fee of $80. The program is in its twenty-fifth year. A winter version of the camp, called the Vermont Winter House Party, is offered by the Champlain Valley Area Agency on Aging in Middlebury, Vermont. Some 70 campers attend, and engage in group discussions and indoor activities. In North Dakota a statewide camping program for elders is sponsored by churches of various denominations from across the state. Camping programs last up to a week, and may include swimming in heated pools, dance instruction and music. Approximately 60 elders attend annually for a modest fee. The program is in its fourteenth year.

Nutrition and Social Interaction Programs

Senior centers and nutrition programs operate as "community focal points" for activities involving older people in many rural communities. These centers vary widely in days and hours of operation, physical facilities and staffing. Some occupy a single room of a church, while others occupy entire abandoned schools or armories. Staff may be completely voluntary or may consist of a director, program director, nutrition director and assorted aides. Programming may be as simple as offering a place to gather, with an occasional guest speaker, to completely programmed centers offering a variety of recreation, education and social-welfare programs.

Numerous recreational programs for the rural aged are provided as part of these coordinated nutrition and social interaction programs. The Goldenrod Hills (no date) program is one such example. In this program, named Project Rural A.L.I.V.E. (Americans Living in Varied Environments), recreational opportunities are provided for rural elderly Nebraskans as part of a nutrition and social interaction program. Recreational activities in this program include group discussions, games such as bingo, and watching movies. The effects of this program on the physical and psychological well-being of its participants were examined, and it was found that program participants have higher life satisfaction (as measured by Life Satisfaction Index-Z) and higher levels of social interaction than a control group of subjects *not* participating in the program. Kohles (1973) also describes the rural A.L.I.V.E. program in Nebraska. According to Kohles, programs of nutrition and social interaction "decrease the amount of medical care and increase the life satisfaction of senior citizens." The rural A.L.I.V.E. program described in these reports serves elderly Nebraskans of east Thurston County, Nebraska.

A similar program for elderly residents in a rural area of Kentucky is described by the Northeast Kentucky Area Development Council, Inc. (1971). This group reports that recreational activities and nutrition programs can be means of fostering social interaction and enhanced well-being among the elderly. Recreational activities in this program include listening to records, oral reading, discussions, live music by seniors, poetry reading, art demonstrations, social events, hobbies, discussions, and holiday celebrations. According to the authors, recreational activities help to attract people to the meals program; they also state that participants are happier and socialize more as a result of the program.

Similarly, Simonsen (no date) highlights some of the recreational aspects of meals programs for elderly persons in rural Idaho. The report indicates that the provision of meals may not only promote proper nutrition, but may also be a form of social recreation for people. According to Simonsen, the meals program helps alleviate the problems of isolation and loneliness for many rural elderly persons in Idaho.

In Washoe County, Nevada, native American elders at a nutrition project funded by the Older Americans Act began teaching Indian dances, songs and rhythms to native American children in the evenings at their senior center. A local elementary school applied for and received travel funds for cultural enrichment under Title IV of the Older Americans Act. The children have the opportunity to learn and increase appreciation of their culture, while the elders contribute valuable knowledge that preserves the culture.

In rural southern Mississippi, programs are offered in centers located in various locations in the fifteen county area serviced by the Southern Mississippi Area Development Council. Participants are involved in the Older Americans Act funded nutrition program, as well as in a cultural enrichment program funded by the National Endowment for the Humanities.

The Kentucky River Area Development District has engaged itself in several programming efforts that benefit its elderly citizens. Using Heritage Conservation and Recreation Service funding, the district has constructed swimming pools, community centers, and parks that are used extensively by the elders of the area.

Also in Kentucky, the Northeast Kentucky Area Development District has embarked on numerous innovative projects to benefit their elderly. Drawing on the natural resources of this farm area, transportation is now provided in vehicles that are run on 90% alcohol, at approximately one-half the price of gasoline. Local corn is purchased and distilled into fuel, and the remaining mash sold to feed companies. In addition, senior centers in the area are partially heated by solar greenhouses. Drawing again on the natural resources of the area, older men and women grow vegetables and houseplants in these greenhouses. Not only do these provide productive activity for the participants, but the operation actually makes money for the centers. These programs are indicative of how local talents and resources can be mobilized to provide affordable, dignified, leisure activities for the nation's rural elderly.

Community Service Programs

In addition to combined nutrition and social interaction programs, recreational programs are also provided as part of community service programs for the rural aged. An example of such a program is the C.A.S.A. Project (Community Activities for Senior Arkansas). Arkansas Scientific Associates (no date) describe their extensive senior center and outreach services, noting that recreation is an important service for the rural elderly. In a similar vein, Ford (1976) weighs the merits of a coordinated service program for elderly residents of rural Gadsden County, Florida. Recreational activities provided in this program serving over 500 persons include dancing, cards, and other games. The author concludes by recommending that the program be continued and expanded.

Norris (1978) describes senior center programs in rural Franklin County, New York, where there are eight full-time multi-purpose adult centers. Reed (1970) outlines a community activities program for aged persons in a five-county area in rural Idaho. Recreational activities provided in this program include dances, bus trips, picnics, parades, and pot-luck dinners. Thompson (1976) details the HOPE (Helping Older People Enthusiastically) program of predominantly rural DeSoto County, Florida. Holiday celebrations and other parties are a significant part of this program and comprise part of the recreation component.

Germane to community service programs serving the recreational needs of the rural aged, the West Virginia Commission on Aging (1977) presents a progress report on senior centers in West Virginia. In 1977, West Virginia had 216 satellite centers. This report documents an increase in use of senior center services. As an example, Marion County Senior Citizen Centers experienced a one-year increase in membership from 1,429 to over 2,000. The report also describes the role of senior centers in providing recreational activities such as games, parties, and trips, as well as in providing other services such as transportation, legal aid, and health care.

Other reports describe more specific recreational programs provided to the rural elderly. Stough (1974) discusses recreational programs provided by churches. Stough describes a church program labelled "adult education" in rural Oklahoma, with over 700 enrollees and thirty volunteer instructors participating in activities with a heavy emphasis in the arts. Beaver and Elias (1980) assess a twelve-week experimental painting class for community-based marginal elderly. According to the authors, the art activity helps these relatively shy and isolated older persons by increasing social interaction, feelings of self-worth, senses of increased confidence and independence, and by stimulating creativity and sensory awareness.

Yet another focus of recreation-related programs for the rural aged has been on reaching isolated older persons. Along these lines, Burkhardt (1970) describes a free bus system provided for rural aged persons in West Virginia. Burkhardt reports that the number of trips made for social and recreational purposes increased due to the implementation of the transportation services. Hirzel (1977) describes a senior companion program being implemented in the rural counties of St. Mary's, Calvert, and Charles in Maryland. In this program, elderly volunteers work with frail and ill elderly persons in order to stimulate interest in new activities and hobbies as well as to provide companionship for these frail older persons. In addition, the volunteers benefit from the program by getting out and keeping busy themselves. Volunteers are paid and receive compensation for transportation costs.

Labanowich and Andrews (1978) detail the development of a model for the delivery of leisure services to the homebound elderly. The authors discuss a program conducted in Fayette County Kentucky, in which leisure services appeared to contribute toward an improvement in the quality of life of the homebound aging.

FACTORS AFFECTING THE PROVISION
OF RECREATION SERVICES TO THE RURAL AGED

Transportation

Transportation is one of the single most influential factors affecting the success of recreational services to the rural aged. Miko (1980) and the National Association of Area Agencies on Aging (1978) declare that adequate transportation is vital to the success of recreation programs for the rural elderly. According to the Carter Administration, (1979) transportation is a particularly significant problem to the rural elderly, as "45% of the rural elderly do not own an automobile." Grant (1980), studying the recreational interests of older people, finds safety and transportation as the major concerns of the potential elderly participants. Furthermore, Kivett (1979) cites transportation deficiencies as a major obstacle to social activity intervention programs for the rural aged.

Larson and Youmans (1978) also point out the importance of transportation in providing programs of recreation for the rural aged, particularly to women who live alone. In a survey of 200 elderly households in rural Powell County, Kentucky, 50% of the survey respondents maintained that if a senior center were to exist, they would need transportation in order to reach the facility. Similarly, Loveland (1979) identifies transportation as a high priority area for recreation programs for the rural aged. Means, Mann and Van Dyk (1978) also report that 50% of their study's subjects cite transportation as a barrier to the use of human services.

Notess' (1978) study focuses specifically on rural elderly transportation markets. Notess points out that a significant proportion of the elderly in rural areas are isolated from social service and recreation centers, yet special transit vehicles serving the elderly carry only a small percentage of those in need. A useful handbook, *Rural Rides,* is published by the United States Department of Agriculture, describing the operation of rural transportation systems.

Attitudes

The attitudes of rural older persons also affect the provision of recreation services to this population. Indicative of rural attitudes, in a study by Auerbach (1976), 45% of a sample of urban elderly indicate a need for money, while 85% of a sample of rural elderly maintain that they need nothing. Notess (1978) reinforces the meaning of this discrepancy by stating that an obstacle to recreation services for the rural aged is their tendency to reject anything considered to be charity, such as free rides and free meals. Similarly, Nash (1977) and Reiss (1979) refer to the rural older person's suspicion about government intervention programs as a barrier to service provision. The National Association of Area Agencies on Aging (1978) also cites mistrust of federal programs as an obstacle to providing leisure services for the rural aged.

Berry and Stinson (1977) point out a peculiar twist in how attitudes of the aged affect recreation service provision to this popula-

tion. In this study of 185 service providers and 751 elderly consumers in 15 states, 78.4% of the elderly stated that they get enough
recreation, whereas only 12.4% of service providers said that the
elderly in their area get enough recreation. Perhaps an obstacle to
many recreation programs for the rural aged is that the rural aged
have different views on their recreation needs than do the service
providers. This raises the issue of recreation providers being sensitive to local values, needs and attitudes.

Another aspect of rural elderly's attitudes meriting consideration
is the degree to which they perceive activities as being meaningful.
Ward (1979) assesses the attitudes of older persons and the affect of
these attitudes on recreation service provision and participation. According to Ward, perceived meaningfulness is a determining factor
of the older person's participation in activities.

The recreation needs and interests of the local older population
are certainly important elements in recreation program design. As
referenced earlier, the recreational interests of the rural aged may
vary from area to area. It is, consequently, very difficult to make
generalizations about leisure interests for *all* rural elderly persons; it
is all the more important to examine the activity interests, and
underlying values and attitudes of a population before initiating a
program of activities for them.

Publicity

Berry and Stinson (1977) and Miko (1980) note that the degree of
the older person's awareness of services is a factor affecting the provision of these services. Inadequate publicity of available problems
can often lead to the demise of recreational programs for the rural
aged. Of course, effective publicity depends upon client identification and outreach. The ability of service providers to locate older
persons in need of services can be most difficult. Resistance to intervention programs and the geographic dispersion of the rural population are two significant problems related to locating rural older persons in need of recreation services.

Socio-Economic Status and Life Situation

Living conditions and socio-economic status also affect the provision of recreation services for the rural aged. While approximately
one-third of America's elderly live in a rural environment, almost

half of all elderly citizens who live at or below the poverty level are rural residents. In 1975 it was estimated that approximately 50% of the rural elderly existed on an income of $5,000 or less. The median income of a rural family with an elderly head-of-household was only $5,136 in 1975, compared to $6,436 for their urban counterparts (Harbert and Wilkinson, 1979). Improvements to social service programs and facilities are slow because of these economic circumstances, and the generally low tax base on rural lands. Complicating prospects for improved programming and facilities is the relatively simpler local governmental structure in many rural areas. As Steinhauer (1980) observes, local jurisdictions tend to lack the bureaucratic "sophistication" necessary to seek and administer outside funds, and to handle the enormous paperwork obtaining these funds entails. Moreover, improvements to social service programming and facilities are unlikely to come about through outside funding, i.e., state and federal governments, because of a fairly pervasive (though not universal) antipathy toward "outside intervention."

Nor should one overlook type of residence as a factor affecting the types of recreation services to be provided. In addition to farm and non-farm rural aged, institutionalized rural elderly need to be considered. Unfortunately, scant research has been undertaken on the recreational needs of this sub-population. Murray (1979) examines the reading preferences of institutionalized and non-institutionalized rural elderly people. He finds, not surprisingly, that the institutionalized aged are more restricted in their reading pursuits because they are unable to obtain suitable reading materials. This is the more unfortunate because these elderly tend to undertake recreational reading as a primary means to fill time.

Ethnic-Cultural Diversity

Ethnic and cultural differences as factors affecting the provision of recreational services have not been extensively explored. The limited research available serves to underscore the need to clarify the roles ethnic and cultural differences may play as determining factors of recreational programming for the rural elderly. Lambing (1972) investigates the leisure-time activities of 101 Black retired Floridians, ages 78-105, and is especially concerned with the effects of socio-economic status on their activities. Lambing reports that the number of leisure activities engaged in is related (r = .59) to socio-economic status, meaning that leisure activities tend to increase or decrease as socio-economic status increases or decreases. This study also indicates that the leisure pursuits of Black and Caucasian elderly within socio-economic levels are very similar. The one exception is that Black retired professionals tend not to participate heavily in sports, while other studies show that retired Caucasian professionals do participate in sports.

Watson (1980) provides an interim report on an on-going study of 1,783 frail Blacks and Whites, 80 years of age and older, living in what he calls the "Black Belt" of the United States (Virginia, South Carolina, Georgia, Alabama, Mississippi and Louisiana). He says that these states, plus North Carolina and Tennessee which he omitted from his study for fiscal reasons, account for nearly two-thirds of all Black Americans. Watson is examining the relationships between activities of daily living (ADL), age, agitation, loneliness, morale, and other personality dimensions. He finds no significant relationship between age and agitation and loneliness. Rather, ADL is the more important predictor of signs of frailty. With decreasing ADL is associated declining morale, increasing negative attitudes toward self and greater expressed life dissatisfaction. Race differences within these findings have not yet been determined.

According to Bastida, (1980) the rural minority aged are in greater need of community services than urban minority elderly. Bastida bases this conclusion on a study of 300 minority aged persons from an urban area and two rural areas within the same region in the midwestern U.S. The Goldenrod Hills Community Action Council (no date) also alludes to the effects of race and ethnic background on recreation services for the rural aged. In a recreation program for the elderly in rural east Thurston County, Nebraska Caucasians, Winnebago Indians, and Omaha Indians each show different activity interests. This corroborates Vinson and Gallagher's (1980) assertion that ethnic and cultural traditions should be considered in planning recreation programs for the rural elderly.

Further research is needed on the rural minority elderly, especially on rural Hispanic and Asian elderly where research is particularly scarce. We do not know the importance of ethnic and cultural differences on recreational programming for the rural elderly. Inadequate information about minority rural elderly populations can lead to no program designs or inappropriate program designs or the adoption of those programs serving Caucasian rural elderly without consideration of differences. Inappropriateness of activity programs for rural minority elderly might be a factor contributing to this population's observed underutilization of recreation services.

Sex Differences

Women can be viewed as a "minority" group, even though in number they represent the majority of elder persons. Several studies indicate that the recreational needs and interests of older rural women differ from those of men. In this regard, Hooyman and Scott (1979) state that rural older women are disproportionately more likely to suffer from social isolation, inadequate transportation, and other problems. Recreation has been shown to play a major role in alleviating such social isolation. Interestingly, Youmans and Larson's (1977) study of 399 older persons in Powell County, Kentucky indicates that 45% of female respondents emphasize a need for recreational activities compared to only 29% of male respondents.

On the other hand older men are sometimes functionally a minority. Jacobs (1974) focuses on the special problems of involving men in senior center programs. According to Jacobs, there are aspects of senior centers that inhibit male participation, including a predominately female orientation, with programs catering to female interests and the center's emphasis on the "leisure ethic," which may conflict with the "work ethic" that many older rural men identify with.

Educational Level

Education level of service recipients is also a factor affecting service provision. It has also been relatively overlooked in the literature, and there is scant information from which to derive generalizations. The Goldenrod Hills Community Action Council (n.d.) alludes to the problems of attempting educational or cultural activities that are inappropriate to the local citizenry, in this case working class Native Americans and Caucasians. On the other hand, such activities can be beneficial to the participants if carefully implemented with sensitivity to the local culture. Overall, while the degree of its importance has not been firmly established relative to recreation for the rural elderly, it seems reasonable to suggest that the educational attainment levels of would-be participants constitutes an important design consideration.

Health Status

Health status of service recipients does affect recreation service provision to the rural aged. Activities and programs need to be adapted to the functioning level of participants. In this regard, Burch

(1966) and Vinson and Gallagher (1980) mention that architectural barriers can inhibit the participation in recreation services of rural older persons who are less healthy. Burch discusses the exclusion of the elderly from participation in wilderness camping because of the lack of planning in adapting these areas for the handicapped and the aged. However, such retrofitting is sometimes cost-prohibitive, and the 1979 Rural Strategy Conference recommended that compliance with section 504 be waived in such circumstances to prevent bankrupting existing programs.

Geography

As mentioned earlier, population dispersion and distance are realities of rural living. The geographic dispersion of the rural elderly is a prohibitive factor in the provision of recreation services. The National Association of Area Agencies on Aging, (1978) and Israel and Landis (1926) cite substantial problems in providing recreation services in rural areas due to the lower population density of these areas. Israel and Landis (1926) noted that the lower population density of rural areas increases the costs of recreation programs over 50 years ago. Hunter, Macht and Mahoney (1980) and the National Association of Area Agencies on Aging (1978) concur, and note the shrinking tax bases of many rural areas.

Climate can affect recreational programming directly and indirectly. Snow and icy roads may inhibit many rural older persons from attending recreation programs during the winter. On the other hand, warm weather in rural areas of the sunbelt makes a wide range of activities feasible for older persons to engage in year-round. Of course, the popularity of various sports and activities also differs from region to region.

System Considerations

Even the bureaucratic climate can affect program provision. Both Steinhauer (1980) and the U.S. Senate Special Committee on Aging's (1977) hearings list several problems in the use of Older Americans Act funds which relate to providing recreation programs for the rural aged; among them are: cumbersomeness of program rules and regulations, fear of elimination of programs if federal funding ceases, and inadequacy of programs to meet the needs of all rural elderly persons.

In addition to these considerations, characteristics of staff also affect recreation service provision to the rural aged. According to De-Jong and Bishop, (1980) rural service providers differ from their urban counterparts in terms of level of training and size and variety of functions. Although an abundance of research on this topic does not exist, attitudes, education, socio-economic status, sex, and race and ethnic background of service providers are all factors which potentially can affect recreation programs for the rural aged.

APPROACHES TO MEETING THE RECREATIONAL NEEDS OF THE RURAL AGED

Transportation

As noted earlier, transportation is a fundamental concern in providing recreation programs for the rural aged. Provision of transportation has been shown to promote the rural aged's use of recreational services (Burkhardt, 1970). Several studies and articles have set forth recommendations for transportation for the rural elderly which, if enacted, would facilitate more effective provision of recreational services.

The 1979 National Rural Strategy Conference (Ambrosius, 1979) recommends the enactment of legislation to coordinate transportation services, including school buses, in order to facilitate maximum use of limited transportation services in the rural environment. Arkansas Scientific Associates (no date) recommend the development of efficient transportation systems to bring rural elderly persons to and from senior centers. Another suggestion from the Arkansas study is that senior centers be located in downtown areas which are most accessible for people. The U.S. Department of Agriculture has issued a booklet, *Rural Rides,* which provides detailed suggestions for the initiation and operation of rural transportation systems.

Notess (1978) presents an informative discussion on transportation and its impact on providing recreational services to the rural aged. According to the author, many rural older persons desire to ride on vans or buses only with people they know. Notess states that sociability among van riders is a factor which can increase participant enjoyment and the use of a recreation program.

In addition to the creation of bus or mini-bus routes to address the transportation needs of the rural elderly, alternative designs should be considered. The coordination of elders who own and drive cars with those who do not has proved successful in many areas. Furthermore, funds not specifically directed toward addressing transportation needs might be available as a corollary to other programs. An example of this is the provision of transportation funds for "Senior Aides" by some of the national organizations who operate Senior Adult Service Employment programs under Title V of the Older Americans Act. A demand transportation service has been successfully implemented in five rural counties in Maryland, employing fifteen "Senior Aides" to drive their private automobiles. Mileage reimbursement is provided as part of the Title V grant.

Another approach to addressing the need for adequate access to recreation programs by the rural aged is the use of mobile centers to provide recreational services. Recognizing the problems of transporting rural aged persons to and from recreation centers, it is often desirable to have mobile centers that serve different areas within a region during different days of the week. Relatedly, Murray (1979) recommends bookmobile visits to nursing homes in order to better serve the recreational reading needs of rural institutionalized elderly.

A parallel concept is that of roving activity specialists. Due to the geographic dispersion of the rural elderly, programs are often conducted on a small scale, i.e., a relatively low number of participants and staff. For programs to be conducted on a larger scale, they would often have to include a geographic area so large that transportation to and from the center would not be feasible for intended service recipients. One disadvantage of the small scale programs is that program participants may oftentimes be exposed to only a limited range of activities, given the limitations of a small staff. A solution to this problem is to have activity specialists who visit different centers within a region on different days of the week. In this way, centers might have a music specialist one day, an art specialist another day, and so on. Roving activity specialists could help enrich the lives of the rural aged by exposing program participants to a wider range of activities than would otherwise be possible.

Citizen Input and Natural Focal Points

A recommended approach for dispelling negative attitudes toward recreation services is to give the rural aged themselves a greater voice in planning, implementing, and evaluating recreation programs. Bley, Dye, Jensen and Goodman (1972), Hoffman (1979), Ansello (1980), and Windley and Scheidt (1980) all emphasize the desirability of giving the rural aged a greater voice in planning and evaluating recreational services. Grant's (1980) study demonstrates the importance of obtaining feedback from planners, community members, and other professionals in planning effective recreational facilities and programs for the aged. Coward (1979) recommends that in delivering services, people significant in the lives of rural elders be included. The inclusion of family members and close friends can increase the impact of the services and make them more efficient, and so Coward discusses the desirability of family-oriented programming for the rural elderly.

Another approach to better meeting the recreational needs of the rural aged is to elicit the cooperation of churches and religious organizations. Karcher and Karcher (1980) state that the church is the most trusted institution of the rural aged. The authors state that outside programs need to tie in with the rural church. Many community activities are church-related, and the church is the most widely participated-in social organization for the rural aged. Though Karcher and Karcher speak to church-higher education cooperation, their recognition of the vital importance of the rural church is instructive. They outline several cooperative roles for the rural churches to stimulate the development of leisure activities for the rural aged, to assist in grant solicitation, and to use college students as volunteers in providing services to the elderly.

Studies and articles by Auerbach (1976), Thompson (1976), Reiss (1979) and Pihlblad, Hessler, and Freshley (n.d.) support the observation of the importance of church and religion in the lives of the rural aged. Stough (1974) presents case studies of church-sponsored recreation programs for the aged. According to Stough, religious institutions are a convenient meeting place, a location for social contacts and recreation, and oftentimes a sponsor of senior citizens clubs. Murray (1979) recommends that large print books of light spiritual reading be available to satisfy the reading interests of the rural aged, and that these be developed in conjunction with church-sponsored programs. Reiss (1979) states that rural people tend to congregate in churches, fire departments, grange halls, county fair grounds, town commons, and community centers. These places would appear to be natural focal points for the delivery of leisure services to the rural aged.

Publicity and Outreach

Means, Mann and Van Dyk (1978) maintain that the rural older people in greatest need of services may not be receiving them. The authors discuss the need for service providers to "reach out" to the isolated rural older persons. Outreach services have been one approach that has been helpful in attempting to increase program usage. Outreach can be useful in increasing isolated older people's awareness of recreational opportunities. Notess (1978) recommends that outreach programs are more effective when the service provider visits the client's home and wins the trust of the client and his family. The Voice-a-Gram Program (Administration on Aging, 1976), a program whereby isolated elderly and their families exchange prepared messages on tape cassettes, is an example of an outreach service which can help reduce the loneliness of isolated older people and increase their awareness of recreational opportunities. Hirzel (1977) describes a senior companion program conducted in three rural counties of Maryland in which elderly volunteers visit frail and ill elderly persons in order to stimulate the isolated elderly's interest in new activities and hobbies as well as to provide companionship to these persons. Clearly, outreach services can be helpful in attempting to meet the recreation needs of the isolated rural aged.

Other means of program publicity were suggested at a 1979 rural strategy conference (Ambrosius, 1979). These include radio interviews, speeches, news articles, and regular columns in rural newspapers.

A related concern is publicizing programs, both through the use of mass media, and the use of community groups. Effective program publicity can help eliminate wasteful duplication of services caused by lack of awareness of existing programs. In addition, effective publicity can help increase the rural aged's use of recreation services. Perhaps the most effective means of publicity is the establishment of sound, meaningful programs, such that participants are motivated to recommend the services to their peers.

Related to publicity and increasing participants' awareness of existing programs is the need for preretirement leisure counseling for the rural aged. Nash (1977) cites the need for comprehensive preretirement counseling to prepare the rural elderly to avail themselves of opportunities. Vinson and Gallagher (1980) also cite the need for leisure counseling for rural older persons. Such counseling can serve several purposes, helping rural older people become more aware of existing recreational opportunities, and also assisting people to make appropriate choices in use of leisure time and to remove psycho-social barriers against engaging in leisure activities.

System Improvements

Overcoming bureaucratic constraints, and for that matter related fiscal constraints, can be accomplished at times through greater cooperation among agencies, the sharing of resources, human and material. Coward (1979) proposes the coordination of different communities and different agencies within a community in providing services. In a related vein, Vinson and Gallagher (1980) state that communication between public and private recreation service providers should be improved.

A study by Hughston, Axelson, and Keller (1979) suggests that senior centers provide more activities during early morning hours. In this study of older persons in a small Virginia community, 20% of the subjects indicate that 7 a.m. to 9 a.m. is the best time for them to be out.

Myths held by service providers concerning the capabilities of elders can also be a barrier to the provision of recreation services to the rural aged. Coward (1979) maintains that myths about rural people tend to prevent service development. Berry and Stinson (1977) recommend that there be a "consciousness raising" among providers of services to the elderly to dispel myths about aging.

Program Design

Jacobs (1974) sets forth suggestions regarding the involvement of men in senior center programs. Jacobs suggests that activities be provided that are related to male interests (e.g., sports), that opportunities for volunteer work be provided, and that craft cooperatives be developed (so that older men can sell wares made at the senior center).

Loveland's (1979) study of elderly participants in a rural recreation program also suggests areas for improving such programs.

Those interviewed in this study recommend that rural recreation programs include physical activity, offer more constructive sedentary activities so the handicapped can be better involved, and include more "useful" activities.

The National Council on Aging (1972) asserts that although it may *not* be feasible to replicate urban senior centers in rural areas, it is possible to adapt the basic concepts of senior center programming to rural areas through a network of clubs and programs over a county or multi-county area. Also related to rural recreation programs is Vinson and Gallagher's (1980) suggestion that ethnic and cultural traditions of the target population be considered in program planning.

Reed (1970) reports several observations from a recreation program in Idaho related to fostering an improvement in the quality of rural recreation services for the aged. According to Reed, activities at the Idaho centers seem to be geared more to the healthiest members. The report proposes that programming be more diversified, and more small group activities be conducted to better meet the needs of the less healthy aged. The report also recommends the use of professional consultants to help upgrade activities and to help staff deal with problems in interpersonal relationships. Yet another suggestion made by this report is that senior centers be used as casual gathering places, not just for planned activities. The implementation of this suggestion could help senior centers fill the need of rural older persons for a meeting place, a need that for many used to be filled by the rural general store.

Architectural Barriers

Not only is it important to remove psycho-social barriers to leisure activity, but it is also important to remove physical barriers to leisure activity. Vinson and Gallagher (1980) say that architectural barriers to recreation participation should be removed in order to insure that impaired persons can use recreation resources. Burch (1966) suggests that wilderness recreation areas be planned to take into account the special needs of the rural aged.

Regarding accessibility of programs and facilities, several pieces of federal legislation in recent years have helped to improve the accessibility of recreation programs for the handicapped aged. PL 90-480 (Architectural Barriers Act) and PL 93-112 (Rehabilitation Act) are two such laws. However, a yet unanswered question is the extent to which natural outdoor recreation areas, such as wilderness areas, need to be adapted for the handicapped. A paradox exists: the need to keep wilderness areas "untouched" and natural, yet the need to adapt them for the handicapped. Related to this issue, as an outgrowth of PL 93-112, over $4 million has been awarded to the Wood County West Virginia Parks and Recreation Commission for the development of a comprehensive recreation complex that is almost totally accessible to the handicapped. Accordingly, the 1979 rural strategy conference has recommended the waiving of section 504 regulations when compliance would be cost-prohibitive.

Funding

A very critical concern of recreation programs for the rural aged is the existence of adequate funds for program operation. One perhaps overlooked source of operating funds is the service recipients themselves. In a study conducted by Youmans and Larson (1977), 43% of 399 survey respondents say that they would be willing to pay to help support a center that would provide recreational services. Indeed, as the rural elderly have been shown to be reluctant to partake in anything viewed as charity (Notess, 1978), the provision for payment could *increase* usage. Related to the notion of self-support of programs, Norris (1978) discusses money raising events for centers such as rummage sales, raffles, and craft and bake sales.

Government funds are vital to the existence of many rural recreation programs serving the aged. According to Hunter, Macht and Mahoney (1980), the 1978 amendments to the Older Americans Act legislate that state agencies spend in rural areas 105% of the amount spent in fiscal 1978 for social and nutrition programs, and multi-purpose senior centers. In that multi-purpose senior centers play a substantial role in providing recreation for the aged, this may mean more available funds for recreation programs for the aged in rural areas.

Of particular interest to recreation programs for the rural elderly are the White House Rural Development Initiatives, which provide funds for ten demonstration congregate housing projects that include community space and social programming; also, other recent efforts include a demonstration project to deliver social services via satellite service centers; an increase in public service employment opportunities from 93,000 in 1977 to 225,000 in 1979 (for needed staff); federal support for rural downtown revitalization; and provisions for improved public transportation in rural areas.

Funding remains basic to the provision of recreation services to the rural elderly not only because such provision is more costly in a rural area, but also because the local tax base is smaller. These conditions necessitate imaginative use of public and private resources, and thoughtful, and innovative coordination of existing resources and programs. Such efforts require community involvement. Local resources that should not be overlooked include churches, banks, merchants, ceramic clubs and shops, police, community colleges, boards of education, libraries, undertakers, insurance salespersons, farmers, grain cooperatives, and volunteer fire companies. On the national level, resources can be obtained through the Department of Agriculture, the Department of Transportation, the Department of Energy, the Department of Education, the Department of Commerce, the Department of Labor, the Department of Interior, the Department of Health and Human Services and the Administration on Aging. When addressing the recreational needs of the elderly in a rural environment, it is important to mobilize the resources of local elders, community leaders, family and the kinship network as planners; to coordinate any and all acceptable public and private, local and national resources; and to develop innovative uses of existing resources to address issues which may be peripherally related to their mandates, but which can be channelled to serve the recreative needs of the rural aged.

SUMMARY, CONCLUSIONS AND RECOMMENDATIONS

Studies on the recreational interests of rural elders demonstrate the awesome diversity of these people. The various studies cited in the first sections of this chapter substantiate that the recreational pursuits of rural elderly persons vary in different regions and according to sex, different socio-economic, racial, and ethnic characteristics. The primary conclusion to be drawn from these studies is that the rural elderly comprise a heterogeneous population. In planning recreation programs for a given rural aged population, it is imperative, therefore, to conduct a thorough needs assessment before initiating any program and to involve local citizenry in the planning process. It is dangerous to make gross generalizations about the activity interests of such a diverse group. The characteristics and quirks of each group and community being served need to be considered.

Several studies refer to the resistance of some rural elderly to any program that they consider charity. In addition, some researchers state that some rural elderly are suspicious about any government intervention programs, no matter how well-intentioned. The authors recommend that sincere efforts be made by outreach workers to win the trust of rural older persons, their families, and their close friends. Such outreach efforts can aid in the success of activity programs for rural elders.

Frequently, recreation programs for rural elders are provided in conjunction with established nutrition or community service programs. Descriptions and evaluations of these programs indicate that recreation can have a significant impact on the well-being of rural older persons. Although a number of evaluative studies are of limited significance due to constraints in the research methodology they employ, the composite picture these studies present is that recreation participation can help improve the lives of rural older persons in various self-conceptual and functional ways.

Senior centers play a major role in the provision of recreational services to the rural aged. The Older Americans Act and its amendments continue to be important in providing funds for senior centers in rural areas. Likewise, churches in the rural environment seem to have major roles in providing social and recreational outlets for the rural aged. Several studies indicate that for many rural elderly, church-related activities are their only form of social participation. Thus, several reports recommend that recreation services can have a greater impact on rural elders if recreation programmers cooperate or tie in with local churches and religious organizations.

Transportation remains an over-riding issue in recreation programming, being repeatedly cited as a significant or the most significant factor in the provision of recreation services to the rural aged. Inadequate transportation is oftentimes a major obstacle to the provision of recreation services to rural elders. In order to alleviate transportation problems, it is recommended that: public transportation in rural areas be expanded; wherever possible, rural senior centers provide door to door transportation for program participants; and all of the community's transportation services, including school buses, be coordinated to meet the transportation needs of the rural aged.

The geographic dispersion of rural elderly persons poses several problems for service provision: difficulty in transporting persons to and from centers; difficulty in obtaining adequate funding for programs for a given area due to the low tax base provided by a lightly populated area; and, difficulty in providing varied programs for a small target population. Recommendations to alleviate these problems include: the use of mobile centers as opposed to stationary recreation programs housed in a particular building so as to increase program accessibility; the use of roving activity specialists so that varied programs can be offered; and the use of fund-raising activities to supplement government funds for programs.

In addition would-be participants should be made aware of recreational opportunities. Rural elders need to be made aware of recreational possibilities and service providers need to be able to locate persons in need of services. A variety of outreach mechanisms exist. Preretirement leisure counseling is one such mechanism which can further assist in meeting these needs.

Physical and architectural barriers inhibit the rural elderly's participation in some recreational programs, particularly outdoor recreation programs. Facilities and programs should be adapted as much as possible to facilitate their use by frail and handicapped senior citizens.

In general, the provision of recreation programming for the rural elderly would be enhanced by the increased competency of those responsible for designing and administering such programs. Specifically, the local citizens who are responsible for the provision of services should receive training in resource development, interagency cooperation, senior center management, program development, use of planning committees, and in mechanisms for obtaining local input. This training would help to insure that local needs are being met, that local resources are being most effectively and imaginatively used, and that those responsible for programming would be able to compete effectively (should they desire to) with their urban counterparts for the scarce resources that are available. Further, training of these local residents would, de facto, introduce local values, needs, and attitudes into the system, eliminating the need to hire outside personnel potentially unacceptable to that rural environment.

In summary, recreation needs of rural elders has been a topic of increasing concern in recent years, due to the growth in this population. Continued attention to this topic will hopefully narrow the gap between recreation's potential and its reality with respect to rural elders.

BIBLIOGRAPHY

Administration on Aging. *Let's end isolation* (Publication No. 129). Washington, D.C.: U.S. Department of Health, Education, and Welfare, n.d.

Administration on Aging. Voice-A-Gram: Prescription for loneliness. *Aging Magazine,* 1976, *5,* pp. 261-262.

Ambrosius, G.R. *A report on national rural strategy conference to improve service delivery to rural elderly.* Spencer, IA: Iowa Lakes Area Agency on Aging, 1979.

Ansello, E.F. Special considerations in rural aging. *Educational Gerontology: An International Quarterly,* 1980, *5*(4), pp. 343-354.

Arkansas Scientific Associates. *An evaluation of C.A.S.A. project (Community Activities for Senior Arkansans).* Arkansas Farmers Union. (National Clearinghouse on Aging. SCAN Social Practice Resource Center, CF 000 135).

Auerbach, A.J. The elderly in rural areas: Differences in urban areas and implications for practice. In L.H. Ginsberg (Ed.), *Social work in rural communities: A book of readings.* New York: Council on Social Work Education, 1976.

Barnett, G. A comparison of leisure activity preferences between residents of a senior citizen's housing project and members of a senior citizen's club. *Master's Abstracts,* 1975, *13,* p. 190.

Bastida, E. The rural minority elderly: In greater isolation and need. *Gerontologist,* 1980, *20*(5), p. 62. (Abstract)

Beaver, M., and Elias, B. Enhancing the well-being of the marginal elderly through art appreciation. *Gerontologist,* 1980, *20*(5), p. 63. (Abstract)

Berry, C.G., and Stinson, F.S. *Service consumption patterns and service priorities of the elderly* (Administration on Aging, Department of Health, Education and Welfare, Contract No. HEW-105-74-3104). Washington, D.C.: Lawrence Johnson and Associates, Inc., June 1977.

Blake, B.F., and Lawton, M.P. Perceived community functions and the rural elderly. *Educational Gerontology: An International Quarterly,* 1980, *5*(4), pp. 375-397.

Blazey, C.H. *An analysis of the relationship between health and medical costs and leisure time activities of aged residents in South Dakota.* Unpublished doctoral dissertation, University of Oregon, 1971.

Bley, N., Dye, D., Jensen, K., and Goodman, M. Clients' perceptions—key variable in evaluating activities for elderly. *Gerontologist,* 1972, 12, p. 79. (Abstract)

Burch, W.R. Wilderness: The life cycle and forest recreational choice. *Journal of Forestry,* 1966, *64,* pp. 606-610.

Burkhardt, J.E. Transportation and the rural elderly. In E. Cantrill and J. Schemelzer (Eds.), *Transportation and aging: Selected issues.* Washington, D.C.: U.S. Government Printing Office, 1970.

Carter Administration. *Small community and rural development policy.* Washington, D.C.: The White House, December 20, 1979.

Chapin, R. (Producer). *Serving the rural elderly.* Minneapolis: Minnesota Resource Center for Social Work Education, 1980. (Film). Abstract in *Gerontologist,* 1980, *20*(5), p. 282.

Coward, R.T. Planning community services for the rural elderly: Implications from research. *Gerontologist,* 1979, *19,* pp. 275-282.

DeJong, F.J., and Bishop, C.J. The view from the country. *Gerontologist,* 1980, *20*(5), p. 91. (Abstract)

DiGrino, B.N., and McMahon, M.M. The Adlerian theory of early recollections: Its relationship to leisure attitudes and participation among the elderly. In R.O. Ray (Chair), *Leisure and aging.* Symposium presented at the National Recreation and Park Association Annual Congress, New Orleans, 1979.

England, J.L., Gibbons, W.E., and Johnson, B.L. The impact of a rural environment on values. *Rural Sociology,* 1979, *44,* pp. 119-136.

Ford, Q.E. *A model project for aging: Coordinated service program for senior citizens in a rural county.* Quincy, FL: Gadsden County Senior Citizens Council, Inc., 1976.

Frekany, G.A., and Leslie, D.K. Developing an exercise program for senior citizens. *Therapeutic Recreation Journal*, 1974, *8*, pp. 178-180.

Gissal, M.L. The effect of a twelve week progressive walking and exercise program on morale for adults sixty years and older. In R.O. Ray (Chair), *Leisure and aging*. Symposium presented at the National Recreation and Park Association's Annual Congress, New Orleans, 1979.

Goldenrod Hills Community Action Council. *Project Rural A.L.I.V.E. (Americans Living in Varied Environments): A comparative study of older Caucasians, Omaha Indians, and Winnebago Indians in no cost, nutritious meals and socialization*. AoA grant 93-P-75025, National Clearinghouse on Aging, SCAN Social Practice Resource Center, CF #000 357, n.d.

Goldenrod Hills Community Action Council. *Project Rural A.L.I.V.E. (Americans Living in Varied Environments): An evaluation*. AoA grant 93-P-75025. National Clearinghouse on Aging, SCAN Social Practice Resource Center, #CF 000 387.

Grant, E.A. A survey of the recreational interests of older adults. *Gerontologist*, 1980, *20*(5), p. 114. (Abstract)

Gullie, R. Cohoes elderly swim their way to fitness. *New York State Recreation and Park Society Journal*, 1978, *1*, pp. 8-10.

Gunter, P.L. The rural aged and leisure activities: Problems and issues, a research study. In R.O. Ray (Chair), *Leisure and aging*. Symposium presented at the National Recreation and Park Congress, New Orleans, 1979.

Harbert, A.S., and Wilkinson, C.W. Growing old in rural America. *Aging*, January 1979, pp. 36-40.

Hirzel, D. Elderly will help elderly. *Washington Star*, March 7, 1977, p. 19.

Hoar, J. A study of free-time activities of 200 aged persons. *Sociology and Social Research*, 1961, *45*(2), pp. 157-63.

Hoffman, D.H. Arts and the rural elderly. In D.H. Hoffman and H. Lamprey (Eds.), *Rural aging*. Lexington, KY: University of Kentucky, 1979.

Hooyman, N., and Scott, N. A mutual help model for rural older women. *Gerontologist*, 1979, *19*, p. 91. (Abstract)

Hughston, G., Axelson, L., and Keller, J.F. Leisure time preferences of the elderly: Family ties, responsibilities, and reflections. In R.O. Ray (Chair), *Leisure and aging*. Symposium presented at the National Recreation and Park Association Annual Congress, New Orleans, 1979.

Hunter, J.B., Macht, M.W., and Mahoney, K.J. Amendments to the Older American's Act: Focusing attention on rural elderly. *Gerontologist*, 1980, *20*(5), p. 130. (Abstract)

Israel, H., and Landis, B.Y. *Handbook of rural social resources*. Chicago: University of Chicago Press, 1926.

Jacobs, B. *Involving men: A challenge for senior centers*. Washington, D.C.: National Council on Aging, 1974.

Jirovec, R. Self-help programs among the rural aged. *Gerontologist*, 1980, *20*(5), p. 131. (Abstract)

Kamaiko, J. *Camping with the elderly person*. Unpublished manuscript, 1965.

Karcher, C.J., and Karcher, B.C. Higher education and religion: Potential partners in service to the rural elderly. *Educational Gerontology: An International Quarterly*, 1980, *5*(4), pp. 409-421.

Keating, N., and Marshall, J. The process of retirement: The rural self-employed. *Gerontologist*, 1980, *20*, pp. 437-443.

Kim, P.H. The low income rural elderly: The undeserved victim of public inequity. *Gerontologist*, 1980, *20*(5), p. 138. (Abstract)

Kim, P.H., and Lamprey, H. *A bibliography on rural aging*. Lexington, KY: University of Kentucky, 1979.

Kivett, V.R. Discriminators of loneliness among the rural elderly: Implications for intervention. *Gerontologist*, 1979, *19*, pp. 108-115.

Kivett, V.R., and Orthner, D. Activity patterns and leisure preferences of rural elderly with visual impairment. *Therapeutic Recreation Journal*, 1980, *14*(2), pp. 49-58.

Kivett, V., and Scott, J.P. *The rural by-passed elderly: Perspectives on status and needs.* (Technical Bulletin 260). Greensboro, NC: University of North Carolina, 1979.

Kohles, M.K., Nordin, S.R., O'Connor, R.J., Patterson, R.L., Smith, P.E., and Stringer, P.R. *Project Rural A.L.I.V.E.: An Evaluation.* Lincoln, NE: University of Nebraska, 1973.

Labanowich, S., and Andrews, N. *Development and field testing of a model program for the provision of leisure services to the homebound aging.* Lexington, KY: University of Kentucky, 1978.

Lambing, M.L. Leisure-time pursuits among retired blacks by social status. *Gerontologist,* 1972, *12*, pp. 363-367.

Larson, D.K., and Youmans, E.G. *Problems of rural elderly households in Powell County, Kentucky.* Washington, D.C.: United States Department of Agriculture, 1978.

Larson, O.F. Values and beliefs of rural people. In T.R. Ford (Ed.), *Rural U.S.A.: Persistence and change.* Ames, IA: Iowa State University Press, 1978, pp. 91-114.

Loveland, N.J. Rural aged and leisure activities: Providers, a report. In R.O. Ray (Chair), *Leisure and aging.* Symposium presented at the National Recreation and Park Association Congress, New Orleans, 1979.

MacCullum, M. Outdoor recreation and the senior citizen. *Leisurability,* 1978, *5,* pp. 16-19.

Means, G., Mann, J., and Van Dyk, D. Reaching out to the rural elderly: Services to rural America. *Human Services in the Rural Environment,* 1978, *3*(2), pp. 1-6.

Miko, P.S. *Addressing the recreation needs of the rural elderly.* Unpublished manuscript, 1980.

Murray, M.S. Variables affecting the reading preferences of institutionalized versus non-institutionalized rural elder adults. (Doctoral dissertation, North Carolina State University at Raleigh, 1979). *Dissertation Abstracts International,* 1979, *40,* p. 1815A.

Nash, B.E. *Rural elderly.* Unpublished manuscript, 1977.

National Association of Area Agencies on Aging. *Rural affairs committee report.* Washington, D.C., 1978.

National Council on Aging. *A comprehensive program for the elderly in rural areas.* Washington, D.C.: National Council on Aging, 1972.

Norris, J. Multipurpose centers in a rural county. *Aging Magazine,* 1978, pp. 18-20.

Northeast Kentucky Area Development Council, Inc. *Country gathering: A nutrition demonstration project, final report.* AoA grant 93-P-75021 National Clearinghouse on Aging, SCAN Social Practice Resource Center, CF #000 351, 1971.

Notess, C.B. Rural elderly transit markets. *Journal of American Institute of Planners,* 1978, *44,* pp. 328-334.

Pihlblad, C.T., Hessler, R., and Freshley, H. *The rural elderly, 8 years later: Changes in life satisfaction, living arrangements, and health status.* University of Missouri-Columbia. AoA grant 93-P-57673. National Clearinghouse on Aging, SCAN Social Practice Resource Center, #CF 000 136, n.d.

Reed, G.R. Survey of elderly participation in community activities for aged. Western Idaho Community Action Program, Inc. (National Clearinghouse on Aging, SCAN and Social Practice Resource Center, CF 000 233), 1970.

Reiss, E.R. *Rural residents and their recreation: Observations from the country.* Unpublished manuscript, 1979.

Simonsen, I. *Senior meals: Improved nutrition and social association in rural America.* Western Idaho Community Action Programs, Inc. (National Clearinghouse on Aging, SCAN Social Practice Resource Center, CF 000 232).

Steinhauer, M.B. Obstacles to the mobilization and provision of services to the rural elderly. *Educational Gerontology: An International Quarterly,* 1980, *5*(4), pp. 399-408.

Stough, A.D. *Brighter vistas: Church programs for older adults.* Washington, D.C.: U.S. Department of Health, Education and Welfare, Administration on Aging, 1974.

Thompson, E.A. *Planting a seed of HOPE for older Americans in DeSoto County, Florida,* Arcadia, FL: Evangeline Lodge, 1976.

United States Department of Agriculture. *Rural rides.* Washington, D.C.: U.S. Department of Agriculture, 1979.

United States Senate, Special Committee on Aging. *Older Americans Act Programs: A rural perspective.* Huron, SD: U.S. Senate, 1977.

United States Senate, Special Committee on Aging. *The nation's rural elderly.* Washington, D.C.: U.S. Government Printing Office, 1978.

Vinson, E.A., and Gallagher, F.M. *First report: National Resource Committee for the rural and small communities recreation assessment.* Unpublished manuscript, 1980.

Ward, R.A. The meaning of voluntary association participation to older people. *Journal of Gerontology,* 1979, *34,* pp. 438-445.

Watson, W. Older frail rural blacks: A conceptualization and analysis. *NCBA Quarterly Contact,* Fall 1980, *3*(4), pp. 1-2.

West Virginia Commission on Aging. *Off our rockers: Annual progress report.* Charleston, WV: West Virginia Commission on Aging, 1977.

West Virginia project backed by physicians. *Chronic Disease Management,* April 1973.

Wilkinson, C. *Comprehensive annotated bibliography on the rural aged.* Morgantown, WV: West Virginia University Gerontology Center, 1978.

Windley, P.G., and Scheidt, R.J. The well-being of older persons in small urban towns: A town panel approach. *Educational Gerontology: An International Quarterly,* 1980, *5*(4), pp. 355-373.

Winfrey, C. For the aged, camp life's slower; but much like that for young. *New York Times,* July 16, 1977, pp. 23; 26.

Youmans, E.G. *Leisure-time activities of older persons in selected rural and urban areas of Kentucky.* Lexington, KY: Agricultural Experiment Station, 1962.

Youmans, E.G., and Larson, D.K. *Health status and needs: A study of older persons in Powell County, Kentucky.* Lexington, KY: University of Kentucky, 1977.

Chapter 17

Sexuality in Later Life

INTRODUCTION

Sexual activity has been well-documented as a uniquely beneficial leisure activity for elders (Weg, 1983). Unfortunately, myths and stereotypes regarding sexuality in later life are very prevalent, and have inhibited the free sexual expression of elders (Robinson, 1983). According to Weg (1983), one means of enhancing the sexual expression of elders in the future is to ensure that health professionals (including recreation therapists) working with elders be well-informed on this topic so that they will be able to effectively advise elders in sex-related matters. Furthermore, educating health professionals regarding the sexuality of elders can help to improve their attitudes toward sex for senior citizens, an important concern in that the negative attitudes of staff in settings such as nursing homes have been cited as contributing to an atmosphere which inhibits the free sexual expression of elders (Corby and Zarit, 1983). Therefore, the purpose of this chapter is a very important one: to provide information on sexuality in later life, in order to educate present and future recreation workers with elders on this topic to enable their counseling of elders on sex-related matters, and to enhance their attitudes regarding sex for elders, in the hopes that positive attitudes of staff toward sex will result in a more conducive social environment for elders to sexually express themselves.

In the first section of the chapter, the value and benefits of sexual activity for elders are discussed. In the second section of this chapter, the current status of sex in later life is examined, including a discussion of research studies on the sexual behavior patterns of elders. In the third section of the chapter, factors affecting the sexual behavior of elders are explored, including an examination of physiological considerations and psycho-social factors. In the last

The authors wish to thank Gloria Leitner for her contributions to this chapter.

section of the chapter, a variety of ideas are presented regarding how to improve the ability of elders to sexually express themselves, including a discussion of both treatments to alleviate physiological limitations, and solutions to psycho-social limitations on the sexual behavior of elders.

VALUE OF SEXUAL ACTIVITY FOR ELDERS

According to Weg (1983), sexual activity can be physically, psychologically, and emotionally beneficial for elders. One physical benefit of sex is improved circulation. Another physical benefit of sex is reduced tension, as documented by Dr. West's experience in a rural nursing home (Weg, 1983).

The psychological and emotional benefits of sexual activity for elders are also very impressive. According to Weg (1983), sexual activity can enhance an elder's sense of well-being, and provide elders with a unique, pleasurable experience which is shared with another individual. The psychological and emotional lift which sex can provide is especially important to elders, in light of the loss of life roles many elders experience (Weg, 1983). For men, sex can counteract a loss of prestige and self-confidence in the work world. For women, sexual activity can enhance one's self-esteem by reaffirming one's physical attractiveness and desirability after menopause (Weg, 1983). Thus, with the elimination of some of older person's outlets for pleasure, ego satisfaction, and sensual expression, sexual activity can be even more vital to the well-being of elders than to that of younger persons.

SEXUAL BEHAVIOR OF ELDERS

According to research studies cited by Weg (1983), interest in sexual activity is maintained throughout the life span to a greater degree than is commonly believed. Although interest in sex does decline, it is a *gradual* decline, and many people in their 90s still report to have sexual desires (Weg, 1983).

However, elders' interest in sex seems to be greater than sexual activity. Weg (1983) cites a study by Kinsey which found that 70% of older married men in the study had a mean frequency of sexual intercourse of .9 times per week, although the frequency of activity was as high as three times per week for some men. Weg (1983) also discusses a study of 250 black and white elders 60-93 years old which found that 54% of the married subjects were still sexually active, but only 7% of the unmarried subjects were sexually active. Blacks in this study were more sexually active than whites, and less affluent subjects were more active than wealthier subjects. However, regardless of color, sex, and economic status, the level of sexual activity earlier in one's life seems to be the most accurate predictor of the level of sexual activity in later life (Weg, 1983).

Another interesting study on this topic was conducted from 1955-1964 with 260 persons ages 60-94 by the Duke Center for the Study of Aging and Human Development (Weg, 1983). The major findings of this study were: (1) interest in sex declined, although 50% of the people age 80 and older interviewed still had an interest in sex; (2) approximately 20% of male subjects age 80 and older remained sexually active; (3) approximately 14% of the males and 24% of the females cessated. The most common reason cited by males for cessation was health; females most commonly attributed cessation to the lack of a male partner.

With regard to the sexual behavior of elders, it is also interesting to note findings on the prevalence of masturbation among elders. Weg (1983) cites a study which found that for males, masturbation peaks in the teenage years and declines thereafter, but for women, research findings indicated that 58% of older women masturbate while only 20% of younger women masturbate. The explanation of these findings is that the socio-sexual outlets for older women tend to be limited, and that possibly older women have profited from their experiences and understand the pleasurableness of masturbation. According to Weg (1983), masturbation is an important sexual outlet which can help reduce stress, stimulate sexual desires, and contribute to well-being.

Another form of sexual behavior which can stimulate sexual desires and heighten pleasure is sexual daydreaming. Unfortunately, research indicates that the prevalence of sexual fantasies and daydreams declines in later life (Weg, 1983).

However, a very positive aspect of sexual behavior in later life is the seemingly prevalent trend toward being less goal-oriented toward orgasm but rather being more gentle, caring, warm, and loving during sexual intercourse (Weg, 1983). Therefore, even though the frequency of sexual activity might be lower for elders than for younger people, the enjoyment of sexual activity might be even greater for many elders.

FACTORS AFFECTING SEXUAL BEHAVIOR

The previous section presented an overview of sexual behavior patterns of elders. It is important to understand the factors affecting these behavior patterns, which is the purpose of this section of the chapter. Physiological factors which affect the sexual behavior of elders are discussed first, followed by an overview of psycho-social factors.

Physiological Factors

It is very important to be aware of the common physical changes related to sexual functioning which are commonly associated with aging, and to understand that these physical changes should *not* cause one to cease sexual activity. It is very unfortunate that the physiological changes discussed below have caused many elders to mistakenly believe that they should cease physical activity.

Physical Changes in Women

According to Weg (1983), the following are sex-related physical changes which most older women experience:

1. Significantly lower levels of estrogen are produced.
2. Fullness of breasts is diminished.
3. The cervix and ovaries become smaller.
4. Vaginal capacity for expansion is reduced, and elasticity diminishes.
5. Less vaginal lubrication is present.
6. The clitoris becomes slightly smaller.
7. Due to a depletion of sex steroids, vaginitis (an infection caused by yeast organisms) becomes more prevalent after menopause. Vaginitis can cause one to experience pain during intercourse.
8. A thinning of the vaginal walls, combined with decreased lubrication not only causes sex to be painful, but it can make penetration difficult and cause bleeding.
9. Painful cramping becomes common.
10. The bladder and urethra become more susceptible to inflammation and irritation.
11. Intercourse sometimes causes urination and a burning sensation.

12. Intensity of physiological responses to stimulation are decreased.
13. The duration of the orgasm is reduced.
14. Resolution after orgasm is faster.

On the other hand, two physical characteristics of older women which contribute to their enjoyment of sexual intercourse are:

1. The multiorgasmic capacity of the younger years is retained.
2. Because older women are released from the fear of pregnancy, they often experience a heightened interest in sex, and reduced inhibitions.

One should not despair at the long list of negative sex-related physical changes older women often experience. According to Weg (1983), sexual disorders and dysfunction among elders are just as treatable as those among younger persons. Furthermore, as discussed in the last section of the chapter, there are specific treatments (e.g., hormone replacement therapy) which can partially prevent, reverse, or retard the aforementioned physical changes.

Physical Changes in Men

According to Weg (1983), the following are sex-related physical changes which most older men experience:

1. Fewer sperm are produced due to lower testosterone levels.
2. A reduction in sex steroids causes a reduction in muscle tone and strength.
3. The testes are smaller and more flaccid.
4. The prostate enlarges.
5. Contractions are weaker.
6. Aching testes or sharp discomfort at the distal end of the penis may be experienced.
7. The force of ejaculation is weaker due to a reduction in the viscosity and volume of seminal fluid.
8. A longer period of time is needed for the penis to become erect.
9. More direct stimulation of the penis is generally required to reach an erection.
10. The loss of the erection after orgasm is faster.

11. A positive change is the ability to maintain an erection for a longer period of time, thereby increasing the potential for arousal and orgasm for the partner.

Again, the reader is reminded not to despair at the long list of negative changes, because there are specific treatments to prevent, reverse, or retard many of the aforementioned physical changes. These treatments are discussed in the last section of the chapter. Also, it is important to remember that it is often people's despondency over the physical changes which inhibits their sexual activity more so than the changes themselves.

Physical Conditions Affecting Males and Females

Weg (1983) discusses the effects of common physiological problems on the sexual activity of elders:

1. Diabetes can affect sexual activity in several ways:
   a. Vaginal lubrication is sometimes delayed and more scant.
   b. The diabetic male sometimes has less control over ejaculation and will occasionally ejaculate prematurely.
   c. The diabetic male sometimes is unable to attain an erection.
2. Pelvic surgery's effects on sexual activity appear to have the potential to be either positive or negative. Weg (1983) cites a study in which 34% of the women studied had heightened sexual responsiveness after a hysterectomy, while 37% of the women studied felt that their sexual relationship deteriorated after the hysterectomy. Although the removal of prostate tumors and hysterectomies sometimes depresses sexual desires and interferes with the capacity for climax, these are *not* inevitable results of surgery. Also not inevitable, but a very serious problem, is the feeling of some women after surgery that they have been defeminized.
3. Cardiovascular disease and hypertension often inappropriately inhibit elders from engaging in sexual activity due to myths about sex being a strenuous and dangerous form of exercise. In reality, only between .3% and 1% of all sudden coronary deaths are caused by sexual activity (Weg, 1983). Furthermore, sex can probably do more to prevent heart attacks (due to its stress-reducing effects) than to cause them. However,

drugs commonly taken for hypertension can cause a loss of erective ability.
4. Drug use can have a negative effect on sexual capacities. Tranquilizers commonly used by elders (e.g., Librium® and Mellaril®) often weaken the erection and delay ejaculation. Continued use of these drugs can result in impotence. Similarly, the use of alcohol, marijuana, and other drugs can adversely affect sexual capacities.

Psycho-Social Factors

As mentioned previously, one's attitudes toward sex-related physical changes can inhibit sexual activity more so than the actual changes themselves. According to Weg (1983), changes in reproductive functioning are especially ego-damaging and feared. These changes tend to have a more negative impact on one's self-concept than most other types of physical changes (Weg, 1983).

Furthermore, Weg (1983) asserts that elders have been assigned to a special category—"sexually inert, uninterested, and dysfunctional." As a result, elders who want to fulfill their sexual desires often feel apprehensive and guilty, because of the societal attitude that sexual activity among elders is abnormal.

Robinson (1983) identifies several psycho-social constraints on the sexual behavior of elders:

1. Stigmas commonly attached to old age;
2. The negative attitude of adult children toward their parents engaging in sexual activity;
3. The barriers imposed by institutional living arrangements (over one million elders are institutionalized); and
4. The numerous obstacles women face, such as the unbalanced sex ratio (149 females for every 100 males), the high proportion of older women unmarried and thus without a sanctioned partner, the poor chances of remarriage, the tendency of husbands to be older than wives (thus often leaving women without a partner or one with limited sexual capabilities due to health problems), sex roles (especially those of previous generations) which discriminated against women freely expressing their sexuality, and the double standard of aging which portrays the aging men as sexually desirable and the aging women as sexually undesirable.

Corby and Zarit (1983) focus on the constraints imposed by attitudes. For example, they cite one study of 124 nursing home residents in which 50% of the residents agreed with the statement "sex over 65 is ridiculous." Corby and Zarit (1983) also express concern that the attitudes of nursing home staff and the nursing home environment in general are not supportive of sexual expression.

In a related vein, Kassel (1983) expresses concern that elders in institutions are very deprived of outlets for sexual expression, even though they are greatly in need of such outlets. Kassel (1983) cites horrible stories of nursing home personnel seriously threatening elders caught masturbating. According to Ferdinand, nursing home personnel tend to view sex as ugly and try to ignore it (Kassel, 1983).

It seems that part of the attitudinal problem regarding sexuality in later life are the myths about sexuality and aging which younger persons, as well as elders, believe to be true. According to Croft (1982), these myths include the following:

1. Sexual intercourse is harmful to one's health and can cause death.
2. One can stay sexually active later in life through abstinence when one is young, and inactivity in later years.
3. Only disturbed elders masturbate; it is a childish activity.
4. Coital satisfaction decreases after menopause.
5. Older women who enjoy sex were probably nymphomaniacs when they were younger.
6. Most older men lose the ability and desire to have sex.
7. Older men tend to be sexually deviant (e.g., child molesters and exhibitionists).
8. Sexual ability and performance remain the same throughout life.
9. A person cannot have sex if they have not engaged in sexual activity for several years.
10. A senior citizen who has a chronic illness or disability should not have sex.

In summary, many of the factors affecting the sexual behavior of elders which were discussed in this section are limiting factors. The next section of this chapter focuses on how some of these limiting factors can be counteracted.

SUGGESTIONS FOR ENHANCING SEXUAL EXPRESSION IN LATER LIFE

This final section of the chapter has been divided into two sub-sections: in the first sub-section, suggestions for overcoming some of the psycho-social limitations on sexual expression in later life are discussed; in the second sub-section, treatments designed to counteract specific sex-related negative physical changes associated with aging are discussed.

Overcoming Psycho-Social Barriers

In the previous section of this chapter, the environment of institutional settings was identified as a barrier to the free sexual expression of the over one million institutionalized elders in the U.S. Corby and Zarit (1983) write that the creation of a "heterosexual living space" within the institution is an excellent solution to this problem. In addition, the creation of the heterosexual living space in one particular nursing home was documented as resulting in men grooming themselves better, and limiting their use of profanity (Corby and Zarit, 1983). Furthermore, Corby and Zarit (1983) claim that institutions which permit the free expression of sexual behavior have less of a problem with inappropriate behavior.

Croft (1982) identifies several suggestions for enhancing sexual opportunities for elders:

1. Communal living, in which groups of elders band together to share housing and form a family unit. This banding together of peers could facilitate outlets for sexual expression as well as improving other aspects of life (e.g., shared responsibilities in cleaning, cooking, etc.). This concept has already been implemented by a Florida organization called Share-A-Home, and by an apartment building in San Francisco called Merrill Court.

2. Polygynous marriages, according to Kassel (1976), would have many advantages for elders such as:
   a. The uneven sex ratio would be somewhat remedied;
   b. Women could be a part of a meaningful family unit;
   c. Elders could pool their incomes and thus live better;
   d. Better nutrition would result (more incentive to cook for several people than for just one or two people);

  e. Older women would have a regular sexual partner;
  f. Older men would have a variety of sexual partners;
  g. Better grooming and appearance would result from the competition for attention; and
  h. Loneliness and depression would be reduced.
3. Greater acceptance of women fulfilling their sexual desires through sexual relationships with other women.
4. A greater acceptance of masturbation as a sexual outlet.
5. A greater societal acceptance of older women marrying younger men.

Weg (1983) offers some additional suggestions for enhancing sexual capacity in later years:

1. Sex counseling can help remove inhibitions restricting an older person's sexual behavior.
2. Sex education throughout the lifespan will improve the sexual capacity of future generations of senior citizens.
3. Placing emphasis on the quality of the sexual relationship, rather than performance, will make the experience of sexual activity more enjoyable for elders.
4. As identified at the beginning of the chapter, one means of improving the sexual expression of elders is the education of health professionals in this area, in order to improve their attitudes toward sex in later life and facilitate their ability to counsel elders in sex-related matters.
5. Greater research efforts to extend the male's lifespan, in order to reduce the eight-year advantage of women over men, thereby reducing the problem of older women not having a partner for sexual activity.

Overcoming Physiological Barriers

There are several ways to prevent, treat, or reduce the effects of common negative sex-related physiological changes associated with aging, such as:

1. Hormone therapy in women to correct vaginal conditions which may inhibit intercourse (Weg, 1983).
2. Hormone therapy in men to treat gonadal problems (Valenta and Elias, 1983).

3. Surgical procedures to overcome erection problems (Valenta and Elias, 1983).
4. An intriguing hypothesis has been presented by Leiblum, et al. (1983), who state that their studies "suggest that women who tend to be more sexually active have less vaginal atrophy." In other words, continued sexual activity throughout life may prevent undesirable changes in the vagina. Leiblum, et al. (1983) point out that while a cause and effect relationship has not yet been proven, their test results "should stimulate further investigation."
5. Other possible methods of overcoming physiological obstacles to sexual performance and enjoyment in later life include nutrition, vitamin supplementation, and the use of drugs (Pearson and Shaw, 1982). These alternatives will undoubtedly be researched and tested in the coming years.

SUMMARY

Recreation therapists should be aware of the various medical, psychological, and social approaches to maintaining and enhancing sexual activity in later life. If recreation therapists are more knowledgeable in this area and thus can help enhance sexuality in later life, they will be making a great contribution to improving the life satisfaction and general well-being of elders!

BIBLIOGRAPHY

Corby, N., and Zarit, J.M. Old and alone: The unmarried in later life. In R.B. Weg (Ed.), *Sexuality in the later years: Roles and behavior.* New York: Academic Press, 1983, pp. 131-145.

Croft, L.H. *Sexuality in later life: A counseling guide for physicians.* Boston: John Wright, 1982.

Dailey, D.M. Sexual expression and aging. In F.J. Berghorn and D.E. Schafer (Eds.), *The dynamics of aging: Original essays on the processes and experiences of growing old.* Boulder, CO: Westview Press, 1981.

Falk, G., and Falk, U.S. Sexuality and the aged. *Nursing Outlook,* 1980, *28,* pp. 51-55.

Fox, N.L. Sex in the nursing home? For the Lord's sake, why not? *RN,* 1980, *43*(10), pp. 95-100.

Horn, P. Sex for senior citizens. *Psychology Today,* 1974, *8,* pp. 51-54.

Kassel, V. Long-term care institutions. In R.B. Weg (Ed.), *Sexuality in the later years: Roles and behavior.* New York: Academic Press, 1983, pp. 167-184.

Kassel, V. Sex in nursing homes. *Medical Aspects of Human Sexuality,* 1976, *10,* pp. 126-131.

Leiblum, S., et al. Vaginal atrophy in the postmenopausal woman: The importance of sexual activity and hormones. *Journal of the American Medical Association,* 1983, *249,* p. 2195.

Ludeman, K. The sexuality of the older person: Review of the literature. *Gerontologist,* 1981, *21*(2), pp. 203-208.

McCarthy, P. Geriatric sexuality: Capacity, interest, and opportunity. *Journal of Gerontological Nursing,* 1979, *5*(1), pp. 20-24.

Pearson, D., and Shaw, S. *Life extension: A practical scientific approach.* New York: Warner Books, 1982.

Pfeiffer, E. Sexuality in the aging individual. In C. Gordon and G. Johnson (Eds.), *Readings in human sexuality: Contemporary perspectives* (2nd ed.). New York: Harper and Row, 1980.

Robinson, P.K. The sociological perspective. In R.B. Weg (Ed.), *Sexuality in the later years: Roles and behavior.* New York: Academic Press, 1983, pp. 82-103.

Stinson, A., Wase, J.F., and Stinson, J. Sexuality and self-esteem among the aged. *Research on Aging,* 1981, *3*, pp. 228-239.

Sviland, M.A. Sexuality and intimacy in later life. In R. Kastenbaum (Ed.), *Old age on the new scene.* New York: Springer Publishing, 1981.

Valenta, L.J., and Elias, A.N. Pituitary-gonadal function in the aging male: The male climacteric. *Geriatrics,* December 1983.

Wasow, M. *Sexuality and aging.* Philadelphia: Plant Reproduction, 1976.

Weg, R.B. The physiological perspective. In R.B. Weg (Ed.), *Sexuality in the later years: Roles and behavior.* New York: Academic Press, 1983, pp. 40-80.

Index